Yes,

I'M A WOMAN
AND I'M TRAVELING

Alone

Struggles and Successes of
a Solo Female Traveler

Alyssa Ramos

To request permissions, contact the author/copyright owner at alyssa@mylifeisamovie.com.

Paperback: 978-1-7371382-3-5
Ebook: 978-1-7371382-4-2

Author Contact:
Alyssa Ramos
alyssa@mylifeisamovie.com
Instagram: @mylifesatravelmovie

Published By:
Journey with Jo Publishing
www.journeywithjopublishing.com

TABLE OF CONTENTS

Preface

Writing books about travel was actually one of my initial dreams, and somehow I ended up as an "influencer" instead. Not that I'm complaining, it's how I've been making a living for almost ten years. But a lot of people have always asked me how this Cuban American girl who grew up poor ended up being a successful, world-traveling, entrepreneur. So finally, I decided to write my books, and it was relatively easy because I lived the story in real life first.

Actually, I wrote what will be the second book first. The second book explains how I ended up going nomadic, how I finally started getting paid for travel collaborations, and how I went to about eighty countries in just a couple of years, mostly by myself. But when I posted preview chapters for feedback, many people said they wanted to know what happened *before* I became successful and nomadic.

They wanted to know what made me start traveling solo in the first place all those years ago and how I figured out how to be a blogger/influencer. So I decided to start a new book and completely spill the tea.

Although my social media posts are very honest, I won't deny that you only see the tip of the iceberg. You only see the epic travels, awesome photos and videos, and endless travel tips. What many don't see is the extreme life that goes on behind it all. The risks we take, what we give up, what we endure, the extreme struggle to remain confident and not let others break us down or get discouraged by followers or like counts.

Then there's of course, all the secrets. I'm pretty sure no one knows about the four-year non-relationship that I was in, which actually pretty much forced me to continue traveling solo; how heartbroken I was a lot of the time and how that is one of the many things that encouraged me to continue being the most badass solo female traveler. How the reactions I got from my audience fueled me to keep going, and still to this day, make me feel like I should never stop.

This book is very raw and not so happy at times. I hope you won't think of me as a downer, but it's the reality of being a full-time solo female traveler. It's not always pleasant; in fact, in the beginning, it mostly isn't! But I will tell you right now that once you get the hang of traveling solo, you won't be able to stop. It's the most liberating thing you can possibly do, and it truly will make you a better person.

Traveling solo, as cliché as it may sound, really did help me find myself. I discovered that I love people, culture, and history. I became an advocate for human and animal rights and global warming awareness. I found happiness and love for myself so deep that I could be alone for weeks and never get lonely, sad or bored. Plus, I realized that it attracts people with the same mentality, and those are truly the ones you want to surround yourself with.

I only hope that reading about my struggles and successes will encourage you to discover the world, and yourself, like I did and continue to do. It's my greatest achievement in life and something I value more than anything money can buy.

By the way, I wrote this entire book during the three months that I was in one of the World's strictest Covid19 lockdowns in Barcelona in 2020. I wasn't allowed to leave my apartment unless to get groceries (so obviously, I went every other day), and it was the first time I was in one place for more than a couple of weeks. I feared my travel career was going to be over and had to spend the money I had finally saved to buy a villa in Bali, to eat and pay rent. Writing this book about how I got started almost ten years ago gave me a lot of comfort, pride, and hope, and kept me sane.

When I finally finished it, I paid a woman who another blogger referred to me a lot of money to edit and self-publish it. But she never did. Months went by, and she gave me more and more excuses, which made me more and more discouraged, not to mention being angry, since that was money spent that wasn't coming in. By the time I finally couldn't give any more hard deadlines, I had pretty much given up, especially since there were so many other things happening.

Spain had finally started to open up, so I went on a road trip rampage and traveled most of the country, plus the French Riviera. I was also in a verbally-abusive relationship that I was constantly running away from, but we'll save that story for another book. This book was officially on the back burner of 2020 as I desperately tried to gain as much content as possible for social media and my blog to make up for what was lost, including my sanity.

We moved to Mexico, one of the few places that was open for U.S. Citizens, and I continued to forget about my book mostly because I was too afraid to pay a lot of money for another editor after being screwed over by the first one and not having much of an income due to Covid.

Before I knew it, it was 2021. I had broken up with my boyfriend finally and was living in Sayulita when suddenly travel started to pick up again, but under the radar. I ended up getting an amazing deal for an Antarctica group trip, and low-key started planning my group trips and personal travels again, which left hardly any time to think about the book.

Overall, miraculously, in 2021, I went to about fifteen countries and hosted six group trips, including the largest ever influencer-hosted group trip to Antarctica with 64 people. I made more money than I've ever made in my life, and in January of 2022, I had six figures in savings and zero dollars in debt for the first time.

So, I decided to give myself some much-needed time off. After Antarctica, I went to New York to see my family for Christmas and had my mom fly my dog Oscar to me from Florida. I then flew with him for New Year in Barcelona with my friends, where this book began, and it reminded me finally that I needed to get serious about publishing it.

I realized I was able to write it so quickly because I was literally locked in a cage with nothing to do, nowhere to go, and no one to socialize with besides my rain-cloud of a boyfriend, who I would typically try to avoid. But now, it was nearly impossible for me to be anywhere where I didn't have at least one friend or person to socialize with. I'm not joking. I could land on the most random remote island in the world, and someone will still DM me saying they're there and asking if I want to meet up, and I likely won't say no. There's also the problem I have where if it's warm and sunny out, I automatically have to be outside having fun or exploring.

So I decided to go somewhere away from friends, and also somewhere cold. Paris sounded perfect. It's where some of the most famous authors wrote their books and found inspiration, plus it's literally my dreamland of cute sidewalk restaurants.

Now that I finally had money, I splurged on a nice loft apartment in Le Marais and spent every cloudy or rainy day inside of my Parisian oasis, working first on my regular back end work of being a blogger/influencer/entrepreneur and then whenever I could, on the book.

It still took me a full month to go through all the edits from the second editor (who by the way, I found through a woman who attended one of my Bali Blogger Boot camps, and now helps people self-publish books! Thanks Jo!). It wasn't that she had a lot of edits, it was that I couldn't stop adding or taking things out. I was so nervous about how much I should or shouldn't share. Would people think differently of me after reading the truth?

When I was finally done with my own edits, I then felt obliged to let one of the main characters read the damn sob story I wrote about him to ask if he was Ok with me publishing it. Imagine pouring your heart out about how much you loved someone and then letting them read about it. The day I sent it to him, I nearly had a panic attack. Although it has been almost a decade since it all happened, I still have the same heartstring pull for him that I had when I was younger, and I seriously feared that he would never speak to me again. But instead, he told me I was a good writer, thanked me for letting him read it first, and told me he really did not want to be in it but knew it was important to my life's story, so to go ahead.

The day I finally sent the final draft to the publisher, I went out for a walk and a victory wine in Paris. As fate would have it, I randomly went to Shakespeare and Company, one of the oldest and most notorious bookstores in Paris. I randomly also bought a first edition Hemingway book called A Moveable Feast, which in his preface also states that it took him forever to actually get the book published and that he worked on it in several locations, including Paris and Spain, like I had.

So here's me hoping I'll one day continue to follow in the footsteps of great writers like Hemingway! Except maybe be more on point about getting the books out faster. Don't worry, book two is already written and I have about four more in the works!

Oh! For those of you who don't know me, I would highly recommend looking at my social media and blog (@mylifesatravelmovie) first to see where I'm at now in life and travel. So far, I've been to 115 countries, all 7 continents multiple times, 7 World Wonders, and have climbed Kilimanjaro (and soon will do Everest Basecamp). I was one of the first ever "travel influencers," and am one of the most well-known "original travel bloggers." This first book explains how it all started, almost ten years ago!

Dedicated to my mom, all my friends and followers who always believed in me from the moment I posted my first back-of-head selfie.

Chapter One

Everyone Said No, So I Went Solo

"If you want to go volunteer in South Africa, then just do it." It was the verification I had been praying for that could have only come from my mom. She had passed the secret test I made per usual when I was trying to gauge how crazy of an idea was that I had.

"By myself? Isn't that weird?" It was my main concern. I was twenty-six and a half as of January 4th, 2013, and convinced that I was "too old" to go traveling solo. It was nowhere near a popular trend then. More like something awkward and embarrassing that only people without friends or a partner do. That was technically half true for me. I had plenty of friends in LA, just none that wanted to randomly go to Africa.

Most of the girls my age that I went to high school or college with back in Florida were getting engaged and thinking about babies. Meanwhile, I was running around LA like Peter Pan in Neverland, writing about things like getting invited to sit at Miley Cyrus' table at a new club while she got a lapdance from a girl wearing a giant bear head on my new blog that I appropriately named 'My Life's A Movie.'

My toxic, mentally abusive relationship was nowhere near marriage material, especially after he shoved me out of his car and left me on the side of the road on Sunset Boulevard last weekend. This was after I told him I was thinking about traveling solo to South Africa, and he said that if I went by myself, without him, he would break up with me. You can probably guess what my decision was. I should have known better than to date a guy who was on a highly dramatic reality show anyway, especially one who ended up in the tabloids for allegedly physically abusing his girlfriend on the show. *I swear I found this all out later.*

I just needed something *more.* I'd been gallivanting around LA for four years already, somehow magically getting thrown into the "Hollywood scene" the second I arrived. It was seriously crazy. I mean, who the hell goes to LA for the weekend because they just broke up with their serious perfect-on-paper boyfriend and quit their well-paying office job in Florida, then ends up living with an actress, hanging out at Zac Effron's house (because they were hooking up), and after-partying at Ryan Phillipe's mansion within the first few weeks?

Who on earth completely abandons the Bachelor of Science biology degree they just spent four years getting and randomly figures out how to be a freelance writer in a place where the competition is the highest? And on top of that, how is it even possible that said person ends up becoming best friends with a literary agent at one of the top talent agencies?

Who, during one of their typical work-on-laptop-by-his-pool sessions, gives her the life -changing advice, "Why are you working your ass off to write for other people? You're a good writer, and you live a dope life in LA ; you should start a blog and write about that. We get requests for bloggers all the time."

And on that fateful afternoon, with a glass of prosecco in hand, 'My Life's a Movie' was born.

This new blog, however, is also what got me fired from my last in-person job as a personal assistant to a wealthy marketing firm owner. It wasn't a job I ever wanted or thought I'd have anyway, especially since I went to school to be a veterinarian and now wanted to be a writer, but it paid extremely well and the perks were things many women would kill for; for example, any time he was mad at his "girlfriend" (AKA girl who was with him but wouldn't admit it in public), I would get a new designer purse. If I had to go grocery shopping for him, he would tell me to get some things for myself as well. Oh! And when he would go out of town, I would *have to* house-sit his mansion in the Hollywood Hills while also dog sitting his designer Goldendoodle. Sounds fabulous, except he also wanted full control over my personal life, and I'm the kind of woman who wants much more than to just do household tasks for a man and refuses to be controlled by one. *This is probably why I'm still not married.*

In my down time, which was a lot of time, I would write about all the things happening in Hollywood, including the extravagant things my boss would do, anonymously of course. It was after I wrote about how he asked me to arrange a private jet to Vegas with three girls, book a table at one of the best day clubs, and take them and myself shopping to all get Louboutins and Herve Leger dresses that he told me to either stop the blog or stop working for him.

Something inside me told me I should give up the glitz, glamour, and money and go for the blog. So I hit publish on my next post and ran off to Mexico for the weekend with some friends so that he couldn't keep calling me incessantly. Then I picked up about eight freelance writing and virtual assistant jobs to attempt making a fraction as much money as what he was paying me to basically do nothing. Every day I'd work all of the freelance jobs during the day, then write on my blog all night, hoping one day it could be my main source of income. But exactly how long that would take, I didn't know, and I was getting a bit tired of LA life.

Four years of non-stop partying and shocking shenanigans later will have me craving a change. A big change; I hadn't traveled much aside from a couple of vacations with previous boyfriends, and to be honest, I didn't really even want to go on a trip with them. One of the trips actually resulted in the guy holding me hostage in a hotel room in Dublin for a few days because I tried to break up with him after he mixed Xanax and whiskey together and went completely psychotic on me. In fact, I wrote an entire psycho-thriller screenplay about it, and when my literary agent friend read it, he literally told me to "stop writing Titanic-length thrillers, and write about 'the cool parts of my life'" instead.

This time traveling would be different, though. It would be *my* decision, *my* trip, and *my* itinerary. Without anyone to tell me what to do or make me feel like I need to act a certain way around them. I could be whoever I wanted to be without anyone in LA or Florida judging me. Well, except for the people who follow me on Facebook and enjoy commenting things like, "Still in LA? Isn't it time to settle down?" Again, that's what I was most worried about. What would all of my married highschool friends and engaged sorority sisters think when they saw the photos of me by myself in Africa? Would they think it's pathetic that I had no one to go with? Would the arrogant guys in LA accuse me of having an older man paying for my travels? *Most likely.*

"People travel by themselves all the time. I mean, it's mostly people from other countries who do it; it's not that popular for Americans." It was rare that I actually took advice from my mom, being the stubborn person I am, but she was a flight attendant in her twenties after all and did a lot of traveling that she neglected to really talk about up until I finally showed interest in traveling myself.

"But what if I come back and I'm broke?"

This was my other main concern. I had only been able to save $2,000 from the personal assistant job since my freelance writing and virtual assistant jobs leave me overworked and underpaid. Not to mention, most of my money goes towards the expensive West Hollywood rent, mine and my dog's food, and maybe a bottle of wine if anything is left over. I was never really sure what exactly I was saving the money for, but I certainly wasn't expecting to blow it all in one month on traveling.

"You have enough money saved, and you can make more when you come back." She said casually. Ok fine. *Twist my arm, mom.*

After we said our goodbyes and hung up the phone, I went straight to the computer to look up flights. I typed in the information for a round trip flight from LA to Cape Town for some random dates in August, exactly three months from now, and almost barfed on my computer.

Over one thousand dollars just for the roundtrip flight? I couldn't afford that! The volunteer program alone is eight hundred dollars! My heart sank, and the vision of me teaching English to little kids started to dissipate. Longingly, my eyes wandered over to the beat-up world map I had taped to my wall. It was from when I took a student Euro-trip in college, and my mom had hung it up in her office and highlighted everywhere I texted her I went each day.

The distance from California to the bottom tip of Africa was far. Like halfway around the world far. So it made sense that the flight was so expensive. I kept staring at the invisible flight route as if the map would magically show me a shortcut.

Everywhere else is so close to it; why does the US have to be so damn far from everything. I thought shamefully, with my privileged American mind. My eyes flickered over the countries to the east of Africa. So many places I had never been, and names of countries I'd never even heard of before. One stuck out to me; Thailand. *I've always wanted to go to Thailand.*

My brain and eyes suddenly went on a rampage, scouring and analyzing the map as if it really were magically showing me the way to go. I jumped up off my flimsy second-hand bed to get a closer look at it. I wasn't exactly sure if it was right since it wasn't an actual globe, but Australia looked a lot closer to California than it did to Africa.

I remembered the cute blonde guy I met during my escape to Cabo last summer. He was saying how he had lived in Sydney for a year and now dreamed of living in LA, and I was saying how I lived in LA but dreamt of going to Sydney. Long story short, I ended up convincing him to move to LA and even merged him into my social circles seamlessly. But I never went to Sydney. I wondered if now was an opportunity to make that happen as well.

I threw myself back onto the bed and opened four more tabs on my laptop. *Please, please, please*, I thought, manifesting as hard as possible that my sudden idea would prove to work.

On the first tab, I typed into the cheap flight finder website: *Los Angeles to Capetown*, selected one way and any date in August so that it would show the cheapest date to travel. In the second tab, I typed from *Cape Town to Bangkok*, one way, any date in August. The third was *Bangkok to Sydney*. And the fourth, *Sydney to Los Angeles*. I waited with extreme anticipation for all of the results to load. Forcing myself not to look until the cheapest flights had fully been reported.

I grabbed a pen and paper off my nightstand and carefully wrote out each of the legs. Then starting with the first flight to Cape Town, I found the cheapest do-able dates and wrote them next to the corresponding leg. The flights to Thailand and Australia were surprisingly cheap, both only about two hundred dollars each. I wondered if it was because the airline offering the cheapest flights was Malaysia Airlines, which had just had one plane "go missing," and another one shot down near Russia, both of which I had suspicious theories about.

Once I had all the prices, I obviously knew it wasn't going to be cheaper than the initial round trip flight I found. But for some reason, I wasn't let down or disappointed. Like most over-the-top ideas I get, once I've set my heart on it, I end up stopping at nothing to do it. The total cost of the flights was about twelve hundred dollars. Two hundred dollars over, and most of the cash I had in my savings. But a sneaky little idea that had been lingering in my mind the whole time made its debut.

I opened a new tab and looked up how much a rare black and white Celine purse sells for on eBay. It was basically enough for the amount of my trip, plus rent for a couple of months afterwards since I wouldn't be working during the trip. Considering I've never felt any real fulfillment from having designer things, the decision was easy. *Thanks boss.*

Click, click, click. Confirmed.

Once my flights were officially booked, I did what any normal person would do; obnoxiously announce it on social media. I posted multiple times on Facebook and Twitter, suddenly not caring what people would think about the fact that I was going alone.

Well, at least I tried not to care. There were definitely several comments from people that were absolutely appalled that I was going to "such dangerous places alone." Many were curious about how I was paying for it all, and some were pitying me that I had "no one to go with." *Cue the tiniest violin that they can all play from their boring couches while I explore the world.*

I decided to answer all the "Why's" with "because I want to travel," and leave out the tiny major detail that I secretly hoped to transition my LA blog into a travel blog. Mostly because I felt like no one takes my blog seriously anyway and just sees it as, "Just another one of Alyssa's crazy, non-substantial ideas."

Little do they know that bloggers make money. Something I learned over the years of ghostwriting blog posts and content for other people's websites. Once it clicked in my head that the more traffic you drive to a website, the more product sales you get, and the more ad revenue you get, I had gone gung-ho on my own blog and started writing entire blog posts almost every day for it.

I knew it would be a while until I got enough traffic to actually make money, though, but money wasn't exactly what I was after. So far, I used my blog to get free meals at restaurants that wanted a review, for red carpet events that wanted coverage, and products that wanted more customers. It was a long shot, but I hoped I could eventually do the same type of leverage with travel. An idea that was very new, especially since there were only a couple of known travel blogs out there, and the only thing similar was getting press trips for journalists. I had learned that concept from my very first "job" in LA, where

I worked ridiculous hours under an absolute tyrant for a digital magazine, and in exchange, I got free room and board in their "artists' house." The bigger exchange of course was the press trips, where I would get sent places in exchange for writing about them in the magazine. Well, I guess the biggest exchange of all is now using that knowledge and what I learned about these barter deals for my own business. If you can even call it that at the moment.

My days leading up to August were a complete whirlwind. I'd get up at nine every morning, have some yogurt and tea, then binge-work for my freelance clients until my stomach reminded me that I needed to eat lunch. I had lessened the amount of content-writing gigs I took on in order to work harder for a part-time virtual assistant job I had gotten for a C-list celebrity publicist in Hollywood. I absolutely loved the job, even if it meant having to do tedious peasant tasks like responding to direct messages and writing Tweets for a musician who apparently has no time to do it on his own with all of his partying and whatnot. By the way, said-musician is also one of my Tween-age celebrity crushes. Talk about a Florida girl coming full circle in Hollywood. Kind of.

That's how I learned all about the techniques behind social media posting, engagement, and content creation, plus how to pitch for publicity or whatever else you want. I got so good at it that my boss actually promoted me to Junior Publicist, officially fulfilling my career goals of being both like Carrie Bradshaw and Samantha Jones. The promotion came with the task of escorting our reality show client on red carpets, which she hated because photographers would mistake me as the "talent" and her as my publicist, and emailing to get her into gifting suites; two things that I had no idea I would be getting invited to because of my own brand three years later.

Then there was the rich asshole who I won't name, but you might remember him for being famous for no reason on Instagram other than his obnoxious macho complex and tendency to post photos of himself with guns and naked models. My boss straight up told me that as both my boss and someone who has two daughters, that I was never allowed to go to any of the events or meetings with him, and I was completely fine with that.

Anyway, around four or five, I'd switch to trip planning, which included figuring out how to apply for visas, get travel insurance, and which vaccinations I needed. I'd never had to do so much planning in my life, but the process was exhilarating.

South Africa needed the most pre-arranging. The volunteer company I was going through had a page-long checklist of things I needed and needed to do. I applied for the free visa online and painfully forked over a total of about $200 for the required vaccines and background check.

Having to get multiple shots was not exciting at all. But getting a little booklet to carry with my passport was. I got vaccinated for Typhoid, Hep A, and Hep B, which were the bare minimum of the requirements, but if I could have afforded it, I would have gotten Yellow Fever as well. Mostly because some countries require you to have it, which I would find out later in life in the most unfortunate ways. *You do not want to get a vaccine at a border airport in Africa.*

Malaria pills were recommended for Thailand but not required. My extensive research had informed me that most people who take them end up getting sick and even hallucinating, so I decided just to get some strong bug spray and take my chances. I also found out I could get a visa on arrival there for thirty bucks, which wasn't ideal but not entirely out of the budget.

Australia nearly gutted me, though, when I realized I needed to pay over one hundred dollars for a visa to go there. But it was too late to turn back now; I already had the non-refundable flights.

I posted updates on Facebook and Twitter each time I did the tiniest thing for my trip. Sometimes even to Instagram, though it was still so new that I didn't see a point in using it that much. I even uploaded photos of me getting shot in the arm with vaccines and doing a thumbs up with my clean background check. The judgy comments had diminished, I assumed either because I was proving that I was being safe and prepared, or they were just annoyed with my constant excitement about the trip.

About one month before my epic adventure, something extremely strange happened. Old friends started reaching out to me, asking me about the trip. As in...they wanted in on it! For an entire year, I had begged people to come with me, anyone, just one person, so I wouldn't have to go alone, and not a single person gave it a thought. Yet after posting incessantly and showing how possible it was to plan and how epic it was going to be, people wanted to go. I realized I should probably write about the process on my blog as well.

But did I want people to come with me? I had already wrapped my head around how glorious it would be not to have to act in a certain way around people or entertain conversations. But on the other hand, I would feel a lot safer and comfortable with someone I knew with me. After chatting with the three people who had said they were one hundred percent interested, I decided to help them plan to meet up with me for parts of the trip.

For South Africa, my fabulous gay best friend (AKA my "GBF") since middle school and a guy I actually dated in Florida in my early twenties but never worked out because he was too much of a "Party Boy," would meet me there for a week of volunteering. If you're thinking right now that inviting an ex to travel with you for a week is a bad idea, you are one million percent correct, and I have no idea why I didn't think of that at the time.

A cool girl who was a year older than me in my sorority and from the same hometown (except the nice area, not the lower middle-class farm area where I was from) was interested in Thailand. I was definitely happy to have her come since it would be my first Asian country, and I was extremely worried about the culture shock and language barrier.

My plan with her was that she would fly to meet me in Bangkok from New York on the same day I flew in from Cape Town. Then we'd explore Bangkok the next day before heading down to go island hopping in Ao Nang. While planning those arrangements, I experienced my first travel predicament: There was something I'd never heard of before called a Military Coup happening in Bangkok, which resulted in a nightly curfew for the whole city.

I was bummed because we literally only had one night in Bangkok (like the song), and we both wanted to make the "world our oyster." AKA experience the famed Bangkok nightlife. Luckily though, my Hollywood-state-of-mind thought of a solution thanks to the movie, *Hangover II*. We would splurge to split a room at the famous *Lebua Hotel* as they do in the movie, and that way, we could at least have cocktails at their notorious rooftop bar. It definitely wasn't in my budget, but of course, I had to keep the mindset that it was also for my blog and that the blog would eventually make money. *I hope.*

Sydney was the only place I didn't have someone to meet up with. It was also the place I didn't really have a plan for aside from staying in Bondi Beach, where the hot surfers are. And of course, seeing the Sydney Opera House. I figured I had plenty of time on my twenty-eight hour flight to Cape Town to do some research though.

On the nights that I didn't get peer pressured into going out to the Hollywood clubs, which were increasing thanks to my new passion for planning the trip and sudden lack of funds, I wrote blog post after blog post until I couldn't stay awake any longer. More than once, I laughed to myself, thinking, 'You stayed in LA partially to avoid a 9-5 job, and now you're working 9 to12 am!' and reveling at the determined little hustler I had become.

Chapter Two

Screw Society, I'm Traveling Solo

It took all the confidence I had to ask the flight attendant to take my photo on the stairway that led up to the second level of the Emirates 747 jumbo jet, even though my seat was in economy. It made me feel extremely embarrassed, especially since the entire economy cabin was watching me do it. But I didn't care ; I'd never seen a two-level plane before. I felt like I really was in a movie.

As I made my way to my seat, I realized I was one of the very few non-Middle Eastern people on board, which was another thing I'd never seen before. It made me feel good that I didn't have any negative stereotypes poking their ugly heads into my mind, especially with all the hate and terrorist talk on the US news. But I also wondered what they thought of me traveling alone. No one knew I was heading to South Africa to volunteer. The first leg of the flight was stopping in Dubai, so for all they knew, I could be some American gold-digger going to look for a rich sheik or something.

Hollywood was too much in my head. I reminded myself that it doesn't matter. I paid for the $500 economy seat ticket, and I was going to enjoy the shit out of it by my damn self. I settled into the aisle seat of the middle row, next to a man in a turban and his wife. They stared at me like they were evaluating my entire existence and did not stop until I finally turned to them and said, "Hi, how are you guys today?" About two hours into the thirteen -hour flight, I could tell that the man's initial appraising look was not a good one. Because he decided to take off his shoes and fold his right ankle over his left knee so that his crusty, rancid smelling bare foot was just inches from my thigh. To make it worse, he started picking at the crust on his toenails, causing me to automatically gag and almost cry.

I didn't want to be rude and didn't know how to ask a stranger to please move their gross foot, or at least put it on the side their wife is on. So I did the next best thing; took out my travel -size Lysol spray and created a cloud barrier of disinfectant between my leg and the foot. He looked at me with disgust, as if my desire to be clean was grosser than him picking dead skin off his foot, and turned to complain to his wife in Arabic. At least he put his foot down though. When the flight attendants came by with the food and beverage cart, I asked for two much -needed mini bottles of wine (which also seemed to offend him) and quickly dozed off after downing them.

When I woke up, I was in a brand new country, the UAE. Even though my layover in Dubai was only for three hours, I was still overly excited about "being in a new country." I explored the airport as if I was exploring the actual markets in the city and even bought a souvenir lamp that looked like the one in Aladdin. Ironically, when I got on Wi-Fi to text my mom that I had made it to Dubai, she informed me of the sad news that Robin Williams, the original genie of the lamp, had just died. I decided to take a selfie with my lamp in front of a sign that said Dubai to post in his honor. Almost immediately, I got my first comment regarding my solo travels, but it wasn't a good one. It was from a cocky thirty-something bartender in LA who thought he was famous because he worked at one of the hot day clubs and was considered better looking than the other guys that worked there. He was also my ex's brother, the one that held me hostage in Ireland, so his thoughts about me were not the best. And it showed in his comment.

"Who's taking the picture? What guy is paying for you to go on a trip to Dubai?

Tag your sponsor!" It said, with multiple laughing emojis. Reading it gave me a sharp jab in my chest, and I was embarrassed that other people would see it and assume that some rich older guy was paying for me to travel with him. I was also hurt that even after spending all of my savings and mustering the courage to even fly to another country solo, I was still stereotyped as just a gold-digging girl who gets to travel because of a man.

I considered deleting the comment for a moment, but then a notification popped up. It was a response to his comment from my GBF, who will be meeting me in Cape Town in a week; *"Have you just been ignoring all of the hundreds of posts she's made about planning this trip and patiently waiting for one that you can try to troll on? She's by herself, and she paid for the whole trip."*

A massive smirk crept onto my face, and suddenly, I got a strange surge of confidence. *Yeah, asshole, I'm my own sponsor! Oh, that's a good one!* I typed furiously in response, and before I knew what I was even saying, I had posted, *"Sponsored by #AlyssaRamos AKA #MyLifesAMovie. And PS, stop hating just because you're jealous of older rich dudes who can afford to take the girls you want traveling, and because independent women like me don't need someone like you to take us somewhere."* My response got thirty-two likes and an *'OMG; I can't believe you called him out like that!!!'* direct message from one of my friends who had gotten played by him in the past.

Feeling triumphant but still fighting off the sting of the stereotype comment, I decided to put my phone away, order one glass of wine, and observe the passengers traveling in and out of Dubai.

My first impression of Cape Town was honestly depressing and a little scary. But that's because the very first thing I saw was the decrepit, tin-roofed township that exists right next to the airport. I immediately felt the shame of being a privileged American, especially as I cruised by with my personal driver that the volunteer company coordinated. I assumed the inclusion had something to do with why it costs so much to volunteer. For some reason, I had expected volunteering to be something you get for free since you do it for free, but the company had sent a breakdown of what the money went towards. Not surprisingly, not much of it went to the actual school where I was supposed to be volunteering. This is why I purchased an entire duffel bag full of school supplies to bring to them.

The drive from the airport to the outskirt city of Muizenberg took several hours. By the time I finally arrived, it was dark, and I worried that there wouldn't be anyone there to let me in. That idea was definitely wrong.

From the moment I walked through the doors of what they called Albertyn House, I knew that this was one of the greatest ideas I've ever had. I found myself standing in the middle of the Albertyn House's bright and bustling hallway, surrounded by the friendly and excited faces of people from all over the world who were all there for the same reasons as I was. Granted, I was definitely older than most of them, but they didn't seem to care as one after another, they grabbed my hand to shake it and introduced themselves in accents from at least six other countries.

"Hey! We're going to Primi to get drinks and Wi-Fi, wanna come?" A petite brunette girl from Canada asked before I had even put my luggage down. Without question, I threw my stuff in what was designated as my room (I lucked out with a single room instead of the girls' dorm after pulling the blogger-card with the volunteer company) and appeared back in the hallway in seconds.

"Oh no, no, you can't take that." She said, pointing at my black Harvey's Seatbelt Bag. I had heard it wasn't safe at night in Muizenberg, so I wasn't surprised at her remark and had actually been planning on using the slash-proof bag made of recycled seatbelts as a weapon. I shrugged, and reached for my bag to grab my iPhone and wallet, then threw my purse in the corner. "Here, you can put your stuff in my backpack; let's go!" She said, opening her bag for me to throw my wallet in while following the rest of the group out the door.

As we strolled and shuffled around the corner, down one narrow street of little houses, then another, I did my best to take in my surroundings and comprehend what this new type of life was. We walked across a busy street next to a bridge sheltering homeless people that I was warned was very dangerous, and finally, down another road that led straight to the beach and Primi – the local restaurant they all go to that stays open late. I tried to absorb all of the "new people" tips that they excitedly had to offer as we clamored inside the adorable beach-chic yet modern restaurant. I continued to listen to stories, advice, and gossip while trying to figure out who was dating who since it seemed like many of them were. I quickly realized that I forgot about the natural phenomenon of a trip-relationship – someone you meet on a trip and have a passionate, die-hard, week-long relationship with, only to have to say goodbye (possibly forever) at the end of it.

I quickly scoped out the table, just in case there were some potentials, but immediately felt creepy and refocused on my conversation with the Sams (two girls both named Sam who had already been in the program for weeks). They were talking about how one of their phones got stolen earlier at Mzoli's – an *extremely* local Sunday Funday spot in a township where fights and theft are the norm.

After everyone was done eating, drinking, and Wi-Fi binging, we stumbled obnoxiously back to the Albertyn house, where some of us sat in the living room, where I figured we'd watch a movie. "We only have these two, and we've seen them a million times, so you guys can pick, and we'll play it on the tablet ." *Tablet?* I thought to myself. "What's wrong with the

TV?" I asked in confusion, examining the turned-off TV on the cabinet next to the non-working fireplace. It was so cold that I could see my breath in the living room since the house had no heat, and I considered attempting to force the fireplace to work. "We don't have any cable. Someone bought a DVD player, but they took it with them when they left".

I could hardly see the screen because I was tired, tipsy, and freezing, but I didn't want to seem rude to my new friends. I was about to stand up and sneak off to bed when a tall, dark, and handsome guy came walking into the room. "Can you make a seat for me?" He said in a thick, foreign accent to the Sam on my right. *Maybe I'll stay a little longer.* I thought to myself. But he didn't so much as glance at me, and my eyeballs couldn't even focus on the screen anymore, so I headed off to bed, making a mental note to get up early to actually do my hair in the morning before orientation, just in case we were assigned to the same school.

Monday morning came quickly, and I woke up thirty minutes before my 7am alarm to the dark, freezing cold two-person room that they had assigned me to. It was smaller than the two rooms on either side of it, but I was beyond happy to have it since the girls' room had three bunk beds and six people in it. I had already done the whole living in the sorority house thing, and at twenty-six, I wasn't about to regress back. All of the girls had to share the bathroom at the end of the hall, while the boys had their own in their four-person room, along with a full-length mirror, which makes zero sense since those are both things that girls *need*.

My roommate was older as well and actually works for the volunteer program at their headquarters in New Zealand. She was sent to check out the accommodations and programs, likely due to the girl getting stabbed while sleeping and then volunteers getting robbed by machete a few weeks ago. *To be fair, they weren't following the safety rules.* I quietly picked out an outfit, which consisted of about three layers of clothing, and crept down the silent hall to the stone -cold bathroom. After showering, getting ready, and eating, I hung around in the kitchen, talking to everyone else as they scrambled to get ready. *Does this make me an adult?*

"Karl's here!" Someone yelled from the girls' room. At once, everyone started running around like the house was on fire, throwing dishes in the sink, grabbing bags, and running outside. We piled in his van with some other volunteers he had already picked up from the other volunteer houses and set off for the first school where our orientation was. I was a little shocked but extremely happy about the raging music video mixes he had playing on a screen at the front of his van. They were like music videos for people with severe ADD, flashing literally one line/scene from each video.

He took us to orientation, which, like any orientation, isn't worth even saying the word 'orientation,' so I'll just leave it at; it wasn't that bad of an orientation. We got to hear where everyone was from and what they do. Demographics ranged from China to Wisconsin and from recent highschool grads to us old working folk who had to sneakily take off a few weeks "for a double wedding in Florida."

Afterwards, we were taken to what would be my favorite place to be for the remainder of the week; Muizenberg Primary School. There wasn't much to it, just an old building with about five or six classrooms, a couple of detached portable rooms, and a grungy-looking dirt play area.

I was enrolled in the teaching program, so I was taken to the tutoring room where the volunteers tutor students on Mondays, Wednesdays, and Fridays, and a special needs person works with children the rest of the time. I'll admit that I was a little nervous at first, wondering, *what if the kids don't like me? What if I'm bad at teaching?* But all of my worries dissolved when the bell rang for "interval" (recess) as soon as we walked in. Seconds later, my arms, hands, and waist were suddenly engulfed in little arms and hands, pulling and pushing me outside.

"What's your name?" They asked in their adorably tiny voices. "I'm Alyssa ; what's your name?" I would reply slowly, watching their wide eyes filled with wonder and excitement. *"Ah-liss-Ah,"* they would repeat, sounding out my name before resuming the hugging and handholding. There was so much love that I could hardly contain myself from smiling and laughing as they jumped, tugged, hugged, and pulled. Many of them had American names like Susan, John, and Ashley, while others had to teach *me* how to say and spell their names so I could pronounce them correctly, like Sinsile and Khotah.

They all spoke English as well as Africans, and I could tell what grade they were in by how advanced their English was. It was beyond impressive that these little kids with nowhere near as much school funding as kids in the U.S., could speak two languages. They were like most elementary school kids with their curious questions and the way they played and fought, except for one very big difference. They didn't have most of the things that other kids had. There were no balls or toys for them to play with, and there was no playground, although they seemed perfectly content running around on the dusty dirt.

They all wear uniforms, which may make it seem like there is some money, but a closer look will show that if they *weren't* required to wear matching slacks, white button down shirts, and navy sweaters every day, they wouldn't have any thing else to wear. Many of their shoes were worn down or broken, and the zippers on most of their pants were broken as well. While all of the snotty noses could be written off as normal, the dozens of black teeth gave a glimpse into what their lives were really like outside of the sanctuary of the school.

'Township' is a new word I learned that day. A township is what they call all of the areas I had seen where the town was made up of tin shacks. At first, I thought it was just where all of the homeless people lived, but I learned that they are actual towns where families live and even work in tin-shack shops inside of it. Most people would look at it and see it the way I did at first, but this is where the kids at the school live with their families. And by *families*, I mean anywhere from four to seven people living in one little tin shack. For me, it was heart-wrenching to hear and see. My American privilege automatically made my brain think, "we need to help them." But I would quickly learn that that actually was White Savior Complex and that the majority of people who come to volunteer unknowingly have it. This made me strongly reconsider how I felt about voluntourism.

When the bell rang again, all the kids scattered to their classrooms, but not without taking my hands, legs, and waist first and pulling me along with them, saying, "Come to class with us!" and "Can you bring me to class?" But we were stationed in the tutor room to teach the students whose teacher was out sick. We helped them with worksheets and math and spelling games, which I would never have imagined I'd be teaching to a second grader or anyone for that matter, but seeing them not only pay attention but actually trying and then looking to me for help and approval was beyond incredible. I wondered how much we were actually "helping" them though. Being there for a week really couldn't make much of an impact unless there was a way to keep giving after you're gone. My mind wandered to how I could do a fundraiser back home for things like new T-shirts for their physical education class.

When the final bell rang to send all of the kid's home, I was a little confused because the majority of them had to walk to the places that we weren't even allowed to walk to in groups without a supervisor. I overheard a conversation earlier in the tutoring room with two-second graders playfully arguing about the knives that they had in their backpacks (one was a little girl) and seriously hoped they were intended to protect them from rabid Wildebeests and not people.

I should have been exhausted from playing with, carrying, and being swung from all day, but their surplus of energy transferred to me in the form of inspiration, making me eager to come back to school the next morning.

Karl, the driver, picked us up after volunteering at school and dropped us back off at the volunteer house after dropping off a few others staying at different houses along the way. One of the older volunteers (and by older, I mean in volunteer weeks, not age) offered to take us to Checkers, the main grocery store chain in Muizenberg. Although my inner sorority girl and currently-broke-young-adult-self was perfectly fine with the included meal plan served at the house, I decided to take a stroll into town anyway.

I ended up finding a cheap little clothing store next door to it, where I bought a much-needed pair of boots for only 250 ZAR ($25) and a little knit head warmer for my frozen ears. If you go to South Africa during winter, you will wear the same boots every day, and you will love them dearly. Unfortunately, my not-well-traveled self didn't realize that South Africa was in the opposite hemisphere as America; therefore, I had to splurge on warm clothing to survive. When the guys were done grocery shopping, we took a walk down to the beach, where the volunteers in the after school surf program were just starting lessons.

The tiny beach in Muizenberg is worth a million words. From its vibrantly colored swimsuit-changing huts to the boldly cut mountains providing a picturesque backdrop, it's definitely photo-worthy, especially with the little kids riding the waves in on the designated blue volunteer surfboards aided by the volunteers. Mr. Tall Dark and Handsome (let's call him Mr. TDH) happened to be one of them sitting on a board in the middle of the waves, coaching an excited little kid on what to do next. I nonchalantly snapped a pic...just in case he wanted it to post later or something...

Our next stop was a small café across from the volunteer surf shop, where it was insisted that I try the hot chocolate made from hot milk and a chunk of solid chocolate stirred into it. It was beyond delicious, especially since per usual, I was freezing. It was starting to get dark, so we did one last social media and email check with their free Wi-Fi and headed back to the house. I would have liked to have had more time to finish my blog post about the day at school, but since it's highly advised not to walk alone, I figured I'd just walk back with the group and finish it from my room.

Since it was still raining later that night, we ended up going back to Primi to get some drinks, (more) pizza, and (more) free Internet. I was a bit disappointed that the weather left us with little options for things to do, but at least the company was fun, and the wine was cheap. You could tell that none of us were used to not having constant Internet access because the entire table was quiet and nose deep in their iPhones, tablets, or laptops for the majority of the meal. Mr. TDH was at the opposite end of the table, so I had to figure out a way to talk to him. *Because I was back in highschool and all.* I decided that I would get up as if I just realized I had found an accidental photo of him that he absolutely had to see.

"You're in my picture," I said casually, feeling like one of the second graders. He took the iPhone from my extended reach and examined the phenomenal photo I had *accidentally on purpose* taken of him earlier that day. *Not creepy at all, I swear.* "Oh ya!" He said in his adorable yet extremely masculine and hard-to-understand accent, "Can you send it to me?"

"Just tag yourself in it; it's a photo collage on my Instagram," I said nonchalantly as if any given person should have known what the hell that meant. And thus started my Instagram icebreaker with Mr. TDH. After we maxed out our free Internet usage at poor Primi, we continued our Monday night at the questionable and sketchy local bar two blocks away called The Village. Everyone furthered their drinking while I furthered my obnoxious conversation about conspiracy theories with Mr. TDH, which surprisingly intrigued him. That's how you know they're a good one; any guy who *doesn't* think you're crazy after explaining what you think happened to the missing Malaysia Airlines flight for half an hour is awesome. Bonus points if they agree.

I also learned that Mr. TDH was from Turkey, which explains his dark features and thick foreign accent. He told me he was twenty-seven, which I would learn years later in Budapest, was a total lie, and that he was actually only twenty-two at the time. He looked like he could have been thirty or older, though, so it was an easy lie to believe. I'm still not sure why he'd want to be older, though, unless he thought I wouldn't be into a younger guy.

Anyway, the night didn't end up in any way, shape, or form how I expected it to. Although everyone was falling asleep at the bar, half of them suddenly got a second wind when the party-guy of the group suggested going to some local guy's house to play pool and "hang out ." It sounded like the worst idea I had ever heard of, so a few of us went back to the house, and I hoped Mr. TDH would be one of them (*we would finally have some privacy*). But he opted to protectively accompany others to the potential catastrophe. *Not all heroes wear capes.*

--

The next day, although I was noticeably dirty and smelled like a second-grader, I didn't bother changing or getting ready when we got back to the Albertyn House after volunteering because I was so damn cold. A few of us were talking about going to Boulders Beach to see the penguins but we couldn't tell how the weather was going to pan out. Naturally, the solution was to Google it, but much to our disappointment, the forecast said rain and freezing temperatures.

We decided to walk down to Muizenberg beach for a snack and free Wi-Fi instead. When we got there, it had suddenly cleared up though, so we decided to take a walk along the beach first. It was as gorgeous as the over-priced postcards that they sell at the airport. Soft white sand with gentle waves rolling out onto it after a surfer rides it in and a picture-perfect mountain background with houses sprinkled along its base.

The surf program volunteers were all out in the water, surrounded by kids in the bright blue volunteer rash guards. There was one particularly large, tall-dark-and-handsome figure I did not see amongst the rest of the volunteers in the water, and I wondered where he might be. But it wasn't like I could just text him since our phones only worked using Whatsapp. That is, when both people had Wi-Fi and charged phones (AKA never). We mostly had to communicate by either running into each other, finding each other, or designating meeting times and places.

The spontaneous weather change must have transferred some of its spontaneity to us because instead of setting up camp at our usual table in Primi, we ventured all the way across the street to a restaurant called Knead, which was *exactly* my cup of tea. Or rather, *glass of wine*. The entire front patio was encased in floor -to -ceiling glass windows so that you felt like you were sitting outside without the freeze-factor.

It reminded me of one of my favorite restaurants, Villa Blanca in Beverly Hills. The décor was chic and modern, with all -white furnishings and decorations. Unlike Villa Blanca, though, a glass of wine was only 40 Rand ($4), and my cheese plate was a whopping 60 Rand. Not bad compared to a typical bill in Beverly Hills that's usually a minimum of $50 for the same order. We spent about twenty minutes trying to log on to the spotty Wi-Fi to check the weather, only for it to start pouring rain out of nowhere as soon as we logged on. The solution to that was more wine.

After our bi-polar-weathered happy hour, we headed back to Albertyn House to figure out what everyone wanted to do that night. Since the house was fairly empty, I took the opportunity to take a hot shower without having to worry about the hot water running out during or after it for the people waiting. It was the first time I was able to shower for more than two minutes, so I took the opportunity to try and wash my hair. I almost succeeded, but the water started cooling down towards the two and a half minute mark, and by two minutes and forty-five seconds, it was back to freezing. I painfully scrubbed the shampoo out of my hair with numb fingers, then immediately turned off the water, not even bothering to attempt the conditioner. The inner privileged American in me wanted to complain, but the new insightful, sympathetic version of me just kept picturing the little kids from school having to bathe using buckets of cold water outside in the freezing cold temperatures. Most of the families from the township didn't even have luxuries like shampoo and conditioner. So who was I to complain about not having enough hot water to condition my hair?

When I finished getting ready in my small but private room, I walked out into the living room to find the majority of the house lounging on the worn-down couches in the living room, *Including Mr. TDH.*

"So, what's the plan?" I asked, casually sitting on the armrest of the couch. He immediately turned to look at me with a glowing smile, "There is a place called Cape to Cuba that we should go to, it's fun, and we can take the train." He said in his perfectly broken English. "Oh, perfect, since I'm Cuban!" I remarked lamely.

Everyone agreed and scurried off to their dorm rooms to get ready. "Will you still do my makeup?" One of the Sam's asked me, as per our earlier conversation, about how she doesn't know how to apply makeup. I wasn't completely confident with my makeup artist skills, but I'm not going to lie, I did a pretty amazing job (not that she needed it). In the midst of my Mac Studio Fix application on Sam, with a few others observing in my tiny two-person "adults' room," who should walk in the door but Mr. TDH.

I froze, my eyes bulging at the thought of how ridiculous we must have looked, "We're leaving in ten minutes, guys," he said with a laugh, locking his eyes with mine after examining what I was doing. *Maybe he thought it was endearing?*

Suddenly the beeping of someone entering the key code to the front door went off, and an influx of volunteers from other houses flowed into the hallway. All of the boys from Recreation House were already drunk and passing around a 2-liter bottle of Coca-Cola, heavily spiked with vodka. We headed over to the train station, but since it's obviously pretty much impossible to get a group that large and that tipsy on the same page, we ended up missing the last train to Kalks Bay, where Cape to Cuba was.

"Primi it is." Mr. TDH laughed before heading off towards the direction of the beach. We started heading in that direction when we noticed music coming from the wide -open doors of a brightly lit storefront just a few blocks from the train station and our house. Excited for a change of scenery, we drifted unanimously towards the festive vibes.

"Welcome! Come in! It is our grand opening!" The jovial and well-dressed Spanish man behind the bar shouted as we all appeared in the 3-meter wide doorway of Ooboola. It was a narrow space with an artistically curved bar downstairs and a winding metal staircase up to an open loft upstairs. Art and photography covered the bright orangish-red and yellow colored walls, and a giant chalkboard displayed the beverage options.

I'm not entirely sure why we went straight for tequila shots, especially considering the conversation earlier about how Little Sam gets drunk off of one beer, but yeah, *that* happened. The tiny little restaurant/bar went from having a small family with a dog as their only guests to a full house of a kaleidoscopic mixture of characters from all over the globe.

I don't remember much after that besides heavily flirting on the walk home. That is until we were about a block away from the house. For some reason, sometimes I think I'm a badass, especially after I've had a bit too much to drink. I had apparently decided to take my badassery to the next level by walking in front and carrying my mini-umbrella like a baton, just in case anyone decided to attack our very large group that included a handful of very large guys.

Along the way, I had also apparently thought it would be fun to whack the innocent blonde German guy with my umbrella-baton...*as if I could really beat up a six-foot-two German guy.* The next thing I knew, I was in mid-whack when he lunged forward in an attempt to grab me to prevent another umbrella blow to the arm, but instead, the metal rod of the umbrella got caught in between my face and his chest, causing it to completely snap in half *on my chin.*

Germany, Mr. TDH, and I all froze, and as I stared at the two broken pieces of the umbrella, they stared at me like I was a ghost. It felt like it had just pinched my chin, but the horrified looks on their faces told me otherwise. I wiped what felt like rain droplets from my face but realized there were more than just a few droplets. I looked down at my hand, and of course, it was covered in blood.

Germany looked like he was about to cry – I spun around, looking to Mr. TDH for help, and in an instant, he grabbed my hand and started pulling me quickly back towards the house. "You're fine, you're fine," he kept saying as I continued to wipe the blood from my face. "I just need Neosporin!" I mumbled repeatedly, drunkenly convincing myself that that would solve everything. We finally reached the automatic gate of Albertyn

House, and he frantically punched in the code to open it. When the slow, rickety thing finally started to open, he yanked me through the opening and repeated the code to open the front door.

"Come in here ; I am going to clean it," he said, leading me into the boys' dorm room. Even though I'm a grown adult, I still felt slightly mischievous going into the boys' room when *the rules* said we weren't supposed to. "It might sting a little, but it will help," he said, ripping open an antiseptic towelette and dabbing it on my face. I could hear the rest of the group drunkenly coming through the doors and hoped they wouldn't come in to see my bloody face and hands.

"There," he said, gently tilting my chin up to examine it. I turned to look in the mirror, expecting to see a minor cut that I could easily cover up with a bit of makeup but *nope.* Hot tears welled up in my eyes as I caught sight of the U-shaped gash that looked like it would scar my face forever. "No, no, no! It's Ok!" He said sweetly, cupping my face gently with both of his massive hands.

But I couldn't help it ; between the wine and the blood, the tears just involuntarily leaked out of my eyes like a hot spring. "Come on, let's go outside," he said, wrapping his arms around me protectively and leading me out the front door to avoid the boisterous "cuddle-puddle" that was happening in the living room.

Once we were outside in the calm cool night, he tilted my chin up to examine it again, but this time in the starry moonlight. "Yah, you're fine," he said softly, slightly laughing at my horrified expression. I was *not* fine. I had a gash on my face and was probably going to get Tetanus or something. *Thank god I got those vaccines. Oh, wait! I didn't splurge for the Tetanus shot!*

Since my mind was distractedly racing with thoughts on what happens when you get a Tetanus infection, I wasn't expecting what happened next. In the middle of my growing anxiety attack, I noticed him looking from my eyes to my lips then back again. Then, before I knew what was even happening, he hoisted me up onto his hips, and we were in the token scene from The Notebook, making out against the brick wall of the back garden area as if we were long lost lovers with only a few days before we never saw each other again....if only that *weren't* true.

This is a terrible idea ; I thought to myself as I scratched my nails along the thick black scruff of his jawline while he easily held me up with one arm. *I'm only here for a week, and he lives in freaking Istanbul.* I reassured myself that it was only a kiss and that it was OK since I was on holiday. But when we finally snuck back inside after waiting for everyone to stop freaking out about one of the girls being in the shower for a long time. (the guys were legitimately worried she had drunkenly fallen asleep in the shower and kicked the door open) he led me back into the freezing living room where we ended up cuddling all night, fully-clothed, including boots, on the gnarly-foot-smelling couch. *How romantic.*

You can probably tell that living in the volunteer house wasn't exactly glamorous or romantic, so you can imagine how excited I was when Mr. TDH said he wanted to take me on an actual date in Camps Bay— the "fancy" part of Cape Town.

To give you an idea of just how big of a deal this was, the entire volunteer house gathered in the living room to see us off. Like we were their teenage children heading off to prom. Actually, it felt exactly like that because not only did I bust out the long -sleeved floor -length Diane Von Furstenberg awrap dress that I had packed in hopes of a fancy date or event, but it was the first time we were going to be alone and unchaperoned. I was actually fairly terrified.

We took a cab there first thing in the morning, which was apparently *too early* because Camps Bay was on the same time schedule as LA; nothing opens until at least 10am. So while we waited, we walked along the fluffy white sand beach and bought handmade paintings on canvas from one of the many local men trying to sell them on the beach.

Despite the massive language and culture barrier, we talked A LOT. Everyone in the volunteer house said they wondered what we were always talking about, but it was anything from the beach trips he took from Istanbul to the coast as a kid to the major job offer that I was debating taking back in LA that he thought I should. I almost think it's better that way because it forces both people to actually listen. There's not a lot of listening and understanding in LA, which kind of makes me want to start speaking in a thick Spanish accent.

Our first official date day was also the first day that it was completely clear and sunny in South Africa for me, and the blue skies couldn't have been a more perfect contribution to the adorably chic and semi-tropical little town. Finally, the first little shop opened, and what could be more perfect on a perfectly sunny day than a perfect scoop of gelato before breakfast?

After we were done with our matching pistachio gelatos, we walked back over to <u>Zen Zero</u>, the restaurant I had chosen because of its chic decor and extensive wine list.   Its atmosphere had my name written all over it. White elegant yet modern decor with perfectly placed tropical plants and chandeliers covered the open patio, where we sat amongst a few other early brunchers who were all already working on their first glasses of white wine.

After I assisted with translating our orders (apparently, I can translate English in a Turkish accent to English in a South African accent), they brought me my 40 Rand ($4) Pinot Blanc and a heaping bowl of pasta.

"What?" He asked, probably wondering why I had such a massive smile plastered across my face.

"I just had gelato for breakfast, got handmade African paintings, and am now having wine and pasta for brunch...in Cape Town," I said, still trying to handle my childish excitement. "Best day ever." I chimed as if narrating an Instagram caption.

"Well, I'm glad, and I'm glad to meet you." He said with a chuckle and a sweet smile that completely contradicted his brawny appearance. I laughed endearingly at his English grammar attempt and took a sip of my wine to avoid having to make a cute response back.

It was literally a perfect day in Camps Bay. There was just one teeny -tiny little not-so-perfect problem with our perfect day that we were both trying to ignore...it was also our *last* day together.

At some point, day turned to night, and we decided to move on to dinner. When it's your first date and also your last day together, you try to squeeze in as many dates as possible. There wasn't much open, so we settled on a place that looked nice and was playing music. Unlike the rest of the day, we didn't talk much. I wasn't sure if it was because we were both pretty drunk, pretty sad, or nervous about what was going to happen in the hotel room afterwards. I'd never had a foreign fling before and wondered if it would be like it is in the movies.

The music ended, and it was time for the moment of truth. He paid the bill, and we walked to what was probably the fanciest hotel in Camps Bay. Making it very clear that his family is rich.

Going from a cold, dirty volunteer house to a luxury hotel with a hot foreign guy after taking me on two perfect dates was admittedly enough to get my panties off. We immediately started making out, and clothes started coming off. I had drunk confidence, but it seemed like he had drunk insecurities. Maybe because he was having drunk issues if you know what I mean. *HOW?* We were both fully naked, making out, and just nothing. Finally, he pulled away and pulled the blanket up over his flaccidness.

"I have to tell you something." He said gloomily. *Dear god, please don't be an STD.*

"Is everything Ok?" I said, trying to sound supportive.

"Well, I have problems, eh, getting an erection. When I said I was leaving dinner to go get gum, I was actually looking for Viagra. It's always been like this." He admitted. My eyes bulged, and I had to try really hard not to let my jaw drop. I'd never heard of a twenty -six -year -old having to take Viagra!

Since that tid bit of information completely killed the mood for both of us, we spent the rest of the night cuddling and watching TV. So much for my epic escapades abroad. As you can probably guess, the morning was slightly awkward. Luckily we needed to be up super early to get back to Muizenberg in time to volunteer, so the urgency made it a little less weird. I slept on his shoulder during the one -hour taxi ride back, enjoying some of the last moments of closeness to him for what I was sure would be forever.

When Mr. TDH and I finally got back to the volunteer house, it dawned on me that I was on a severe time crunch. I had yet to see the cute little Boulders Beach penguins which were on the top of my list of things to do in South Africa, but between volunteering at school all day and joining in on the other volunteers' activities, I found myself penguin-less on my last day in Muizenberg.

"Take the cab ; he'll take you to Boulders Beach and back," he instructed after negotiating a flat fee of 300 Rand ($30) with the driver who had brought us back from Camps Bay. Boulders Beach is the only beach where the penguins live and it's about 30 minutes south of Muizenberg. You can take the train for free, but I heard it was a 45 -minute walk from the station to the beach and cabs were scarce.

"You can come help with surfing when you get back," he added, noticing the sad puppy face I must have been making at the thought of not seeing the kids before I left (and maybe also not seeing him). I ran inside to get my GBF, and Party Boy, except Party Boy had been making plans of his own.

"Ok, so let's take the cab to Boulders Beach, then down to the Peninsula." He announced without asking anyone besides *my* cab driver. The Peninsula was supposed to be a beautiful view and the southern most tip of Africa, but it was an additional two hours to get there and back, which I was planning to spend at the surf program with the kids and Mr. TDH for my last day. "Well, I wanted to do a surf program, so I'll need to come back after Boulders ," I said. "Well, you can take the train back then." He said nonchalantly, completely disregarding the fact that the train is extremely dangerous in the evening, especially alone and if you're a small woman.

I ran to go tell Mr. TDH about the ignorant idea and considered skipping my penguins altogether. He was *not* happy about Party Boy's train suggestion, so he came up with a solution. Since he had been there for three weeks, he was close to some of the volunteers and asked one of the guys from the UK if he would go with us so I wouldn't have to ride home alone. *My hero.*

The cab driver was great, most of them are and are more than willing to give you any information about the area. If you get a good one, make sure to get their phone number because they'll come and get you any time you call!

The drive along the coastline was beautiful, and we got to drive through smaller towns on the way like Kalk Bay, where we went for karaoke the Wednesday before. When we finally got to Boulders Beach, we paid the entrance fee which was 55 Rand and started walking along the wooden boardwalk to the beach.

The little penguins were everywhere! In the bushes along the boardwalk, waddling up and over the dunes and cuddling in the circular man-made nests that were throughout the park. There was a crowd of people at the very end, so we squeezed through to see the picture -perfect little beach that was dotted with the adorable little penguins! They would waddle towards the boardwalk and look at us inquisitively, then waddle away to go join the rest of the penguins who were stand-up tanning in the warm sunlight. *No big deal.*

After watching them for a while and taking our penguin selfies, we headed back on the boardwalk, stopping whenever we would see a few of them running around in the bushes. I wanted to get a closeup, so I decided it would be a good idea to lower my iPhone down to penguin eye-level, but the curious little guy examined it for a few seconds, then pecked at it so hard that I almost dropped it!

When I caught up with everyone else, Party Boy was already in the cab, ready to go. "He said the train station isn't that far, only like ten minutes, you could walk there," he said, opposing my earlier idea to have the cab driver bring us to the station before they went down to the Peninsula. I looked at the driver, who seemed to agree, so I turned to the UK guy for his opinion. "That's fine, I guess," he shrugged.

It was not a ten -minute walk. It was a forty-five minute walk, just like I had thought. There were no cabs to hail, and neither of our phones worked to try and call one. I was beyond irritated that Party Boy and the driver both knew the station was far, but let us walk anyway for the sake of not back tracking. Not to mention, it was more time that I wouldn't have with the kids in the surf program. It was starting to get dark, which was not a good sign at all. Not only is it dangerous to be out at night, but the trains stop running around 6pm.

Of course, when we finally got to the station, a train had just pulled away, and the next one was going to be another twenty-five minutes. I felt really bad that the UK guy had to come babysit me but was extremely grateful to not be alone. When the train finally came, we boarded, choosing a seat at the very front of the graffiti -covered car. Despite the sketchy company and condition of the train, it was actually quite beautiful to watch the sun setting as we rumbled back along the coast.

It took almost two hours total to get back to Muizenberg, all because Party Boy had to change the plans, so by the time I got to the volunteer surf shop, I only had time to help with feeding the kids their late afternoon snack before they headed home.

Mr. TDH and I walked back to the Albertyn House together after sadly saying goodbye to all of the kids to get ready for the Friday Market. I had been waiting for it all week and had watched out my bedroom window as they started setting up for it mid-week in the empty single-story building that took up the entire street corner next door to our house.

All of the volunteers from every house went there every Friday, like how they all went to Brass Belt in Kalk Bay for karaoke on Wednesdays. Food booths lined the walls of the large, festive area, serving everything from sushi to crepes to some famed meatball sub that *this* vegetarian had zero interest in. We ate and drank and ate some more until we couldn't fit anything else in our stomachs.

So what do you do after ten PM on a Friday when you're staying in Muizenberg? Head to the only sketchy hole in the wall bar that's still open. But the less than aesthetic ambiance was never an issue since we went there to hang out and drink cheap drinks anyway. Especially that last Friday night. Instead of playing pool, chit-chatting, and flirting, we were engulfing each other in goodbye hugs and trying to hold back tears from the pleas to stay longer.

But there was one person who wasn't hug-attacking everyone and who was extremely quiet. Someone who had accidentally fallen in love with a Cali girl who he lives thousands and thousands of miles away from. Someone who wanted nothing more than to *not* have to say goodbye...*Mr. TDH.*

We snuck out of the bar, giving the excuse that I needed to go pack and that he was escorting me so I wouldn't have to walk alone. Technically both were true, but the more important matter was that we wanted to spend some last alone time together. And it was obvious everyone knew that because for once, no one opted to head home despite it being late and freezing.

The walk back was awkwardly silent but seemed quicker than usual. When we were finally safely inside the house, he made no hesitation in lifting me up onto his hips so that my face was near his, foreheads pressed together, and my hands automatically griped fistfuls of this thick black hair. Without a word, he pressed his full lips to mine, kissing me like he was never going to see me again. *Because he really thought he wasn't.*

"Should we go to my room? I can't get in trouble if I'm leaving tomorrow." I whispered, even though there was no one in the house. He nodded and carried me into the small icy room, putting me down gently so he could close and lock the door. Meanwhile, I climbed onto the bottom bunk and started untying my boot laces, kicking each shoe off as fast as I could while he did the same standing up.

When we were finally both boot-free and stripped of at least two out of four layers, he bent down to try to fit himself on the tiny less-than-twin-sized bed. It was not ideal. At all. But it

34

was better than the foot-smelling couch or separate rooms. *But like, not better than that fancy hotel.*

We made out for what seemed like an hour, all the while I was questioning in my head when he would finally make a move to do more. When I heard the beeping of the front door code, I realized he knew the rest of the group would be coming back soon and didn't want them to hear us.

"Let's wait until they're in bed." He whispered with that sexy, scruffy voice. I agreed and cuddled up against his massive, warm body as he wrapped his strong arms protectively around me.

I woke up with a jolt so strong that I nearly hit my head on the rails of the top bunk. It was still dark outside, so why the hell was my alarm going off? *Shit!* I had fallen asleep somehow! Now not only was I going to be late for the safari, but I had completely missed my last chance at ever hooking up with Mr. TDH. *Or so I thought.*

He rolled off the bed and turned on the light as I scrambled to get my boots on and shove the remaining unpacked items into one of my bags. This wasn't the first time I had waited until the last second to fully pack before a trip, and it certainly wouldn't be my last. Once I had everything as close to ready to go as possible, including myself, Mr. TDH helped me quietly get it all out of the room and outside where I was supposed to be getting picked up for the safari. There was no one there yet, which meant I wasn't late, and we still had a few moments left with each other. He turned to me and cupped my face in his gigantic hands, looking into my eyes that were just visible with the single yellow light coming from the gate.

"Hey so, listen to me, OK? I..eh..love you, and...I will miss you a lot." Mr. TDH said meaningfully as he hugged me tightly in the cold, misty, dark, early hours of that last Saturday morning in Muizenberg. My response to the L-bomb was nonexistent since I was used to guys in LA avoiding it at all costs. I couldn't even remember the last time I told someone other than my dog that I loved them, so I was really hoping he wasn't expecting me to say it back. Plus, my face and arms were buried in his chest as he bear-hugged me to keep me warm.

"I will miss you too. Keep in touch, Ok?" I sniffled from my warm pouch in his arms. "Oh! Your jacket!" In my rush to get ready, I had accidentally layered on the jacket he had put on me earlier that night. I just so happened to notice it was Versace, so I figured he'd want it back.

"No, keep it. You need it more than I do." He said with a laugh, keeping me in his tight embrace. We stood there hugging until finally, I heard a vehicle clamoring up the dirt road.

'This does not look like a safari vehicle,' I thought, peeking a judgmental eye out from under his muscular arm to observe the dark tinted windows while the seemingly sketchy-looking tour guide loaded my luggage into the weird cargo pod behind the van. I thought I could see people moving inside but wasn't particularly wary of it. I was too focused on my nose freezing off and the fact that in a few hours, I would be hanging out with lions and Crocodile Dundee while Mr. TDH was on a plane back to Istanbul. *Sigh.* At least this would make for a great blog post.

"Err, um, are you guys almost ready?" Safari Guide asked awkwardly, trying not to stare at the scene of The Notebook we were re-enacting in Muizenberg. I pulled away finally and looked around, "Dan's still inside." I said, noticing that Party Boy was finishing loading his stuff, but my GBF was nowhere in sight.

"Oh, I thought it was just you three?" He replied, glancing from me to Mr. TDH to the automated gate of Albertyn House.

"No, I am not going." Mr. TDH said morosely in his deep Turkish accent. *Ouch.* I buried my nose back into his chest for the last few moments. I knew it would ever be there. And by '*there,*' I mean on my face *and* on his chest.

"Hey, uh, nice meeting ya, man," Party Boy said as he shook his hand firmly with the apologetic look of someone who knew how it felt to have to let someone go unwillingly.

"*Sorry!* I'm *so* sorry!" My GBF said from behind the gate as it slowly opened to reveal his perfectly styled blonde hair and all-black ensemble. He rushed to throw his designer duffel bag into the cargo pod, making sure to check that his hair was still as styled as it was before he left the mirror inside.

"Nice meeting you! Have a safe trip home!" He said sweetly to Mr. TDH, following Party Boy into the vehicle.

After they both climbed into the potential murder van, we gave one last depressingly heartbreaking goodbye before I boarded the van in what seemed like slow motion. I couldn't see anything except for the empty seat next to my GBF and took it willingly, leaning on his shoulder for comfort. It seemed like I was literally living in one of those old-fashioned movies where one young lover is forced to watch the other stay behind through a rain-stained window. *I told you, my life's a movie.*

"You totally just broke his heart." My GBF muttered next to me with a sarcastic smile as we pulled away. I shoved him hard with my elbow and for a moment, almost felt a tear in my eye as I watched Mr. TDH wait until the van was far out of sight to turn back into the volunteer house. I held my breath for a moment to gather my composure and took a sip of water out of the self-filtering water bottle I had somehow managed to not lose the entire time I had been there. Normally I'm never so emotional, but it's not every day you fall in love after a week of volunteering with someone in South Africa, then have to leave them to go on a safari. *Could be worse.*

After I finally got my shit together, I took a look around the packed bus. *Oh my god.* My cheeks burned with embarrassment as I realized the bus was full of *highschoolers* with a very wide and clear view out of the windows to the left of the bus where I had been very affectionately and passionately saying goodbye to my one-week-boyfriend. *You have got to be kidding me.* I thought to myself, wondering what the hell I had managed to get myself into this time.

About six hours later, we finally arrived at our "safari" destination. It wasn't a National Park or the jungle. Nope. It was a game reserve, much to my disappointment. But before I could even start to complain to my GBF, he grabbed my arm hard and blurted, "Oh my God! LOOK!"

I followed his gaze, almost as if in slow motion, to discover that the guide who had been driving us in the dark the whole time was incredibly attractive. He had dirty blonde hair that was tousled on top and light green eyes. He had taken off the dorky cargo jacket with the company logo on the back and was just wearing a fitted white v-neck that showed his slender yet defined torso, khaki cargo pants, and black boots. Maybe it wouldn't be such a terrible safari afterall. *But wait, what about Mr. TDH.*

Both my GBF and I couldn't help but casually flirt with him. Especially with that South African accent. *Swoon.* Well, my form of flirting is more like wild-animals; I try to show off. You can probably guess who was first in line to do the "walking with lions." Something that years later I would realize likely isn't too humane for the lions, but at the time, I definitely thought walking only three feet behind two adult lions was amazing.

Safari guide definitely ended up flirting hardcore back, but of course, kept asking about my one-week boyfriend. By the time he finally mustered up the courage to kiss me, it was goodbye at the Cape Town airport.

CH 3: One Night in Bangkok

Twenty -seven hours later, I finally landed in Bangkok. I was half asleep and hangry and had just finally received my friend's message that there's no mini bar in the room and to pick up wine from the airport. I shuffled over to the first Thai ATM I saw and withdrew 5000 Baht (about $156), then dragged myself over to the nearest Duty Free alcohol store.

"HA!" I accidentally said out loud when I read the price on the normally cheap bottle of Yellowtail pinot grigio. They were charging $40 for a bottle of wine that is only about $6 in the States. It wasn't funny anymore when I realized that *all* the wine was around that price. *Damn.*

I didn't want to use my cash, so I went to pay for it with my debit card but then, *wait.* Where the hell was my debit card ? I frantically scoured through the contents of my bag and wallet, but it was nowhere to be found. I quickly paid in cash (*yes, I still got the wine*) and ran back to the ATM.

Of course, it wasn't still there, and of course, the woman working the money exchange booth next to it hadn't had anyone turn in a debit card, so that was just freaking fantastic. I felt a little dead inside and extremely stupid. After twenty-seven hours of traveling to Thailand, I had lost my main source of money within the first five minutes of being there.

By the time I had finally gotten to Lebua at State Tower, Skybar at The Dome was already closed, which was pretty much the only reason why I wanted to stay there. Oh, and not to mention, not only did I lose my debit card already at the airport, but when I told my friend about it, she said, "Oh my god, I lost mine too right before I left!" *Great.*

The solution: Throw away the itinerary and just go with it. Normally I'm a plan-a-holic, but there wasn't even time to attempt re-planning, especially since I hadn't researched anything besides where to eat Pad Thai. The only thing we had planned that day was our flights to Krabi the next morning, which only cost about $40 for the last minute, one-hour flight. After that, we just went downstairs and attempted to ask for recommendations on what to do.

A sweet little Thai woman brought us a tourist map and showed us how to get to the main river that runs through Bangkok called the Chao Phraya River, where she told us we could get on a ferry. We didn't quite understand anything else she was saying besides "temple" but figured it was something important to see. We thanked her with our newly learned *"kap kun kah"* and headed off.

The second we stepped out of the hotel, we both froze, then slowly turned to look at each other with wide eyes and giant smiles. I thought to myself, '*This must be what Culture Shock is.*' I had thought South Africa was a bit different than the U.S., but had never seen anything quite like *this*.

There were people *everywhere*, and different food stands were set up along every square inch of streets and sidewalks. The smell and sound of foods sizzling swirled around every sensory organ I own as my brain tried to register it all and figure out what was going on.

"*This is so cool! Oh my god, look! What's that?*" It seemed like we repeated that sentence in different variations every step that we took. Most of the food looked like weird meat on sticks or bags of liquid.

We weren't ready to try any mystery meat, so we opted for some traditional Pad Thai that was being sold for only 40 Baht (roughly $1.20) near the ferry terminal. The Thai women were more than excited to have us, and although we thought we were supposed to just get it to go, one of the ladies shuffled us inside the little tent behind the cooking area and sat us at a small folding table with two plastic chairs.

After she set the table for us, and by set, I mean brought over the plastic bin of mixed silverware, the cheap napkin dispenser that everyone used, and a massive array of sauces, she shuffled away to the tent next door. I felt a little bit of my normal anxiety about being on time but then remembered that we had nowhere to be, and what an amazing feeling that was.

While we waited for our food, we used my friend's translator app to practice our Thai so that we could say '*thank you,*' '*tastes good,*' and '*what is this.* We also noticed an old photo on the "wall" of the tent that had named them a top restaurant and, of course, a traditional photo of the Queen that everyone had plastered everywhere we went.

A few minutes later, the other Thai lady brought over two heaping dishes of noodles on ceramic plates, while the other lady brought us a water bottle with two glasses of ice (that we didn't dare touch due to the common warning we got in the U.S. that ice will make you sick). Since we both hadn't eaten all morning, we immediately dug into the savory -smelling meal like savages.

Words cannot express the amazing explosion of delicious tastes that occurred in my mouth in that first bite. She made mine with glass noodles, fried egg, bean sprouts, scallions, and peanuts, which all came together to taste so good that I'll never eat Thai food anywhere in America ever again. It seemed like the never-ending plate of Pad Thai, but I got so full that I literally could not eat another bite. Not bad for $1.20.

After we finished our meals, paid, and attempted to say bye and thank you in Thai, we set off again to try and find the ferry terminal, stopping in random spots to examine the peculiar things that were being sold on the street.

Although the lady from the hotel suggested that we get on the cheap "stop-stop" ferry that would have taken us immediately to the temples, we quickly ditched that idea when we saw the pretty, colorful long -tail boats that were also docked at the terminal.

"Excuse me? How much?" My friend asked, pointing to the long wooden boat with strings of flowers dangling from the front. The men at the counter pulled out an old, mildewy-looking laminated paper with different prices for the boats and held it out for us. They somehow suckered us into the 1200 baht (about $40) canal tour that takes you through the narrow canals where locals live and work, and also where there was supposedly a Floating Market, which was one of the things we originally wanted to see.

Let me pause for a moment to explain how difficult it was to pay for things at this point. So not only did we both *not* have debit cards, but we also had a limited amount of cash. The cash comes in bills that are terrible for splitting things, so we pretty much ended up spotting each other for everything. Oh, and sometimes our credit cards wouldn't work for certain things like the flights to Krabi, so I'd put my friend's flight on my card, and she'd owe me cash, except it got more complicated when we started running out of cash. *It gets worse.*

We set off on our private longtail boat tour of the Chao Phraya River with our adorable Thai gondolier leading the way. The second we got out into the middle of the river, the same speechless culture shock slapped silly smiles on our faces again. "*We're in fucking Bangkok!*" was all we could manage to repeatedly say. We drank in the gorgeous views of the buildings, both new and *very* old, that lined the wide river before our boat turned off into the narrow entrance of the canals.

The culture continued to bewilder me as we slowly glided through the calm murky waters of the canal. All along its edges were shack-like houses that were traditionally decorated and held up over the water by unstable-looking stilts, one was even an old wooden boat that was turned into a house. We could see people in many of them, cooking, cleaning, and carrying on with their normal everyday lives, which made me wonder what their lives were like.

We started to approach an area that was filled with tropical palm trees that hung over the water and an area of sticks that held up cloth canopies. Suddenly, a woman on a much smaller boat glided out from underneath one of them effortlessly and used a long stick to direct herself towards our boat.

"Sawadee kah, I have many nice things for you," she said as she somehow docked her seemingly unstable little boat to ours. She quickly began taking out different trinkets and souvenirs from the pile of bags on the front of her boat. I realized that this is what they meant by visiting the '*floating markets*'. It wasn't exactly what I had in mind, but I decided that technically it still counted.

Since I wouldn't be seeing any *real* floating markets, and since I always feel bad not buying something when someone takes the time to pull everything out to show me, I purchased some extremely overpriced little coin bags and a hand-painted fan. Of course, right when I thought we were done, she offered us some cold beers to buy, which we immediately took since it was beyond hot outside. And I mean, why *wouldn't* you have an ice-cold beer on a boat in Bangkok?

"Look! Look!" Our Thai gondolier shouted suddenly from the back of the boat. I spun around to see him pointing to the murky grey-green water, where I thought I was going to see a giant fish or something. But *nope*.

"What the hell is that?!" I screamed, jumping so hard to the left that I made the slender boat sway. It looked like a swimming dinosaur. A giant, slimy, tourist-eating, freaking dinosaur. Like if crocodiles and anacondas weren't scary enough, someone had to go mix the two together to come up with this monstrosity.

42

"Is it a komodo dragon?" I asked him very seriously, even though I was pretty sure those only exist on a certain island in Indonesia, which I'd confirm in person a few years later. I couldn't understand what he was saying, but I later found out they are called Monitor Lizards and that I hate them.

"Oh my god, *ew.*" My friend gasped from a few rows in front of me. I shifted my attention away from the slithering monster and towards the rancid-smelling, bloated object that she had spotted. I gasped and spun back around to look at our gondolier for his explanation of what the giant dead animal bobbing up and down in the water as we passed it was. "Dog." He said half-apologetically.

Just as I was wondering how a dog got into the canal, I spotted another dog on a dock, eagerly watching a very chiseled Thai man who was waist deep in the disgusting water. He suddenly pulled a net up out of the water that was filled with black and grey fish that had been swimming in the same water as the dinosaur and dead dog. Guess who won't be eating any fish in Bangkok? *This girl.*

Next, we passed some beautiful, ornate outdoor temples that seemed to become more common as we approached the opening to the river. We saw school kids, monks in training, adults with small children, and people hard at work, who all enthusiastically waved at us as we passed by.

Suddenly we were back in the middle of the wide Chao Phraya River, surrounded by other boats and the views of the grandeur buildings and temples. "Wat Pho," our gondolier announced, pointing to a dock on the right and steering us in its direction.

The little Thai lady from the hotel had recommended the Wat Pho temple, and since it's where the first original Thai massage school is, we decided it was a good idea. After getting slightly distracted in the dock house that was filled with souvenirs that we couldn't afford after the floating market, we made our way to the street to try to find this giant reclining Buddha.

There weren't as many food stands as there had been near the hotel, and these ones did not smell nearly as good at all. We got distracted again by the clothing stands that were selling beautiful dresses, skirts, and pants that were only about 100 baht ($4) but we *still* couldn't afford to buy them due to our limited cash.

"Do you take credit cards?" I joked to one woman who would not stop trying to sell me something. She didn't think it was funny, but at least she got the point. My friend's cash was completely gone since she used her bills to pay for the boat, so I used my remaining cash to budget out our costs for entrance to the temple, a Thai massage, and emergency money in case we missed the last ferry and had to cab back to the hotel.

"Too sexy! Both! Too sexy!" A Thai lady sitting at the front of the temple snapped. She pointed from our tops to the rack of lime green robes behind us. "You put on, too sexy!" We tried really hard not to laugh, but it was just way too funny. We reluctantly pulled on the questionably clean robes and placed our shoes in the mandatory shoe bags in the bin next to them.

We looked beyond ridiculous and couldn't stop laughing, much to the amusement of some younger tourists ahead of us who asked if we'd take pictures with them. I tried not to think about how gross it was to walk barefoot on the floor where hundreds of other feet walked, but it wasn't like mine weren't already disgusting from wearing sandals all day.

The giant reclining Buddha was exactly that. He laid casually on his side in all of his golden glory, stretching across the entire length of the massive temple. It was actually pretty amazing and so impressive that I didn't feel embarrassed at all taking multiple selfies with him. As I was doing so, I kept hearing a clinking sound that was a little eerie, especially since we didn't see anyone playing a triangle anywhere.

I'm not entirely sure what the fascination with feet is in Thai culture yet, but his feet were the most important part of the statue. They were made from Mother of Pearl, which was used to design hundreds of extremely detailed pictures in a square grid with two giant circles in the middle of each. On the other side of the giant Buddha, we found out where the clinking sound was coming from; a row of tin pots that extended along the length of the building that people dropped coins in as they walked by as a donation to the temple. *We couldn't afford that either.*

I was more than happy to take off the pungent-smelling lime green robe and put my shoes back on at the exit and then look around for where we were supposed to go next. We spotted some buildings that looked like a mixture of Gaudi and Dr. Suess, so we headed over to check it out. It was another temple, which is nice and all, but we were way more amused by the dozens of stray cats that were roaming around everywhere.

"What is that!" I gasped as one of the cats ran in front of us with a large rodent hanging out of its mouth. "Maybe we should feed them?" I wasn't expecting my friend to agree but was happy she did. We spotted some kittens in a bush and tried to get them to come out so we could pet them, but they were too scared. Finally, when we had them cornered for some pictures, a lady came over with a bag of cat food that she sprinkled on the floor in front of them.

Within seconds ten cats came out of nowhere, including the two kittens that we were sure weren't going to be able to get any of the food. We were wrong. The kittens freaked out like they had rabies, hissing and throwing themselves on top of the pile of food, preventing any of the bigger cats from getting any. They weren't so cute anymore after that.

We wandered into another outdoor temple, whose walls were lined with dozens of life-sized golden Buddhas. Each one of them was sitting exactly the same way on their pedestals, but when I looked closer, I noticed that each statue was different from the rest.

By the time we left, we only had about an hour left until the last stop-stop ferry, but we still wanted to get our traditional Thai massages. We negotiated a half-hour massage for 120 baht (about $4) since that's all we had time and money for. We took our shoes off outside and followed the massage lady up to the second floor of the sketchy building. It kind of felt like one of those situations that you were warned to avoid and were slightly scared of, but did it anyway because, well, *why not?*

The room had four bed mats lying next to each other on the floor, separated by cloth curtains. The two Thai massage ladies instructed us to lay face down, then proceeded to manhandle us in a traditional Thai massage manner. At one point, I couldn't figure out which of her limbs were doing what and how they managed to twist me around like a pretzel.

I won't lie. It was painful. But I definitely had zero knots or tightness in my muscles after that! We made it just in time for the last stop-stop ferry that was already jam-packed with locals and tourists trying to get to their final destinations. Of course, our stop was the very last one, so by the time we got close, it was already starting to get dark, which I was slightly worried about.

But seeing Bangkok at night was a totally different experience than seeing it during the day, and we got to see all of the tall towers light up and reflect in the water. The streets looked completely different as well when all of the shops and signs lit up. It was what I expected Bangkok to look like for some reason, and although I thought it would be very dangerous, we actually felt quite comfortable roaming around by ourselves at night.

We were starving again and knew we wouldn't be able to afford eating at the restaurants in the hotel, so we stopped at a small street market outside of the terminal for another plate of Pad Thai. We had to wait ten minutes for her to make it from scratch, but it ended up tasting even better than the first one we had earlier despite the questionable tiny dried shrimps she added.

I wanted to keep exploring the night markets, but it was already 8pm, and we were running out of time if we wanted to get dressed and go to Skybar, so we bypassed the various scents and people and headed back to Lebua.

Since both of my Thailand bloggers recommended Skybar and since I didn't get there in time to see it the night before, I decided to just bite the bullet and book our hotel at Lebua for a second night. There was also no way in hell I wanted to pack up and find another hotel after the long day of exploring we had just had.

I was beyond exhausted and reeked of Thai food and sweat, which I didn't realize until we got to our clean, luxurious hotel room, but I pushed myself to get ready to go see this damn Hangover bar anyway. I didn't exactly pack anything nice to wear, considering that my travel plans included Africa, the beaches of Thailand, and Sydney, so I opted for the nicest thing I had; my go-to black and white striped maxi dress.

As expected, the rooftop bar was packed with tourists, but the view of the city and The Dome was more impressive than I thought it would be. We had to push through the crowd of people to get to the *one* small, circular bar in the corner of the lower terrace that was surrounded by a 360-degree view of the city and The Dome.

I knew the drinks would be overpriced because the stupid movie was shot there, but I definitely was not expecting them to be $32. *And that was for the cheapest one.* I got some girlish martini that had a vodka-infused ice pop in it that I attempted drinking as slow as possible since it would be my only drink of the evening at Skybar.

Since we couldn't afford to continue drinking at Skybar, we decided to go check out the other restaurants in the hotel to see if any of them were more reasonable. We went down a few floors to Mezzaluna, whose interior was a little too old and stuffy looking but got lucky with an opening at the bar on the outside patio.

It was a completely different atmosphere but just as visually enticing as The Dome. We followed the accommodating hostess along the bright blue illuminated glass runway that floated above the outdoor dining area and bar. The drinks were a tiny bit cheaper, but we were still forced to drink sugary cocktails like Mojitos instead of our preferred white wine because of how expensive it was, almost $40 a glass!

A major difference between South Africa and Bangkok was the weather. I went from constantly rainy, freezing cold weather to hot and humid with bipolar rain cloud weather. Although it had been perfectly clear out when we were at The Dome, we were suddenly startled when the entire sky lit up from lightning inside of a cloud. After the initial shock, it was actually really cool to see the bolts of lightning striking sideways through the clouds. I tried to capture it on my action camera, but of course, that was a fail and made me look like more of a tourist than I already did.

When we finally couldn't handle our exhaustion, bar tab, and conversation with the bartenders who thought we were famous (but still didn't give us free drinks), we headed back to our comfy hotel room. Once we were finally all packed and ready, we started embracing our next adventure; getting to Krabi with no cash and finding a Western Union to try and wire ourselves some.

The one -hour flight from Bangkok to Krabi wasn't bad at all, aside from the fact that my friend almost missed it because she was buying makeup at the airport since she left hers at JFK. We booked last -minute flights for only $40 and had planned on meeting up with my friend Nina, who lives in Krabi and was supposed to show us around and tell us where to stay. Ironically, I met Nina on my Eurotrip back in 2008 and managed to keep in touch via Facebook, which is how I knew she was now living in Thailand and working as a freelancer like me, and also as an English teacher. She was also an aspiring travel blogger.

I had interviewed Nina prior to coming to Thailand for a blog post, and she gave me very important tips and insights before I got there. Like that the weather is extremely hot and humid, so wear light clothing, which I wish I would have listened to when I stepped out of the airport in my jeans and double-layered tank tops. I did however take her advice to not book a hotel in advance so I could wait to see which area I liked best. But as we loaded our "glampacks" (rolling luggage instead of backpacks) into the cab, I wondered if that was really such a great idea.

It only took us 30 minutes to get from the airport to the main area of Krabi Town, where the only directions we had to give the driver was the Good Dream backpackers that Nina told us to meet her at since her address was impossible to find. We probably looked ridiculous rolling our luggage into the small cafe of the backpackers, but at that point, I really did not care. The only way I had been able to connect with Nina was through Facebook chat, but since the Wi-Fi of the cafe didn't work, I ordered us two beers to sit and wait for her the old-fashioned way.

When she finally got there, she took us to see her apartment, which I definitely would never have been able to find, where she only pays $300 a month for! She let me drop off my bag of winter clothes from South Africa, then led us back outside to show us around the tiny town

"So you're going to get on one of those things with the blue writing, those are the 'stop-stops,' they'll take you down to Ao Nang for cheap, then you just hop off when you get there." She said, pointing to a questionable little mini-bus/truck-looking vehicle across the street. I planned on just getting another cab, but my friend and I shrugged, said goodbye, and headed off to the stop-stop.

It was the most interesting ride of my life. We shared the back of the cramped, open-air bus with about five school kids, all in different colored polo shirts that indicated what grade they were in. They would hop off one by one as the bus stopped at each of their neighborhoods, while a mother with a baby and then an elderly woman with a small child hopped on.

As we neared the beach, the landscape changed from rural farm areas to lush, exotic jungles and mountains, but then suddenly, I realized that I had no idea where we were. There were no street signs or 'Welcome to Ao Nang' signs, and I had no idea where we were supposed to be looking for a hotel. I started to panic as I tried to turn on data for my Google maps and nothing loaded, especially since we had been driving along the beach for a few minutes.

"Let's just get off," I whispered to my friend, pulling the string above us that requested a stop. We awkwardly pulled our glampacks through the narrow aisle and jumped off the back of the bus, paying the driver 10 baht each (about 30 cents). We wheeled our glampacks to the sidewalk, where we could already see the fun and festive beach street that was filled with restaurants and shops.

"Oh! I think this was one of the places I looked up!" I said, reading the glamorous golden sign for the Princeville Ao Nang Resort and realizing we had happened to randomly hop off at the perfect place. Walking into the tropical, exotic resort made me realize what everyone meant by "*things are really cheap in Thailand,*" It looked like a 5 star resort on a tropical island, yet it was only $40 for the night. Oh, wait. It was a tropical resort on the beach in Thailand, and still only $40. Although it was cheap, our lack of debit cards and the limited amount of cash prompted us to only book one night with the hopes of finding somewhere cheaper the next day to stay the remaining two nights.

After we put our stuff away in our jungle-view room, we headed down to the beach so we could at least see the sunset since we had missed the sunshine. For some reason, I'm like the only female in the universe who doesn't find sunsets that enthralling, but this one may have completely changed my mind.

Where in the hell did all those colors come from?! I wondered as I gazed at the seemingly surreal sight. The sky looked like a fluorescent water painting with only the most delicious shades of pinks, purples, and oranges. To make it even more tantalizing, the entire portrait was mirrored on the smooth, glassy shore of the dark beach. I suppose it would have been nice to have a cute guy to make out with during the sunset, but I didn't, so at least I had my friend take a picture of me attempting to do artsy poses with my action camera.

We didn't have any plans, and like I said before, that's the best way to do it because it forces you to explore, so we wandered up to the lively street to find a place to eat and drink. After reading a few happy hour signs, we finally settled on the one with the cheapest wine specials (90 baht, so around $3 per glass) and the cutest sidewalk promoter. The wine tasted like shit, and we didn't even want to know where they got it from since we knew how expensive wine is everywhere else, but at the end of the day, it was still wine and didn't taste as bad after three glasses.

They also had free Wi-Fi, which is something I desperately needed if I was going to continue my quest to be consistent with uploading to social media and my blog.

"I don't think I've ever seen you eat a full plate of food before ," my friend said suddenly after staring at me strangely for a few seconds. But the red curry I ordered with a side of glass noodles to mix in was by far the best thing I had ever eaten in my life. After we got fat and tipsy, we wandered around some more and realized that there were a ton of massage places that offered even cheaper massages than our "expensive" hotel did at a whopping 90 baht ($3) an hour. Needless to say, we got three different types of massages before heading back to the hotel.

We didn't have much to do back in the hotel room since our "free in-room Wi-Fi" wasn't working, but we found high levels of amusement when it suddenly began to downpour outside, turning our balcony into an exotic rainforest. We stuck our hands in the warm rain and attempted to take pictures of it, laughing hysterically for no particular reason other than that we were so happy to be in that moment.

"Oh shit. Get back inside!" I gasped as the first mosquito landed on my arm. We jumped back inside and slammed the door shut. I had taken every precaution not to get Malaria *except*take the Malaria pills I had been prescribed and advised to take before I got there. I figured dousing myself in mosquito spray was a much better alternative to night terrors and stomach problems, but I wasn't about to test my theory especially when there was a sign plastered to the wall next to all of the doors warning you to keep them shut due to mosquitos.

Once again, we started packing all of our stuff up since we would have to store it at the reception in the morning before we went on the Four Island Tour at 7am. My friend had to pay for mine since I was officially out of cash until I could get to

Western Union the next day and wire myself money, but I was lucky to at least have that as a solution.

We were happy to learn that you don't need to pre-book tours since there are tourist booths on every block and at every hotel, and we made sure to negotiate the lowest price! I think we got down to 600 baht ($21), which I wrote down in my notes as "rip-off" meaning you can probably go even lower.

The tour guide picked us and everyone else up at around 7am from the hotels and took us to the place where the boats were. They then stay with you all day, feed you homemade Thai lunch, then bring you back to the dock, then to your hotel.

For being a total tourist attraction, the tour was actually quite nice. We made friends with a group of young people from Malaysia who requested a rather large amount of photos with us as we hung out on one of the islands. The water was crystal clear, so I went in to attempt an underwater photo. I set my selfie stick out in front of me and dove down after it.

"Holy shit! I can see underwater!" I yelled to no one in particular. It hadn't dawned that after getting Lasik a couple of years ago, I could now also see underwater! Talk about a revelation! By the end of the tour, both my face and my eyes were bright red.

We were so badly sunburnt that my friend couldn't get out of bed the next day, which was also our last day together. I felt extremely bad and offered her what little lotion I still had. She was supposed to be continuing on to Koh Samui, a beautiful island known for its Full Moon Parties, which meant more sun. I was headed to Australia for, well, I wasn't really sure what to expect there, actually.

After helping her figure out how to get back to the airport, we said our goodbyes, and I headed back into Krabi town for a night. I was a little nervous because the only place I could find online to book with my credit card was a single room in a hostel, and I had never stayed at a hostel before, nonetheless, alone. It also had a bar and small restaurant, though, which I prayed took credit cards because the Western Union I had planned on saving me was definitely closed.

While I checked in, my nerves did not subside. I definitely felt like everyone was staring at me, and I definitely assumed it was because I was solo. Thankfully my reservation went through, and I made my way to the tiny single room passed the shared rooms. It was the size of a closet but totally fine for one night.

After changing and using a shared bathroom for the first time since living in a sorority house, I climbed the metal stairs up to the rooftop bar for a much-deserved drink. After, of course, verifying that they accept credit cards. Sitting alone felt strange, especially since everyone else seemed to have someone to talk to or be part of a group. Instead of awkwardly looking around, I decided this was a good time to start editing my many photos and writing my blog post titled "25 Thailand Tips for 25 Year Olds".

I'd edited about three photos when two blonde girls approached me. I tensed up, not expecting the sudden company.

"Hey! Do you want to join us? We're playing cards!" One of them chirped, pointing to the table of people behind them. There were about ten people, they all looked like they were from different places, and some of them waved when I looked over. *So this is why people like staying at hostels, it's easy to meet people.*

Without a thought, I accepted the invitation and joined the table. Everyone introduced themselves and told their story about how they ended up in Krabi. One of the blonde girls and an Indian guy across from me said they actually met in Vietnam and had just been traveling together ever since. I wondered, no scratch that; I straight up prayed I would have a story like that one day. Not like mine, where my travel love either has to go back to their home country or stay in it while I venture off on my own.

After about an hour, they declared that they were all going out to a local bar and invited me along. But, I knew local bars definitely do not take credit cards, so I kindly declined and headed back to my room. With their big group gone, the hostel felt and sounded a lot more empty. I decided that was probably a really great time to shower in the shared bathroom.

I threw my small coin purse on the bed with my credit card and driver's license in it and headed for the showers with my toiletries, towel, and phone...just in case I needed to call for help or something. Of course, it was cold, but that was nice since Krabi is so hot. But it was hard to enjoy it without constantly thinking someone or something was going to pop their head over the stall and see me.

After I finished, I quickly got dressed and headed back to my room. Strangely, the door looked more open than I recalled leaving it. I wondered what the chances were that someone...*FUCK!*

It was gone. My coin purse with my last source of money was gone. How could I have been so naive as to leave my door open in a hostel ? I wanted to cry but for some reason, I remained calm. I immediately cancelled it and checked for charges. None. It wasn't like I'd be able to use the card to take the stop-stop to the airport anyway. Luckily at least I had been smart enough to ask one of the girls in the group if I could pay for their drink with my card in exchange for their cash, so I had plenty to get me to the airport and the flight, of course, was already booked..

Now to just figure out how to pay for a hotel room in Sydney with no credit card, debit card, or cash.

Chapter Three

Solo in Sydney

Everything seemed like it was in slow motion. The cool, crisp airport air stung my eyes as I squinted around to see where the imaginary slow-clap had started from. I made it. I had flown an extremely empty Malaysia Airlines and made it to Sydney without missing. Hopefully, that would encourage others to stop being so scared to fly with them.

After the ongoing obstacle course that was my week in Thailand, things immediately started getting better as soon as I landed in Sydney. I found a Western Union at the airport, so I was able to get cash out, which was fantastic considering the fact that I was officially down to $0.00. My mom was able to convince the short-term apartments I was supposed to be staying at in Bondi Beach to let her pay for it via email with her credit card since they don't accept cash. All was looking up for my final destination on my first big international adventure!

Of course, I had chosen the few days of the year that it rains in Sydney to go there, but I was so happy to have made it there in general that I really did not give two shits. It sucked a little that I couldn't check in yet when I finally got to the Beach Apartments since it was only 8am, but at least they let me store my luggage. Although, showering off the stench of Thailand and Malaysia Airlines would have been amazing.

So off into the freezing cold, dreary morning I went, wearing the same outfit I had worn almost every day while volunteering in similar weather in South Africa. First, I went to go see the famed Bondi Beach, which was only a few blocks from where I was staying. It was completely empty. So I kept moving. I bought an umbrella, which inverted within ten minutes, so I bought another one, along with some Red Bull.

Suddenly, a giant red double-decker sightseeing tour bus rolled up to a stop outside of the shop I was exiting. '*Perfect!*' I thought triumphantly, deciding it was a genius idea to ride around the bus for a few hours to get the touristy stuff out of the way. I sat on the open-upper level so I could get good pictures, which would have worked had I not been so freezing that I couldn't even hold my phone. But I saw all of the major sites and noted what I wanted to go back to see later after I became human again.

"Do I need to change buses to go to the Opera House?" I stuttered through chattering teeth to the jolly-looking bus driver downstairs. He seemed to be evaluating me for a moment, which I automatically assumed was due to my disheveled, zombie-like appearance.

"Yes, you'll get off and in ten minutes get on the next bus, there will be a guy named Sam at the stop, he'll help you, he *loovvesss* the young blonde girls." He snickered, revealing an English accent. *Great.*

The bus pulled to a stop, and I hopped off, trying to quickly walk in the opposite direction to avoid whoever this creepy Sam person was. I spotted a young, fairly good-looking guy standing near the back of the bus, but before I could register anything, the jolly man shouted, "Hey Sam! This young lady has some questions for you!" *Awkward.*

Turns out Sam was cool. He was around my age and lived just outside of the main area of Sydney. He even wrote me a list of non-touristy, local things to do, and we exchanged Whatsapp's in case I wanted to meet up for drinks later since I was by myself and didn't know anyone else in Sydney. *Totally safe.*

The entire bus tour ended up taking about five hours from Bondi Beach to Sydney and back, so it was more than past the check -in time when I got back. My room was cute; it looked like a small studio with a kitchenette and a little living room nook. The sign on the shower said to limit water usage, so I apologized to it because it took me a good twenty minutes just to defrost and scrub all of the accumulated international grime off of me.

When I was finally re-grouped and wearing the only outfit I could pull together that was both appropriate for the trendiness of Sydney and the forty-degree weather, it was already 4:30pm. Since I only had three days in Sydney, I had to get everything out of the way as quickly as possible in order to cover it on my blog, so I decided to ride the tour bus back into town to knock out the indoorsy touristy things then check out some nightlife.

Sam had been Whatsapping me non-stop about things to do, tour times and prices, and in general to get my ass moving since I didn't have much time, which I appreciated since my ADD is equivalent to a Koala bear's. I had thirty minutes until the next bus, so I searched the main street in Bondi Beach for something quick to eat.

'Happy Hour Special – 1 Slice of Pizza and 1 Wine $9AUD' ...*JACKPOT!* It was at that very moment that I decided I should move to Bondi Beach. It was a small little café in a nook, one block from the beach, and the owner/only staff there was a very attractive man in his late 30's. I couldn't tell if he was shocked or impressed that I ate my pizza and drank my wine in 7 minutes, but I was too shy and awkward to stick around to find out.

I ran to catch the bus just in time, which was now packed with people doing touristy things like standing up to take pictures on a moving bus. I reveled at the moment when they finally got whacked in the head with low tree branches. I had somehow memorized the bus route and the city layout, so I knew to get off at Central Park and walk the six blocks to Darling Harbor instead of having to change buses.

It was starting to get dark, so I walked quickly, noticing the uncanny amount of young, attractive men in suits walking importantly in every direction. I immediately regretted not bringing any sort of heeled shoe. I kept my focus on my pre-determined path since if I took one wrong turn, it would result in me having to pull out my map and look like a tourist.

I finally made it to Darling Harbor, exasperated and aching from the walk and carrying around my ten pound Harvey's travel bag for the last twelve or so hours. It was around 6pm which was perfect since the website said the Sydney Aquarium closes at 8pm, and I had pre-bought my ticket on the bus.

The doors to the aquarium were open, and there was a boisterous family of about twelve sitting around a table in the concession area and another approaching the ticketing desk. However, there was no one there to sell or take tickets. Being as impatient and practical-minded as I am, I decided it would be fine if I just slipped through the rotating metal entrance bar since I could just show someone my ticket if they asked me inside.

The place was completely empty! It was amazing! Kind of boring, but still better than pushing through a bunch of people and dodging little kids. Suddenly I saw a worker cleaning one of the tanks and froze, fearing that I'd get in trouble. *By the fish police?*

"Sorry, ma'am!" He said as if he were in *my* way. Now I felt all VIP and badass, like I owned the aquarium or something, and carried on my merry little way through the rest of the exhibits. I passed another aquarium keeper, who just smiled and nodded at me as she continued in the opposite direction until I finally got to the exhibit I wanted to see the most, the sharks.

The exhibit required me to go outside the main area, up a ramp, and into a glass tunnel where a bunch of terrifying sharks were swimming. Since my great white shark-diving excursion had gotten canceled in South Africa, I figured taking safe selfies with these sharks would be the next best thing. Except I may have gotten a little carried away with the selfies.

It suddenly dawned on me that I had been taking shark selfies for about ten minutes and was in a separate part of the aquarium where no one could see or hear me. I started speed walking back to the ramp and may or may not have even started to run a little bit, half expecting to be locked out of the main hall.

The doors were still open. *Obviously, they have to check to make sure no one's still inside.* My anxiety subsided as I followed the remaining "Exit" signs through the rest of the last exhibit.

"*No!*" I literally gasped out loud as the last "Exit" sign pointed to a padlocked metal gate. "*No, no, no!*" I whimpered to the fish, who now all seemed to be jeering at me.

I spotted another Exit sign above two double doors and ran to push them open, begging the universe to let them be an exit. But the blinding white tile hallway behind the doors only led to the "behind the scenes" area of the giant fish tanks for employees only. There was another set of double doors at the opposite end ; I ran over to them and pushed them open, but only to reveal an even shorter hallway and a second pair of double doors that said: "EMERGENCY EXIT ONLY, ALARM WILL SOUND."

'I'll just go back the way I came and leave through the front." I told myself, trying to be reasonable. As I retraced my steps, I turned on my data roaming so that I could Whatsapp the only person I had contact with in Sydney, Sam. After sending about five texts with no responses, I suddenly looked up to discover that I had walked in a circle and was back at the exit doors that led to no open exits.

At this point, I started to panic. Like, stomach-twisting, heart-pounding, lack-of-oxygen-feeling, panic. "HELLO?!" I shouted as I started to run through the dark, empty, extremely eerie aquarium. But again, it somehow led me to another circle. Sam had finally written back, confused by "what I meant by being locked in the aquarium," but I had no time to explain since I was about to have a heart attack and die.

I ran back to the double doors that led to the emergency exit and popped them open. '*Just do it.*' I thought to myself, imagining the entire aquarium erupting with sirens and flashing lights, likely killing all of the fish. It was only about a ten-foot distance between the two doors, so I decided to just go for it. But as I was halfway to the second pair of emergency exit doors, panic struck again as I heard the first set of doors clank shut.

"*Shit!!!*" I huffed, spinning around to confirm the thought that the first set of doors would be locked from the outside. They had no press bar, no handle, nothing. I turned back to the emergency exit and, disregarding its warning sign, went in for the push. "*No, no, no, no, no!*" I said out loud to the empty ten-foot by seven-foot hallway. It didn't open. I thought for sure I was going to have to sleep in the hallway dungeon.

'*Maybe Sam can call someone!*' I suddenly thought, unlocking my phone. No service. I was literally about to start crying. It was my first night in Sydney, with only two nights left, and I was going to have to spend it locked in a hallway with no phone service. *Could be worse ; the plane could have gone missing.*

In one final fit of anger, anguish, and adrenaline, I launched my shoulder into the metal rod-handle of the heavy door and gasped as it flew open and sent me tumbling down onto the hard wet asphalt. I'd never been so happy to be lying on the disgusting floor of an alley in Australia in my life. I almost didn't notice the loud alarm that had immediately started going off as soon as the door opened.

Although I had a perfectly legitimate reason for setting it off, I also didn't want to take my chances with the law, so I got up and started running down the dark alley to the metal stairs that led up to the street. I was immediately back in the bustling blocks of business professionals, locals, and tourists, blending in like nothing had happened aside from my lack of breath and flushed cheeks.

Exasperated and annoyed that no one understood why I was so upset (my mom accused me of getting locked in on purpose), I started walking towards my next intended destination, the Sydney Opera House, for my one glass of wine (because it was all I could afford) at the Sydney Opera Bar.

There was a live band playing inside, but I couldn't pry myself away from the iconic view of the Sydney Harbor Bridge across the bay and the smooth white sails of the Opera House that were jutting out into the dark night sky right in front of me. I got my one glass of Pinot Grigio from the bar and went outside to stand at a table next to a heat lamp.

Since no one was that close to me, I discreetly slipped my tour guide books that I had picked up on the bus out of my bag and started flipping through them for the tenth time. But of course, the second I try to be discreet about anything, someone notices.

"Excuse me? Sorry to bother you, but would you mind taking a photo for us? My friends don't know how to use a camera." The cutest guy in the group finally asked with an Australian accent. I had been watching them in my peripheral vision as they attempted to take a photo in front of the bridge with a regular camera whose flash was way too bright to capture anything in the background.

"Sure, but I think you should use your phone's camera ; otherwise you won't be able to see the bridge ," I smirked, watching all of their eyes widen as they considered my suggestion. It worked, *obviously,* and for that, I was rewarded with my second glass of wine!

The guys were from Tazmania, as in, where the Tazmanian Devil lives, and *yes,* it's a real animal. They were visiting the younger, cute one, who lives in Sydney, and who was overbearingly interested in knowing *everything* about me. So much so that the rest of his "mates" left him to go to the seedy nightlife area in Kings Cross while he stayed behind and blindly committed to doing anything that I wanted to do.

I wasn't in love, but at least I had someone to hang out with. *He,* on the other hand, was very in love. He reminded me of a little puppy...I guess that's why they call it puppy love? Either way, the term is appropriate because I found out he was about as young as a puppy. We went to a local bar in Surry Hills, where everyone stared at me like I was an alien. Tazmania boy later admitted that it was because I was American and Aussies love Americans. Well, some of them anyway.

It took me a while to detach him from my hip, but I finally was able to slip into a taxi and take a painful $30 AUD ride back to Bondi Beach. Basically, I paid a fortune to *not* have to avoid him trying to hook up with me. And it was a glorious solo night indeed.

On the very last day of my extremely long three -week journey around the world, I found myself half pouting, half googly-eyeing the massive waves the surfers were riding at Bondi Beach. I sighed as I took my last attempt at a photo of a message I had written in the sand for a highschool friend whose wedding I was missing in Florida that day, "*Congrats M&B, Sending Love From Sydney – Alyssa.*" I couldn't decide if I felt awesome or like an asshole for solo traveling in Australia while so many of my friends were walking down the aisle. *Awesome.*

The massive weather-proof Prada jacket that Mr. TDH in the volunteer house in South Africa had forced me to take so I wouldn't freeze to death made me move robotically. The 200R ($20) flat boots I had bought because I was so cold there didn't help me move much either. I knew I stuck out like a sore thumb with my dark tan from Thailand, blonde hair, and makeshift *'I-had-no-idea-it-would-be-this-cold* outfit. Which is why I attempted inconspicuously to take my last pictures for the blog before heading back to my short-term apartment rental on O'Brien Street.

Shuffling morosely through the white sand and frowning enough to make a plastic surgeon wince, I made my way across the long stretch of shorefront, mentally saying '*Bye, I love you Bondi*' as I left. I was also thinking, '*Wouldn't it be awesome if I magically met a really hot Australian surfer who swept me off my feet, and then I just stayed?!*' Yes. Women have these thoughts. And don't act like you don't secretly hope to meet someone hot in a foreign country while traveling.

'*Ok, so I can stop by the consignment store on the way back, get souvenirs, grab a bottle of wine, pack, be in bed by 9pm, then get up at 4am for my flight at 7am.*' I rehearsed my responsible plan of action over and over again, trying to decide if I could fit in a pit-stop at Mad Pizza é Bar somewhere in the mix. But I knew it was unlikely.

As I tried to shove my imaginary love story out of my head so that my realistic plans could actually happen, I started to notice something in my peripheral vision. Something that I half didn't want to happen, and half '*holy shit, is this seriously happening?!*'

"Hey! Did you get your shot?" *What. The. Fuck.* He came jogging out of *nowhere*. All six foot five, deeply tanned, salt-hair-tossled, wet-suit clinging, muscular inches of him. I can't even exaggerate that it was literally like a movie. I even looked around briefly, wondering if he was talking to someone else.

"Wh-what?" I mumbled. I looked like shit, I felt like shit, and I was wearing an outfit that someone going camping in Antarctica would wear. "Yeah! I saw you taking pictures! I wanted to see if you got the shot!" He beamed enthusiastically. *WTF.* His freaking pearly white smile was perfect, and so were the deep lines they made in his leathered cheeks.

His green eyes sparkled like the glistening drops of ocean water that were daintily flying off of him in all directions. Speaking of *all of him,* I couldn't help but notice the perfectly defined chest, abs, legs, and *other things* that were protruding out of his very snugly fitting wetsuit. *Not my fault they were at eye level.* But more importantly, I tried to convince myself that there was no way this could be happening in my last few hours left in Sydney. And also, why did nobody warn me that it's highly likely to fall in love multiple times while traveling solo ?

"Oh, um, yeah. I was taking a picture for a friend ; she's getting married in Florida right now." I mumbled. *TMI.* "Cool!" He said, sounding like what I always thought an Australian surfer would sound like. "So, how long are you here for?" He continued.

"This is actually my last day ; I leave in the morning ," I grumbled, hoping the conversation would end and my dreams could just shatter already. "Oh no! Well, do you have any plans for later?" My eyes lit up, and suddenly my Aussie love dream started competing for attention in my mind against my responsibility and safety concerns.

"I was, um, just going to go by a store to get some gifts, then pack ," I admitted, expecting him to be running along soon with his *two* surfboards. But he didn't. "Well, do you want to do something?" He asked hopefully, with a hint of an accent I couldn't quite decipher. "Like what?" I replied, almost too combatively. "What time is it?" He squinted towards the sun before I could even check my phone, "Sunset is at 5:15 ish . Do you want to watch it?"

I blinked at him, trying extremely hard to suppress a laugh. *'Is somebody punking me? Where are the cameras ?'* I thought. There was no way exactly what I had imagined would happen would actually happen. *Is this what manifestation is?*

"Where are you staying? I just need to put these away and change, then I can get you." He said excitedly, nodding at one of the two surfboards he was carrying. The idea of someone being able to pick me up in their own car was strange since I had been used to taking taxis everywhere. It was also slightly worrisome considering that I had no idea who this potential really hot, surfing serial killer may be. "Um, somewhere on O'Brien Street?" I chirped, playing into my *'dumb blond'* appearance.

"Ok, well, do you know where the post office is?" He asked seriously. "Chyeah." I laughed, recalling seeing it but not understanding why it would matter. "Ok, well, can you meet me there in, say, forty -five minutes?" My smirk fell off my face faster than he fell into my life. He didn't ask for my number ; he didn't ask for my Instagram name, he asked me to meet him at a public location at a certain time. *Do I even know how to do that?*

64

Apparently, I didn't. I set my alarm on my phone anyway, and with a sudden rush of adrenaline, excitement, and wanderlust, I raced back into the sleepy surfer town. I needed to pack, I needed to prepare for my thirty-hour journey home, I needed to, *Oh look, there's that really cute consignment store!*

The black crochet shawl I had seen earlier was gone. I searched everywhere for it, but someone must have snagged it when I dashed out earlier that day to catch the bus. I cursed myself for worrying about spending a whole $12 on it earlier. Instead, I settled on a cluster of bangles that I could give to each of my friends and a snapback that said "Sydney Surf Camp" for $2.

Shit! A surge of panic swept over me as I realized I had spent twenty out of my forty -five minutes sifting through hand-me-downs. I dashed out of the quaint shop and past a plethora of adorable cafés before nearing my apartment. I had planned on packing a bit, knowing that now the time to do so was in the running for time to sleep, but by the time I got there, I was already down to fifteen minutes before "meeting time." Shaking my head at the number of people who flake when they actually have phones that work, I quickly freshened up, layered on two more sweaters, and ran out the door.

Out of breath, cheeks flushed, and slightly embarrassed, I stood out in front of the small, historic post office. My Skeletor knees trembled against each other as I squinted my watering eyes around to try to find this mysterious surfer man. '*I'm too late, dammit ; why did I go to the shop first!*' I thought, assuming I had taken too long, '*Whatever, I should just go back ; I need to pack anyway.*'

"Heelllooo!" As I was turning to leave, I heard that same exotic accent from the beach behind me. He was hanging out the window of his jeep wearing a comfortable yet trendy looking hoodie, with his surfboards sticking out the back. I waved back awkwardly and shuffled into the right-side passenger door. I wish I could have greeted him with something more charming than, "Where are we going ?" but I'm not going to lie, I've seen plenty of movies where the hot, sweet, foreign guy ends up being a secret fetish freak or

65

murderer. Not that I'd mind some 50 Shades of Grey action with him.

His response started with a giggle and glorious showcase of that perfect smile. Then he explained that there's a hill above Bondi Beach where the locals go to hang out for sunset. I wasn't entirely comfortable with the thought of driving outside of the little town with a random guy I just met, but your brain does strange things when you're traveling solo, I guess. That or I was just completely hypnotized by this man that I seemed to have manifested out of thin-freezing-air.

On the way up to the lookout point, I learned that he was Bondi's top surfing instructor (according to him) who owned the surf school right across the street from the famous beach. Oh, and that he was originally from Tahiti, which explained his accent and overall exoticness. I immediately wondered if he had any of those sexy Polynesian tattoos like The Rock has but decided it would be best to just go ahead and force that image out of my head. Just in case my manifestation skills were real. I mean, I wouldn't be mad about seeing him naked, but was I really ready for another foreign fling already? *Crap. Image of him naked officially stuck in my head.*

When we got there, he grabbed a dorky-looking cooler from the back seat and motioned for me to wait. "Don't get your shoes wet." He said seriously, easily scooping me up with one arm and taking one massive step over a puddle that I would have probably had to swim through. *Swoon.*

We sat on the only bench in the park as the blazing orange sun began to drift slowly over the perfectly defined cityscape of downtown Sydney, The Opera House, and the Sydney Harbor Bridge. As if he could read my mind, he unzipped the mini-cooler and extracted two bottles of strange -looking beer. "They're from Tahiti," he laughed when he saw me trying to read the label, "They have a little bit of tequila and lime in them." *Please, be more perfect.*

"Do you want me to take a picture for you?" He read from my mind again. I was thinking of taking a picture with my selfie stick but was also thinking of how touristy it would make me look. "I never see a girl using one of those action cameras ; it's really cool that you have one." He admitted, giving me the confidence boost to bust that baby out. *If only he knew I had spent the last of my savings to buy the latest model...from a pawn shop.*

He took sneaky good pictures of me jumping around in front of the sunset and one as I sadly watched my first and last sunset over Sydney. *Or so I thought, I wouldn't have believed it if you told me I'd be back two more times for collabs, one of which involved scuba diving the Great Barrier Reef.*

I didn't want the evening to end, but it wasn't like I could just ask this random hot guy to drop everything to hang out with me. In my perfect fantasy world, he'd ask me out on a date, we'd drink too much wine, then savagely have sex after.

"Do you want to go to dinner?" He asked. *WTF ?* Was I thinking out loud? It was literally the fifth time he had read my mind! "Sure!" I smiled so big that I must have looked like that one smiley emoji that you sometimes send to emphasize sarcasm. I couldn't believe my luck, my very last night in Sydney and the hottest surfer in the world took me to watch a sunset then asked me to dinner.-But I couldn't decide if it was good luck or bad luck.

Dinner made me feel like I was in some strange alternate LA universe. Not only does the main strip in Bondi Beach resemble Santa Monica Boulevard in West Hollywood, but the place he picked for dinner was called "Bondi Hardware," and was strangely similar to the "Laurel Hardware" we have in WeHo. The concept for both is taking an old hardware store and converting it into a trendy restaurant, keeping relics and architecture from the original store to add to the rustic chic atmosphere.

There was lots of wine, just like I manifested, and food, and talking, and coincidentally, our waitress was an aspiring actress working to save up for a flight to LA. *Shit!* That reminded me, I really needed to pack for *my* flight to LA!

"We should probably go soon ; I need to figure out how to get a cab to take me to the airport at 4am." I grumbled, dreading the task and early wake up call. At that point, I'd be able to sleep for a whole two hours. *#worthit.*

"I can take you." He said casually. I stopped wrestling with my five layers of jackets and blinked up at him, trying to decide if he had really said what I thought he said or if it was another one of my preposterous manifestations screaming inside my head. "What?" I asked, a little too accusingly.

"Yeah, I get up that early anyway to go surfing ; I can take you to the airport first if you want." I was so confused. Didn't he have a girlfriend? Why was he being so nice? Well, I obviously was thinking what you're probably thinking, but this guy literally looked like he should be dating a Victoria's Secret model, not a frazzled little girl from LA.

"Are, are you sure?" I stuttered, unable to believe my luck. Normally I would have insisted he didn't have to, but I was literally down to $30 AUD and not entirely sure it would be enough to get me to the airport. "Yeeaahhh, no worries at all!" He said, sounding like a total Aussie surfer.

As we walked up the street to my apartment, he used one of his massive arms to warm my shaking body. One of his hands covered my entire right shoulder while my other shoulder pressed into his rib cage. He must have been at least three times my size. He, of course, walked me to my door like a gentleman and began reiterating his plan to go home and then come back to get me at 4am as I opened the door to reveal my extremely unpacked luggage.

"Oh, no," He gasped. "What? What's wrong?" I jumped back, expecting to see a spider or a shark or something. Or maybe my extreme mess scared him, and he no longer wanted to take me to the airport? "I'm helping you pack." He said sternly, glaring at me as if I was in trouble for not having packed yet.

"No, no, it's really Ok, I've had to pack like fifty times already," I pleaded, but he wasn't having it. "You work on pouring that wine," he waved his massive hand in my face, then motioned to the cheap bottle of wine on the counter that I had picked up earlier, "I'll start organizing." He said, picking up one of my sweaters and examining its small size.

I yanked it out of his hands ; there was no way I wanted the hottest guy in Sydney touching my dirty laundry from Africa, Thailand, and Australia. "YOU pour, and sit there for moral support ; I'll organize," I instructed him, attempting to shove him towards the kitchenette.

He did as he was told, and I took the spare seconds to hide any panties or bras that were lying around. "Cheers." He said sweetly, handing me my very full glass of Chardonnay. "Cheers," I mumbled back, locking eyes with him as we sipped, "it was nice meeting you." His gorgeous smile melted off his face as I said it. Really ? Did I have to be that dramatic ?

"You can always stay longer ; you can stay with me!" He chimed, completely completing my completely irrational daydream earlier at the beach. I chuckled and shook my head, "I'd love to, but I think it's time for me to get back to LA." *And also because I'm now officially broke.*

He hugged me in that same meaningful yet depressing way that Mr. TDH had when I left South Africa. He let go and sat down on the dark blue velvet couch, carefully holding the glass of wine with a few fingers. He didn't take his eyes off me as I scrambled around, attempting to organize the clusterfuck of clothing, gadgets, and souvenirs on the floor. Admittedly, it was probably highly amusing to watch. Once I got to the point of actually cramming clothes into my suitcase, he couldn't just sit and watch any longer and got up to help. The travel space bags that took me both hands and knees to roll the air out of to compress my clothes took him one hand and about two seconds.

The entire time I was wondering the obvious questions like if he was going to kiss me, if he was intending on staying until 4am, what he looked like without his shirt on, if he had that Polnesian thigh tattoo, and so on. Then he finally stood up around 2:30am. "I'm going to run home to shower and get my stuff for tomorrow ; you should try to get some sleep." He said, stretching his arms back so I could just barely see the distinct tan line on his pelvic region. *Ugh.*

"Oh, OK." I stammered, not hiding my sad disappointment at all. *Way to sound desperate Alyssa, good job.* I might as well have said *'Please stay!'* and he could totally tell. He wrapped me in the romantic embrace again, except this time, he leaned back to look down at me, then suddenly swooped me up into the token pose from *The Notebook*, just like Mr. TDH had done, except this guy was half a foot taller. For the first time, I was eye level with his smoldering hazel green eyes, but only briefly before he closed them and leaned in for the kiss. *Insert fire emojis.*

Before my brain could even register what was happening, we were both naked, and his bronzed, chiseled body was positioned over me. Half of me was panicking; I was *not* the type of girl to have a one night stand with an insanely hot and nice surfer from Tahiti that I met on the beach in Australia. And the other half was like; *BITCH BE THAT GIRL! One day you'll write a book about this shit!* And here we are.

He was gentle and considerate, likely because he was fully aware that he was huge and I was small. It was the kind of sex you literally can only imagine reading about in a steamy romance novel or seeing on a telenovela, and once again, I questioned if my life was actually a movie. There couldn't have been a better ending to my trip if I tried.

By the time he left, it was 3:30am. I did my best to casually get him to stay, but he insisted that if he did, I would never pack, and likely miss my flight. He was right. I didn't even start packing until 30 minutes after he left.

As promised, he came back to get me at 4:30am on the dot, and we set off for the Sydney airport in the cold, dreary morning weather. We didn't talk much, and I wasn't sure if it was because there was no point or because we both probably didn't sleep. When we finally approached the airport, it felt like a curtain closing on a theatrical Broadway show.

"Do you want me to wait? Just in case?" He asked as he lifted my carry-on suitcase out of his trunk. "No, it's Ok." I said glumly, "Actually, maybe you should since I don't have any credit cards." I joked, even though I was half-serious. He hugged me again and kissed the top of my head. "Can you come back soon?" He asked seriously. *'Do you have a spare $2k to get me back soon?'* I thought but held my overly sarcastic tongue.

"I wish. Come to LA ; we have waves there!" I said slyly, knowing that probably wasn't a possibility either. He hugged me again and leaned down to kiss me goodbye. "It was nice meeting you ; keep in touch." He said softly. "It was nice meeting you too," I mumbled, "Go on Facebook chat, so I don't get bored on the plane ," I added, trying to conceal my sappy emotions. As in, I was super sad to be forced to leave the hottest, sweetest man I had ever slept with in my life.

After a few more hugs and kisses, I finally pried myself away and set off for the final chapter of what I had no clue would actually be the first chapter of many journeys around the world.

Chapter Four

Transition to Travel Blogger

By the time I landed at LAX, I had at least six blog post drafts written. Somewhere between my fourth and fifth glass of wine, soaring high above the Pacific Ocean, I had made it official. I was going to stop writing about Hollywood and become a full-time Travel Blogger. How exactly I was going to do that, I didn't fully know, but I figured I could use what I've learned through my freelance writing and publicity jobs to make it work.

When I finally reached our shabby-yet-expensive apartment in WeHo, and after excitedly blabbering about the entire month of escapades to my roommate with more animation than a cartoon, I retreated to my mundane second-hand-decorated room, where the familiarity of it made me immediately miss traveling. Before even thinking about unpacking my carry-on, I grabbed a permanent marker from my make-shift dresser and made a stride for my paper map. Carefully, as if preserving the memories from each place, I drew a line from L.A. to Dubai, Cape Town, Bangkok, Ao Nang, then finally, Sydney. I looked at it with contentment and whispered to myself, "*You just went one full revolution around the world!*"

For the next several months, I took on as many freelance jobs as I could in hopes of saving up again in order to go travel. I specifically attempted to get travel writing gigs, but they were scarce and highly competitive, as you can probably imagine. It didn't take me long to realize that getting paid to write about travel was probably a lot of people's dreams. But I was one of those people, and I was determined as all hell.

So I took the boring content writing jobs that would pay, I gratefully continued working part-time as a virtual Junior Publicist, but I had a new job role as well. One that I was the boss of travel blogger. *Even though it didn't pay yet. And there's no way you could have ever convinced me I'd be making six figures doing it in the future.*

I took my experiences and knowledge from that month in three countries and wrote probably twenty blog posts about it. I wrote about travel tips and catchy articles on how to date a girl that travels. Using what I learned from being a publicist, I applied it to myself and figured out how to pitch guest posts to big media outlets, where I'd link my blog to the posts for more traffic and recognition. I even reached out to the few travel bloggers that were already established, asking for advice, but to no avail. That was my first taste of how competitive the travel blogging industry was, and that was before it even became insanely popular.

But I kept trying regardless of the rejection. Not only did my blog traffic start to pick up with the addition of the travel articles, but my social media followings did too. I had started posting regularly on Instagram, using the hundreds of photos I took during my trip. I had purposely made it a point to only post the ones I took with my selfie stick of the back of my head, never of my face or body, so that people would pay attention to where I was, not what I looked like. And also, so they couldn't say that I get to travel or am successful because of the way I look. Since no one but my computer and phone screen see how much work it actually all takes.

Interestingly, I started getting more requests to cover events in LA as well and realized that's what comes with an increased audience. I wondered how big I would need to be before I would achieve my dream of getting sent on a trip for free in order to write about it. At that time, I didn't care about making money from it. I just cared about getting there.

January 1st, 2015, came faster than...I was going to make an inappropriate joke, but nevermind. It had been four months since my around-the-world trip, and I was dying to go somewhere, *anywhere*. I was back in my hometown in Florida for the holidays, hanging out at one of my favorite waterside restaurants called Bradley's in West Palm Beach. Surrounding me was what I guess you would call the local celebrities; a mixture of Palm Beach Island's trust fund babies and the common folk from the city area on the other side of the bridge that connects to the island, who either manage or own a restaurant or bar or have just been deemed cool for one reason or another and accepted into the circle. I fit into the latter category.

I'm not entirely sure what I was talking about or what they were talking about, but my ears zeroed in when I heard, "Yeah, I gotta go do a drop off in the Bahamas tomorrow." and I immediately interrupted b*ecause I'm not rude or anything.*

"You're going to the Bahamas again? What exactly do you do there anyway?" I asked the early-40's, still-beach-bum-yet-also-pilot. I couldn't help but assume he was a drug runner. I mean, why else would you fly back and forth to the Bahamas by yourself almost every week?

"I bring boat parts, construction supplies, fishing bait, anything people who live over there want from the U.S. that they can't get there or get for cheaper here." He explained with an amused smile.

"Like drugs?" I couldn't help but ask.

"That's what everyone thinks, but nope. Tell you what, why don't you come with me? You can write about it on that blog of yours." He smiled smugly, and I couldn't tell if he was joking. I also couldn't tell if he was making fun of my blog or not.

"Really ? I'm down!" I blurted a little too loudly. The group of mostly men had tuned into our conversation at that point, and some were asking if they should take their planes over as well. *Because people in Palm Beach just have their own planes and all.*

Turns out that, to my surprise, I was going to be the co-pilot. The plan was to pick up and drop off both supplies and people to and from seven different islands. Don't worry, by "supplies," I mean parts for boats that aren't available in the Bahamas or American snacks that aren't sold there either. The people he was to pick up are friends of his who pay him a couple of hundred bucks to transfer them as opposed to booking a private jet.

I'm not going to lie, being a co-pilot when you are one-thousand percent *not* a co-pilot, is slightly terrifying, especially when your pilot is an adrenaline junky who flies a plane in flip flops and sees a water funnel reaching down from a storm cloud and immediately reacts with, "Ooh! Let's get a closer look!"

I almost kissed the ground each time we landed. While he was doing his deliveries, I roamed around and used my selfie stick and action camera to get photos on each of the islands, plus of course, a ton of me in the "co-pilot" seat. It was enough content to write two blog posts and have about two weeks' worth of social media posts, but holy shit, was it exhausting. And slightly terrifying.

We got back just in time for my twenty-seventh birthday, which made me feel older than ever. I was fast approaching my late twenties, still single, and still trying to make my dream job happen. After a quick celebration with family and friends in West Palm, I flew back to Los Angeles to get back on track with work. Well. And to have my annual Black Tie mansion soiree birthday party that half of West Hollywood always attended. This year was the best one yet because most of my guests had started asking me about my worldly travels rather than which Hollywood events I had gone to over the holidays.

I wasn't even in LA for a week when one door shut and another opened. My amazing publicist boss notified me that we had lost a few clients over the holidays, and he could no longer afford to pay me. I was gutted, especially since that gig was how I was able to pay rent, but I tried to think of it as having more time to work on my blog. *Little did I know that he would be the last real boss I ever had.*

A few emails after his unfortunate news was the door that opened. A gig I had applied to a few weeks ago had finally gotten back to me. And not just any gig. A travel writing gig. It was for a travel-fashion magazine, and it was run by a fabulous, indulgent Haitian man in Miami. He said he liked the writing samples I sent him and wanted to pay me a whopping $200 to write an article about Cinque Terre in Italy! I nearly screamed when I read it. Granted, I had never been to Cinque Terre (yet), but I had also never gotten paid more than $30 for an article. *This is it!* I thought, *I'm going to be a travel writer!*

After doing extensive research, I wrote a tantalizing tale of the colorful Italian Riviera town. It was so imaginative that a few times, I was actually convinced I had really gone there. The editor in chief told me three times to make it "sexier," which I was slightly uncomfortable with, but I did my best to apply the steamy escapades I had in Cape Town and Sydney to a fabled story of a girl in Italy. He loved the final product, and finally, I was published for the first time, with my actual name on the byline, as a travel writer.

In fact, he loved it so much that he called me a few weeks later with another potential project.

"You're Cuban, right? Have you been to Cuba?" He asked in his smooth Caribbean accent.

"My family is from there, but I haven't been unfortunately ," I replied glumly, remembering seeing the high costs of tour packages required to go there as a tourist.

"I want to do the next destination feature there. Obama just lifted the embargo, and I want to get there before everyone else in the U.S. does, but I'm not sure about the visa." He said excitedly. My heart sank ; I would absolutely cry if I had to write about Cuba without getting to go there.

"Well, I know if you go there with a tour, you can get a visa that way, but you have to stick to their agenda ," I informed him morosely.

"No, no, that won't work. I want to do a casting call for local models, and do a photoshoot in one of the old mansions, and make a video of the whole process." *And I thought I had big dreams*.

I had started Googling information about Cuban visas while he was taking -- an ADHD multitasking trait I tend to do whenever someone requires me to be on the phone. I scrolled through some do-able options and read them off to him, "Support for the Cuban People, Volunteer Work, Cultural Events, and Family Visits can all qualify for a visa for a US citizen."

There was silence on the other end of the phone, and I assumed he was thinking of how to make Support for the Cuban People count if he'd be hiring them as fashion models.

"You said your family is from there, right? Do you still have family that lives there?" He said finally. My heart rate started to speed up. I'd been longing to go to Cuba since my grandmother passed away a few years ago, and I had found a secret journal she had written about her life growing up there. If he was about to ask me to go, I would be able to see where my grandparents were from, not to mention meet her last remaining sister! *Calm down! Don't get your hopes up!* I hissed at myself. *He's probably just going to ask you to ask them how to set up a photoshoot and get a sketchy visa...not that they'd know since they're over eighty.*

"Y-yes. My grandma's sister and cousins live there." I replied carefully.

"I wonder if you got a family visit visa if we could somehow say I'm your husband and my partner is my brother or something." He replied casually as if that was his plan all along.

I couldn't believe it. He was not only giving me a second travel writing assignment but potentially offering to bring me to the actual destination! Even if it was just because he needed me to get him and his partner there.

"I can contact a lady who helped my mom get a visa and find out! Does that mean I'd get to go too?! I'm dying to go ; I would be so happy! I would write the article for free, of course, and I can even write another one about my grandma's journal I fou..." He cut me off abruptly as if he got what he needed in the first sentence.

"Fabulous! Yes, if you can get in touch with your contact and see if it's possible, and also how much it would be for three visas, three flights, and two rooms for two weeks, that would be great. If it's within our budget, we'll make it happen!"

When we hung up the phone, I screamed. So loud, in fact, that both of my roommates came running into my room.

"What? What's wrong?" David demanded with wide worried eyes. That was strange since I always assumed he hated me.

"Are you Ok, girl?" Amanda said with more amusement than concern.

I was jumping up and down on my bed yelling, "YES! YES! YES!" then flopped down on my ass and announced, "I got my first travel writing TRIP! To CUBA!"

David rolled his eyes and turned to go back into his man-cave, muttering, "Oh my god, I thought you were getting attacked by one of the weird guys you date." Again, I was still flattered by his somewhat concern that I knew stemmed from extremely prolonged sexual tension. Afterall, we had drunkenly made out once before we became roommates, and when he accepted Amanda's offer to be our third roomie, we had both just stared at each other, knowing it was going to be either a really good or really bad idea. So far, our interactions consisted mostly of him eyeing me with his icy blue eyes and a raised eyebrow whenever he'd come and go out of the kitchen area where I worked on my laptop or him making a weird cricket noise when he was coming out of his room which was supposed to alert us in case we were naked or something. He "hated" when he'd accidentally walk out and I'd be standing in the bathroom in a towel, and a few times even fell back into his room and slammed the door shut. *A few years later, he would admit all of this to me before finally grabbing a hold of me and kissing me hard like I was about to board a plane to a faraway country and never come back to LA again...which I was.*

"That's amazing, sweetie!" Amanda chimed with a big genuine smile as she leaned on my door frame. "When are you going?" That was a great question. I had forgotten to ask and suddenly feared it would be in a year from now or something.

"I don't know actually. But the editor-in-chief and his boyfriend need me to get a family visit visa so they can go without a tour, so they're bringing me! Can you believe it ? It finally happened!" I got back up and started jumping up and down on the bouncy old mattress again. *"Stop jumping! It sounds like you're having sex!"* David yelled from his room. *Ew. Does that mean he knows when I'm having sex?*

"I know! That's great! I see you working all day on the computer out there, and it's finally paying off!" She beamed. I was touched. I always figured she didn't really know or care about what I was doing on my laptop for twelve hours a day, just as long as I paid the $900 rent each month. Amanda was like a big sister to me.

When I finally got my own place in LA, she was my first roommate, and we had moved into our current place and added a third roommate, AKA David, since then. She had started as a bartender at the trendy Pink Taco restaurant in Century City, but after deciding it was way too much drama (it was made into a reality show afterall), she decided to change her pace. She got connected with a job at an Italian restaurant a few blocks away that Robert De Niro was an investor in, called Ago. The rest of our friends and I went there multiple times a week to see her, and she'd give us bottomless glasses of wine if we ordered something to eat off the bar menu. Needless to say, I ate $6 Margherita pizza and had unlimited wine for dinner almost every night.

"Well, come celebrate at Ago later, bring the crew!" She said with a laugh at my monkey-like behavior before turning to go back to her recliner to watch the next episode of Lost.

Chapter Five

Discovering My Roots in Cuba

I spent the next few days communicating back and forth with a woman who works at a travel agency in Miami that one of my cousins referred me to. It was my top priority to get this trip planned ASAP, not only because I wanted to go so bad but also because they wanted to go in less than two months.

After dropping the name of the magazine, and my hyped-up blog, suggesting we could offer her company some publicity, she was eager to help us out. It was apparently totally possible for me to get a family visit visa and for them to come as my immediate family members. The only problem we started running into though, was that literally everyone in Cuba was after our money. As soon as my contact mentioned that we would be taking professional photos and videos to her contacts in Cuba, there was suddenly a ton of permits and people we needed to pay.

My budget from The Editor for our flights, visas, two-week stay at a casa particular, which is like a bed and breakfast or homestay, and estimate for food was just within the budget of

$800 per person. Still, the addition of not only the various permits but now a photographer and videographer duo caused a severe increase. Throughout the entire process, I was expecting The Editor to say, "Sorry, we can't afford to have you come anymore." But I kept reminding myself that they needed me for the visas. Well, and to write the article. I should probably give myself more credit for that one.

Finally, after what felt like an eternity, our departure date of April 1st, 2015 came. I was so nervous, yet so insanely excited. I had held off on making any announcements about my trip on my blog or social media until I actually stepped foot in Cuba. In case, you know, they didn't let us in or something.

We got our visas cleared at Miami International Airport with ease, and after a short flight later, we landed in Havana!

My nerves didn't stop freaking out the entire time we were in the small Havana airport. The customs officer had asked me multiple questions about what I was doing there and where my family lived, yet ironically didn't even give the slightest thought to The Editor and his partner. I assumed because they were tanner and looked more Cuban than I did. But then also felt like that would make someone get questioned more since it's not exactly easy for Cubans to fly in and out of the country.

I waited quietly at the baggage belt, where I noticed that a ton of people had brought brand new flat -screen TVs and bedding sets over from the U.S. It quickly clicked in my head why that was; with the new relaxed restrictions for U.S. tourists, Cuban-Americans could now come back to Cuba to see family who got trapped there or who they had to leave when Castro and Che Guevara took over. I remembered hearing from my cousin, who was one of the people who left when the Regime took over, that with communism, everyone is forced to be equal. So, not only does everyone get paid the same regardless of their job or education, but everyone is appointed to a place to live depending on family size and I'm pretty sure, class. That being said, there is some loophole where if you run a business out of your home or use your own car, you can keep that money.

So, the Cuban people got smart and started creating Casa Particulars and Paladares (little restaurants) inside their homes. Obviously, with the severe lack of imports to Cuba (hence the cars all being from the 50's when the embargo was placed), it's hard to furnish a room or restaurant for guests. So, when the restrictions on entry from the U.S. was lifted thanks to Obama, the Cuban-Americans started bringing things over to make rooms in their family's homes hospitable, thus helping them earn more money.

Anyway, big money-hungry apps like Airbnb didn't exist in Cuba yet, so I found our homestay through my travel agent contact. Supposedly she had informed the hosts of our arrival time and had also arranged a personal driver in a sexy black 1950's Rambler to take us there and everywhere else for the two weeks. I felt like a movie star getting into the car, especially since The Editor had insisted I sit up front since *"I looked better in the front seat than he would"*. I'm not going to lie, I had purposely dressed the part with my top knot, over-sized black Chanel glasses from my personal assistant days, and a long slim-fitting aqua dress. What's more important though is that I *felt* like a movie star. Starring in my very own travel movie.

Our driver was an enthusiastic middle-aged man named Panfilo who told me in Spanish that his real job is a pharmacist, and he drives tourists in his car as a side job. *Yep. That's Communism for ya.* He also informed me that he doesn't speak a word of English, like most people in Cuba. For the first time ever, I consciously appreciated my grandpa secretly teaching me Spanish when I was a baby. My parents never spoke it to us in Spanish and I always believed it was because my now-estranged father had some weird ego complex where he thought everyone thought of Cuban- Americans as poor immigrants who had to swim over to the U.S., so he tried to make us as "white" as possible. He even moved us away from the rest of our families in Miami to the least-diverse possible towns, including the one we ended up growing up in, where I met plenty of good people and friends but also experienced a lot of racists. Especially when it came to our last name and my two adopted siblings.

Anyway, for the first time in my life, I actually legitimately needed to use my rusty but understandable Spanish , and I absolutely loved it.

My first reactions after the general excitement of actually being there were shock and bewilderment. They came from viewing the multiple billboards of straight -up communist propaganda. I had such a strange and uncomfortable feeling seeing billboards praising Fidel Castro when my whole life I heard nothing but what a horrible person he was from my family members. Did people here really think he was their savior, or was this one of those situations where if you disagree, they put you in jail? I had to assume that the people who were poor or homeless before he took over were definitely a fan of him.

They're the only ones who would truly benefit from the sudden now-everyone-is-equal-idea. For the well-off and wealthy people, especially the ones with big houses, businesses, and assets though, getting everything taken away from you and replaced with the same appliances, pay and housing as the lower-middle -class probably doesn't sit well. Hence why so many Cuban people fled to the U.S. when Fidel took over, including my grandma with my five -year -old mom and her sister.

It took an hour to reach the area called Vedado where our casa particular was. Vedado is just west of the main tourist area called Havana Vieja (or "Old Havana ") and one of the most fascinating neighborhoods I encountered. That was because Vedado used to be a very wealthy neighborhood, and likely where the drug lords, gangsters, gamblers, and other rich - corrupt people from the U.S. used to have mansions. You see, before Fidel took over, and a big reason why he did, was because Havana used to be considered the "Las Vegas of the Caribbean." High rollers, and even powerful political figures, used to take trips there to gamble, get legal prostitutes, do drugs, party, and of course, buy cheap property in a glorious tropical destination. This didn't fly with Fidel, though. And so with the help of crazy guerilla leader Che Guevara, they shut that shit down, abolishing drugs, sex workers (both punishable by jail time now), and the ability to own property in Cuba. The mansions were straight -up taken away from their owners, who had to flee back to the U.S. since the border got shut down as well, and they were turned into multi-family homes under Fidel's new "everyone is equal rule."

What happens when everyone makes the same mediocre salary, and you're designated to live in a mansion that was meant for daily upkeep? It deteriorates. So right now, all of the once glorious, Gatsby-esque mansions in Vedado are broken down and crumbling because the people living in them can't even afford the upkeep, and the government does nothing about it. The same situation exists in Havana Media and Havana Vieja. Except it's much worse because those people live in cramped, crumbling buildings.

It took us several circles around the blocks of crumbling mansions to find where our casa particular was. I secretly hoped it was going to be inside one of the stunning pieces of failed architecture, but lost hope when we turned on a block that basically looked like my grandparent's neighborhood in Hialeah, Florida.

"Ello? Ello? Oye! Estamos aquí en la dirección que nos dio, pero no hay números, ¿por qué no pondría números? Estas loca? ¡Ven afuera!" Panfilo talked loudly into the first-edition-Nokia -looking phone, and I could hear a woman talking equally as loud on the other end. He shook his head, muttering to himself in Spanish about how ridiculous it is to give guests your address but to not have the house number up to find it. A minute later, an older Cuban couple emerged from the pin-pad -locked gate.

"Ah que bueno! Bienvenido! Que tal?" The woman purred, both of them talking so fast in Cuban-Spanish that I could barely understand it. She gave me a hug and a kiss on the cheek, just like my relatives in Miami would have, and tried to take my carry -on bag for me. I insisted against it, but she kept trying and kept saying something about the stairs.

"Mira, esta es para aqui," she said to us carefully, holding up an old school gold key that looks like what you'd see in an old movie, indicating that that key was for the first door. She

84

then continued to explain in Spanish that there's only one key, so we can't take it with us, and instead, we have to push the doorbell to their floor, look up, and wait for someone to drop it out of the window above us. Then we had to unlock the front door, go up the stairs, and use the other key to open the front door to their floor and put the key back by the window. *Fascinating*.

As I huffed and puffed up the four flights of stairs with my bag, she continued to explain that this used to be one house! Can you imagine? A four -story house in Cuba? Then as I was expecting, she went on to explain how when the Revolución happened, the government came in and made each floor a separate apartment so that four families could live there instead of one. I couldn't tell if she was happy about that or not , but when she showed me to my room, which had a similar bedspread and flatscreen TV to the ones I saw people bringing in from the airport, I assumed it was the latter.

Once I settled in and got over the fact that she had laughed hysterically when I asked for the Wi-Fi password, I quickly changed into a floral jumper and headed to the shared living room. The Editor and his partner were already sitting in there discussing something.

"Ah, there you are cariña. We were discussing where to eat . Do you know of somewhere?" I wasn't sure when we started using endearing Spanish nicknames, but I took it as a sign that I was doing good so far. However, obviously I didn't know where to eat as I mentioned, I had never been to Cuba before, but I was determined to be as helpful as possible to earn my keep.

"One second ," I said, quickly spinning out of the classic old Cuban living room to find the vieja (another term of endearment that means "old lady") to ask about food. Again, she spoke so fast that I could hardly understand her, and it must have shown on my face because she said "Esperate" and left the kitchen to get a piece of paper and pen. She drew several lines and little squares on either side of them. It took a second, but I realized she was making me a map.

"Camine hacia la derecha, luego gire a la izquierda y camine dos cuadras. Entonces gire a la derecha y en la quinta casa a la izquierda, hay un paladares." She said slowly. I would have understood her telling me to walk right, then left two blocks, then left again to find a paladare if she had said it that slow in the first place, but I appreciated her map -making efforts anyway.

Following her directions, we found the most massive, gaudy former mansion we had seen yet. It took up two plots of land and had two curving staircases that led up to the front double doors. I made a mental note to Google what it looked like pre-Communism, and before a massive tarp covered its front lawn and served cheap, bland Cuban food out of a makeshift kitchen. We walked past the large empty pool in front that I assumed used to be a grand water fountain and took a seat at one of the many folding tables and plastic chairs. We were all starving and excited for some authentic Cuban food, but I quickly realized it probably wasn't going to be like what we're used to in Miami. Afterall, with barely any imports coming into Cuba aside from the big hotels and restaurants or for the places with family connections in the U.S., that means there's a lack of basic things you probably wouldn't even think of, like salt and spices.

The only thing I could find on the menu that I could eat was black beans and rice, which was slightly disappointing since I was envisioning camarones or at least fish since we were on an island, but I was so hungry that I didn't even care. I assumed we'd be going to better places during the rest of the trip anyway, judging by the editor's desire for all things chic.

But damn was I wrong. It turned out that since they had to pay so much extra for "required permits", and the posh demands of the French videographer, they had hardly any money left for anything else. That meant that they insisted on eating at that same paladare for lunch and dinner for the next three days since it only cost them a couple of dollars per person. This obviously sucked the most for me since the majority of the menu was meat, and I was heavily advised not to eat salads there due to the possibility of water contamination. But I didn't complain, especially knowing that there are a lot of people who only get rice and beans to eat in general. Well, maybe not in Cuba though, since their ration cards are all equal, and that includes at least some sort of meat portion.

Eating the same dish of black beans and rice every day wasn't even the worst part though. Oh no. Not at all. The worst part was that we saw absolutely zero of Cuba in the three days we had been there so far. It dawned on me that either they were solely interested in looking at the models and doing the photoshoots, or they didn't want to spend money doing anything else.

I woke up early on our fourth morning with a plan. I rehearsed it over and over again in my head to make sure I sounded confident, grateful, and not completely pissed that I was in one of my bucketlist destinations and not allowed to even experience it. I put on my same black and floral jumper that ties around my neck and is probably the most modest thing I brought since it covered my legs with loose pants. I tied my hair in the same topknot I always did, which I assumed made me look more professional, and quickly brushed on some mascara and lipgloss.

Quietly opening the heavy door of my room and sliding out into the hallway, I found myself face to face with The Editor who was just coming out of his room next door to mine.

"Cariña, you are so pretty ; why do you never let your hair down?" He said with an exaggerated pout as he squeezed the bun on top of my head with two fingers.

"Because I'm a writer, not a model, so I don't need to be the one looking pretty!" I said proudly, trying not to let my inner feminist bubble up and explode.

"Speaking of which, I wanted to ask if it would be Ok if I went and explored a little bit today. I can't write a good article about Havana if I'm stuck inside a house watching models audition all day." I added honestly, hoping it didn't come off as ungrateful. He raised an eyebrow and looked at me as if it were blasphemous that I *didn't* want to watch the models audition all day.

"Where do you want to go? Maybe we can all go somewhere after the auditions today..." He said, clearly missing my point.

"It's wasteful for you to have me here if I'm just going to sit there all day and do nothing. I could just go to the main tourist area, Havana Vieja. I'll take the double -decker tourist bus that goes around." I had it all planned out. I'd been thinking about it since I first saw the bus go by. I would pay for a day pass, walk to the pickup point at the Presidente Hotel a few blocks away, use it to get a ride into town, and then just come back later.

"Cariña, you cannot go by yourself!" He said with a fatherly tone.

"I travel solo all the time! It's my job, remember?" I had used my articles from traveling mostly-solo on my around the world trip to initially pitch him for the job and hoped he maybe remembered reading them , but in case he didn't, I added, "I went to *Africa* by myself. If I was fine there, I'm sure I'll be fine on a tropical island." It was technically true ; I did fly there by myself.

"Ok." He said finally, "If you are sure you're Ok by yourself, and you promise to take that tourist bus and be back before it gets dark, you can go." I was so happy that I hugged him and then nearly fell trying to get back into my room to pack a day bag. I was free. I was solo. And I was going bask in the glory of every moment of it.

First on the agenda was getting to the Presidente hotel to use the Wi-Fi. I hadn't checked in with my mom, freelance clients, or social media in almost four days, and I was suddenly worried someone may have suspected I died.

It wasn't so easy getting online, though. Data and Wi-Fi are so scarce and expensive in Cuba that there are actual rules and time limits for using them. At the Presidente Hotel, the rule was that you had to order a minimum of 5 CUCs (Cuban tourist currency which equals about the same as the US dollar) at the poolside bar, and you could only use one hour of internet per day. The bar menu again was all meat options, so I asked for a "Cuban sandwich with no meat," which they thought was hilarious, and since that was only 2 CUCs, I spent the rest on a Cuba Libre, also known as a "rum and coke." I always found the name of that drink ironically hilarious and also irritating since Cuba definitely is *not* libre ("free").

Following the instructions for logging onto the internet and entering the code I was given by the bartender was confusing as all hell, but when I finally got on, my laptop exploded with various pinging noises. All my texts were coming through on my computer's iMessage app, and emails from my three different accounts came pouring in as well. The few people sitting at the tables around me all stared at me as I turned bright red and tried to rapidly tap the volume-down button. I looked around and smiled, then jokingly said, "Lo siento, estoy muy popular!" But the looks on their faces didn't seem like they thought it was very funny that I thought I was popular. Kind of like, '*So like, you think you're really pretty?*'

I should have immediately responded to the ten messages my mom had sent over the past three days, but a Seattle area code caught my eye. Could it be? For some reason, the iMessage app on my laptop didn't transfer over the contacts on my phone, so I wasn't certain it was him, but I also couldn't think of anyone else that would text me from Seattle. I clicked open the chat and read, *"How's Cuba treatin' ya? Have you gone to El Nacional yet?*

It was him. I knew it was him. Nate Smith was not only the *only* person from Seattle that I had spoken to recently but probably the only other person besides my mom and family in Miami who thought it was exciting that I was going to Cuba. I was almost certain that after I interviewed the super-successful global real estate developer slash social media celeb on my blog a few weeks ago that he'd be back off into his fabulous world of traveling the world for a living, not interested at all in becoming potential buddies. But then again, it did seem like he kept the video interview conversation going a lot longer than the original twenty minutes he had slotted me for. Something I was *not* prepared for and had to panic-put-on my makeup in about two minutes.

Actually, now that I think about it, of course the ultimate travel bachelor would be hitting up a cute, young, struggling writer whose dream was to travel the world. In my perfect world that exists only in my head, it would be like a Carrie Bradshaw and Mr. Big situation. Preferably minus the lying, cheating, and flakiness, and with more traveling of the world. *If I could only meet my future self to tell me not to get involved or I'd endure nearly ten years of heart breaks, just like Carrie.* Naturally, I immediately responded.

"Hey! It's good, today is the first day I've been able to go off on my own, so I found Wi-Fi now and am going to head to the Nacional later." I hit send and then immediately regretted writing such a long message with too much information. Why couldn't I simply just have said, "Not yet!"?

Embarrassed, I quickly closed out of his chat and clicked on the one from my mom. As expected, she had asked a few times if I was still alive, and then the last one mentioned advice for getting Wi-Fi at hotels. She probably should have told me that before I left, but oh well, I figured it out.

"I'm alive! I'm using the Wi-Fi at the Presidente Hotel where you stayed, and it's next to my casa particular. I WISH we were staying here! The magazine guys only care about the photoshoot . I haven't seen ANYTHING in the last three days! I finally got them to let me go explore on my own today! Did you get a hold of Leny to see what day I can go see them?" I felt extremely bad that I had been there for three days already and hadn't been able to get in touch with my cousin to plan to go see her. The plan was for my second cousin in Miami (her son) to call her to see when is a good time and day, then he would call my mom, and she would text me. But she hadn't mentioned anything about it in her ten "are you alive" texts.

As soon as I clicked over to one of the disastrously full email inboxes, I heard the ping of an incoming iMessage. *She's up early*, I thought, automatically assuming it was my mom. But to my extreme surprise, it wasn't my mom. It was Nate. I couldn't believe he had responded so quickly!

"That's great! Be sure to get a mojito ; they make 'em the best there! I'm stuck on a crappy island near Costa Rica where it's pouring non-stop, so I've just been sitting at the bar watching football." He had said. *Were we...friends?* It sounded awfully a lot like a conversation you'd have with your friend. Maybe he was just bored. He did say he was stuck on an island after all. *Ping!* Another message came through. It was a photo! My heart nearly exploded as the spotty internet slowly revealed a selfie of Nate smiling big with his thumb up at a dark bar with multiple TVs in the background playing sports games. *We're friends, AND we send selfies now? What does that MEAN?!* My heart fluttered. Another three pings came in from my mom. I switched over to her chat while I tried to figure out if I should send a photo back to Nate or just write a friendly response.

"Oh good! I got worried when I didn't see you post anything on Facebook or Instagram!" Her honest yet slightly absurd response made me snort. Mostly in agreement that it was actually strange that I hadn't posted in more than a day. The thought of that made my anxiety start to spike. It was already 11:20am, why was I still sitting by a pool having breakfast cocktails and chatting with people *not* in Cuba? I should be chatting with people *in* Cuba! Then I remembered I actually had clients I needed to respond to, and now only forty minutes to do so.

But first, more importantly, I quickly asked my mom again for details on meeting my cousin and promised Nate I'd send him a photo from the Nacional later. That is...if I could find Wi-Fi there. During the time that I was multitasking, responding to emails, and updating Facebook, Twitter, and even my blog, my mom sent me all of the information for meeting my long -lost family members.

I would need to hire a car to take me back near the airport to a little town called Santiago de Las Vegas, which I remembered from my grandma's journal. The drive would take over an hour, and I was slightly worried about how much that would cost me. She said that I should go tomorrow at 12 pm, and reminded me about the make-shift map that she had given me at lunch in Miami before my flight. I pondered that thought for a second and realized the lack of phone service and language barrier probably causes some confusion when getting around. Either way, I had thought it was super cute when my mom presented me with a map she drew of how to get to the house her mother was born in and where she used to go when she was young.

It was a big deal to my family that I was going to Cuba. Well, not my siblings, who don't seem to care much about my travel escapades and don't feel a strong pull to our heritage like I do. But my mom, grandpa, aunt, uncle, cousins, second cousins, third cousins, etc., were all extremely excited that I was going. So much so that many of them came to meet us at lunch before I left to either give me advice or give me something to bring to their family members in Cuba. My loco uncle who I endearingly call "Tio Feo", which translates to "uncle ugly" gave me the advice not to eat the cheese in Cuba...because it was "made of condoms". Naturally, my 'Tia Bonita" had given him a smack on the arm and told him to shut up as we toasted with bellinis to my adventure.

My grandpa, who is one of my favorite humans on Earth, and the only male-parent figure in my life after my dad left when I was in fifth grade, sat at lunch with a nostalgic smile and whimsical tales of his former home. I asked him for secret places to go to that no one knew about or that were his favorite places. He told me about Cayo Coco; a luxury beach area on the far north-east part of Cuba, and also a lesser -known island called Isla de los Jóvenes, which supposedly is where the original Pirates of the Caribbean hung out when they weren't raiding ships. According to him, that is, but he's definitely loco too. I had actually thought he was messing with me, but I Googled it on the way to the airport and am pretty sure it's true. Well, to an extent anyway.

He also mentioned that he had always said if he became rich, he would want to retire there , which made sense because I knew of his love for the ocean. I also knew of his past; growing up dirt poor in Cuba, and the extreme lengths he went to in order to win my grandmother's love. Like learning English so he could enlist in the U.S. Army, which resulted in him being a prisoner of World War II. I'll get to that story later.

My second cousin, the one whose mom I was going to go visit, secretly slipped me an envelope of money to bring her, taking my hand in both of his massive palms and thanking me profusely. My mom had given me a bulging duffel bag of over-the -counter medicine and toiletries to bring them as well. Apparently, my cousin in Cuba had severe stomach problems that are so painful that they sometimes prevent her from even being able to eat sometimes , but they don't have medicine for it where she lives. So she just suffers.

With all of the items and information I had been given, along with the looks of, "I can't believe you're going there" (both excited and worried), I'm not going to lie, I felt like I was on a secre t mission. I should also probably mention that when I was a little kid, some of my family members would tell me that "if I ever went to Cuba, they'd probably take my passport away and make me a slave." I went ahead and added that to my list of reasons never to mention that I was Cuban American when I was younger.

'Tu sección termina.'

"Dammit!" I hissed a little too loudly at the obnoxious square box that popped up on my screen in the middle of an important email. My one hour of Wi-Fi was up before I could send my jewelry client the three articles about vintage wedding rings I had written while bored out of my mind last night in my Wi-Fi-less room. Well, at least I got the info for my family meeting and got to talk to Nate b*ecause that's obviously a priority over work.*

I shoved the last of my "Vegetarian Cuban Sandwich" (Cuban bread, a piece of cheese, sliced pickles, and mustard) in my mouth and washed it down with the now-watery Cuba Libre. Snorting again with the irony of the name. After gathering my makeshift office back into my black seatbelt purse, I left one CUC coin on the bar, thoroughly shocking the bartender with my apparent generosity, and said, "Hasta manana, mismo tiempo!" since I had already planned to come back at the same time tomorrow.

After walking up and down the blocks outside the Presidente Hotel for twenty minutes or so, I started getting frustrated. There were no signs that indicated where the red double-decker tourist bus stopped, but I had sworn I read it stopped at the Presidente. The idea to just take one of the many taxis lined up outside the hotel started crossing my mind after the ten -minute mark, but I was 100% sure I'd get ripped off if I took one.

In fact, when I asked in Spanish how much it would be to get to the Hotel Nacional, the first driver quoted me 15 CUC. After I argued that the tour bus cost only 10 CUC for the entire day, he said that gas was expensive, and he had AC. As enticing as AC was in the scalding hot Caribbean sun, I only had about 20 CUC on me and was determined to get both a mojito *and* something to eat eventually.

Finally, the bus came, and the driver, seeing me drenched in sweat, laughed and said the buses were rarely on time because they just waited until there were people to pick up. *Noted.*

According to the colorful little map he gave me, the route we were taking would take an hour and a half before stopping at the Nacional. I contemplated whether the overpriced taxi would have been a better deal since it would take me there in twenty minutes, but then remembered again I'd be out of cash. Plus, this was a great way to see the historical sites and make note of what to go back to tomorrow. For only 10 CUCs per day and a pick up/drop off point near my casa particular, I could budget taking that bus every day to different parts of Havana *and* still be able to afford an hour of Wi-Fi, food, and at least two drinks!

I climbed up to the open -air seating area at the top of the bus and joined about fifteen other tourists. For some reason, I was surprised to see even that many tourists. As surprised as I had been to see the tourist bus that you usually see in major cities. Naively, like most Americans, I automatically thought that since tourism wasn't allowed for us, that meant it wasn't allowed for anyone. Once again, I figuratively shook my head at myself for believing what *they* wanted me to believe.

It was a bit intimidating walking down the aisle to an empty seat. Both because almost everyone was staring at me and because I started wondering what would happen if I got caught doing tourist activities without a registered tour group. To be honest, I wasn't entirely sure what all my family visit visa included, but I was pretty sure it did not include solo sightseeing. So I decided right then and there not to speak any English, and if anyone asked, to say I was from Spain. Or, more realistically since I'm a bad liar, Canada.

Once we started driving, I was *so* proud of my little plan. Not only did I get a free history lesson about the country my family originates from, but I had fully planned out where I would venture to each day that I could get *permission* from the editor. The bus route covered all of the major neighborhoods, from mine in Vedado to the main hub of Havana Vieja, and everywhere in between. With logistics taken care of, now all I had to worry about was my confidence, and lack of cash. Did I already mention there are no ATMs in Cuba, and I had only brought about $200 with me for two weeks?

It was evident that there weren't many solo travelers in Havana when I was there. All the tourists that hopped on and off the bus were either couples or families. My self-conscious mind felt like everyone was looking at me strangely and likely wondering why I was by myself, but I did my best to act oblivious to it all. Actually, I did better than that. I kept reminding myself that while all of these people are here on vacation, I'm here on a paid travel writing assignment. Yeah, that's right! I am not only a badass woman traveling solo, but I'm *also* a published travel writer!

When we finally pulled into the massive loop-drive entry of Hotel Nacional, my mind started fluttering with flashbacks that were both real and materialized. The prestigious five-star hotel looked identical to The Breakers Hotel in Palm Beach, which I used to frequent when I was randomly accepted into the elite social philanthropy circle on the island in my early twenties. One particularly obnoxious memory came stampeding ahead of the others; the time when one of Palm Beach's most eligible heirs fell hard for me after I made fun of his expensive clothing.

We started dating basically the next day, and before I knew it, he was taking me to Saks Fifth Avenue and buying me ball gowns to wear at galas he had to attend. One of them was Donald Trump's Mar-a-Lago gala for the LLS, and The Donald himself sat at our table. Well, for a whole five minutes before getting angry at a server and leaving his own event. Anyway, I had worn a gorgeous royal blue gown that had sapphire beading on the bodice, and tiny bows hand sewn all over the entire skirt. His grandmother -- one of the island's most prestigious socialites, had approved of me instantly and urged him to impress me. In fact, during an impromptu live auction of bottles of Cristal, where my date bought two for one thousand dollars each, she nudged him and said, "That's all you're going to get? Buy the whole case!" If that wasn't impressive enough, when we left, we were given gifts that came in a very familiar light blue box with a white ribbon. They were crystal vases from Tiffany's. That was the moment I realized that most of the money raised for charity at galas definitely does not go to the people who actually need it. He wanted to go out on Palm Beach Island afterward, as all the young rich people did after galas, mostly to show that they were at them. The valet pulled up his dad's black lamborghini, and he loaded the case of champagne into the tiny trunk, grabbing one of them out of it for the road. He popped the bottle right there in the driver's seat and filled the crystal Tiffany's vase I was delicately examining in my hands. Scared about getting in trouble for drinking and driving, I asked where we were going. '*The new bar at The Breakers, I bought a table there.*' He had said casually, taking a swig from the bottle and buckling his seatbelt. *So, this is what it's like to be filthy, indispensably rich.* I remembered thinking.

The triggered memory was of us pulling up to The Breakers; young, glamorous, and totally toasted. Valet drivers ran to be the first to open our suicide doors of the Lambo, and all the people who had just stepped out of vehicles themselves craned their necks to see who was getting out of it. I had smiled smugly as he came around and took my arm to escort me up the stairs in his Gucci tuxedo, especially since everyone was gasping, waving, and even sneaking photos. It was like a

Cinderella story ending, considering I grew up poor in an area nicknamed "The Farms." But not really, it turned out he was just another typical rich douchebag who easily replaced me one weekend when I went out of town with my family. At least I got to keep the dresses, which I ended up dragging to the desert years later for Instagram photos.

Suddenly the bus came to a jolting stop, and the memory of my Cinderella story from my early twenties launched out of my mind as my twenty-seven -year -old broke, single self came back to reality. I'd somehow managed to go from Lamborghini and ballgown to sweat-stained jumpsuit and budget-hack bus transportation. I guess that's why everyone says to marry someone rich while you're "young and pretty". Except, if you do that, there's a good chance you'll also end up divorced, miserable, and *not* currently living your best life in Havana. And also like, screw society. Who came up with these rules and standards anyway? *Men. That's who.*

I waited for the bus to pull away and the other tourists to walk up to the glamorous hotel. I was not trying to look like I was just there to gawk . I wanted to appear as though I was a paying guest, even though, let's be serious, I could never afford it. *And by 'never,' I mean 'never until a few years later when I'm getting paid to stay there.'* I ducked behind a bush near the valet parking lot and fixed my top knot so that it looked fresh and free of fly-aways from hanging my face out the top of the bus like a dog in a car with the window down. I moved my heavy seatbelt bag from my shoulder to my elbow, cleaned the smudges from my oversized black Chanel sunglasses, and applied a fresh layer of NYX Butter Gloss.

Envisioning the elite women of the 50's who used to frequent the Nacional, I straightened my posture, held my head high, and gracefully strolled up the marble steps of the grand hotel.

"Bienvenido! Como estas señorita?" A doorman in black tailored pants, white button -down prince-charming-looking shirt, and velvet red cylindrical hat asked as he opened the door for me. *It's working! I totally look like I belong here!*

"Bien gracias, y tu?" I responded in my best native-Spanish accent.

"No me puedo quejar!" He said with a happy smile. No, I guess he really can't complain, considering he's probably getting paid as much to open doors at a fancy hotel as doctors are in hospitals.

The lobby was stunning and again gave me flashbacks of The Breakers. Two- story high ceilings dripping with enormous crystal chandeliers and light flooding in onto the marble floors from outside. There were fancy velvet couches lining the floor-to-ceiling rectangular windows that gave way to a view of the garden area out back. Everything was so elegant, except for all of the people in the lobby. It was immediately evident this was a popular stop for tours and that most of the people on them had dressed for a day of sweltering hot sight-seeing, not an afternoon soiree.

"Hola señorita, ¿estás registrando?" A bellman pulled me out of my mental assessment of my surroundings with his languid words. I smiled wide, maybe a little *too* wide, because he had assumed I was checking into the hotel and asked if I was registering.

"No perdón, estoy aquí para el famoso mojito!" I replied confidently. I had rehearsed saying I was there for the famous mojito in my head on the bus. He clapped his hands together and said, "Ahh si!" with a big smile, then in way-too-fast-Spanish explained to me why theirs is the best as he escorted me into the courtyard. Immediately to the left were several tables with comfy -looking cushioned wicker chairs that were all as-expected, taken. *Although only about half of the patrons had actually ordered something.*

The bellman seemed to have shared my feeling of '*Don't take up an entire table if you're not going to order something* and shook his head with an eye roll.

"Un momento, por favor," He said, taking a step towards one of the waiters while still gently holding on to my arm. I heard him quickly berate the service-tuxedo-clad waiter for allowing people to sit down without ordering something when there are guests like me who would like something, then shooed him off with the order for my mojito and directions to bring it to an area in the distance towards the ocean where he was leading me. I felt a little pang of embarrassment as several non-customers heard the exchange and looked at each other to see if anyone was actually going to get up and make the other look bad, but no one did.

"Allá es la mejor vista!" He assured me, pointing to a row of wooden lounge chairs facing the water. I smiled and nodded, replying that the entire place was so beautiful. Just when I thought it couldn't get anymore *this-place-is-so-me,* I spotted two peacocks casually strolling on the lawn.

"PEACOCKS!" I squealed, which gave the suave Cuban man a fit of laughter. He didn't stop, though, I assumed because he was used to seeing them, so I made a mental note to try to chase them down after my drink for a photo. As we approached the row of lawn chairs, I started to get that embarrassing feeling again. Because it was very clear they were all full, but he wasn't stopping or turning around to look for somewhere else to seat me.

Instead, he announced to the entire row of people that if they were just there waiting for their tour to leave, to please let this hotel guest have their seat. Apparently, now I was a hotel guest...

A group of three middle -aged European men scoffed but stood up and walked back towards the lobby. I definitely did not want to sit there while the rest of the people judged how spoiled I was, but I couldn't deny, the view was breathtaking. As he helped me down into the low seat, I scoured my crap-pocket in my purse (you know the one you throw random small items and trash into?) for some coins to tip him. I came out with a palm -full of either 10 cents or 1 CUC plus a bunch of gross dead makeup crust. One CUC was a lot to tip someone in Cuba, but I was still in my *"pretend you're a prestigious person"* persona, plus I knew a good tip would grant me great service in the future. It definitely worked because less than five minutes later, he had returned to personally deliver me my mojito.

It was a whopping five CUCs, which is expensive for Cuba but absolutely worth it. Not only was the mixture of crushed brown sugar and mint leaves, soda water, white Havana Club rum, and lime the best damn mojito I had ever had, but the view and vibes along with it made me finally feel like I was really in Cuba. Not to mention, it inspired the non-paying patrons near me to at least order a beer.

Naturally, the first thing I wanted to do before sucking the entire thing down was take a selfie. *For the blog,* I told myself, even though I was secretly more determined to send it to Nate whenever the next time was that I got Wi-Fi. I could feel the people near me staring at me taking a selfie with my phone, so there was no way I was going to bust out my action camera and selfie stick. I actually didn't feel much like sitting anyway, so I got up to explore the cannons and ruins leftover from the Cuban Missile Crisis.

I tried to envision how crazy it must have been to have troops using the courtyard of the most famous hotel in Cuba as a base for battle —aiming cannons straight at the United States and hiding in barriers where they were obviously expecting fire in return. I wondered how the owners of the hotel felt about their esteemed establishment being the main target for destruction.

Wandering around the ruins was nice because there was hardly anyone else there. I assumed they had already toured them, and that's why they were now taking over all the seats. I looked around sneakily when I got to a spot at the very edge to see if anyone was around, and when the coast was clear, I whipped out my selfie stick and took an epic aerial shot of the back of my head with the Malecón and ocean far below.

When I sat down to admire the growing sunset and thus the growing number of people heading to the Malecón, I envisioned my grandmother doing the same thing. I'd read in her journal that when she was in her 20's, she escaped her small town to go live in Havana and ended up getting a great job at a department store that paid twenty cents per week. She said that for entertainment, they would go out dancing or simply just sit on the Malecón and talk.

SHIT! Sunset meant it was getting late! And the tourist bus stops running at 5 pm! I jumped up and started speed walking back to the hotel lobby. I would have run except my pride wouldn't allow me to. I checked my phone for the time ; it was 5:12 pm, which made my feet move even faster. Thankfully I didn't see my bellman as I rushed out, that totally would have given it away that I took a bus there, but when I finally got out front, I did see the last flash of the big red bus before it pulled out of the long driveway. *Shit!*

I had only 4 CUCs left, which definitely was not enough to get a taxi. Panic started to build up in my chest, and of course, all the scenarios of what would happen if I couldn't get back before dark started to flash in my mind. *I could call the casa particular from the lobby, maybe the editor is back, and he can send the car.* No, that wasn't an option because then I would for sure not be able to go back out on my own.

It wasn't the safest idea, but I could technically walk along the Malecón until I got to my neighborhood. It would probably take close to an hour, and it would probably be dark by the time I got back, which would also likely get me a big fat "NOPE" on my next request to go out solo. *Think think think!*

Just as I was about to muster the courage to approach the row of colorful old -fashioned 1950's cars-turned-taxis, the street to my right caught my eye. It was lined with funny yellow bubble-looking vehicles that had only three wheels. *The Cocos!* I suddenly remembered hearing my mom talk about these cute little vehicles that were super cheap but not comfortable enough for her to try and take.

Comfort or not, I didn't care . If they accepted my 4 CUCs, I was taking it! I approached the first Coco where a gangly young guy with a deep tan and hard -working hands was lounging in the singular front seat.

"Hola! Cuanto cuesta ir al Hotel Presidente?" I asked nervously, praying to the universe that he didn't say more than 4 CUCs. For some reason, since the taxi earlier asked for 15 CUCs, I expected the vehicle one -third its size to be at least one -third the price.

"Hotel Presidente? Trienta pesos, ven!" He replied, sitting up quickly and starting the shotty little contraption before I could say anything else. While trying to think what the conversion of thirty Cuban pesos was to CUC, I slid onto the small bench behind him inside of the yellow Coco. If my calculations were correct, it was less than 1 CUC, which would also mean that I found a new way to get around Havana that was cheaper and more convenient than the tourist bus.

Sure enough, when we pulled up to the Presidente, I handed him 1 CUC, and he tried to give me change back in pesos. I pushed it back at him with a smile and said, "Una propina", and watched his mouth stretch to show every one of his bright white teeth. For safety measures, I pretended to walk up to the lobby of the Presidente while waiting for him to take off in the Coco, just in case my tip was an indication that I had more money. When he was out of sight, I spun around and made a mad dash for the casa particular. As much as I wanted to use the remaining 3 CUCs of my daily budget to get an hour of Wi-Fi and a Cuba Libre, I wanted more so to be able to explore again on my own tomorrow.

"And then they escorted me to these seats with a prime view of the Malecón, and there were peacocks just walking around everywhere!" I excitedly gushed over the details of my day, but in a way that made them seem like I was solely collecting content for the editorial piece I was writing. To my surprise, The Editor was intrigued and realized he may be missing out on his initial glamorous experience of Havana.

"Maybe we can all go there when we're done with the model castings." He said, "I need to exchange more cash anyway, and I hear they can do it there." *So, he did know there were cool things to be seen aside from the models!*

"Tell me, cariña, when will you go see your family?" He added. I was shocked he remembered or even cared. He hadn't seemed as excited as I was about the pitch I made to 'Trace My Roots Through My Grandmother's Journal,' and I assumed he only said yes because, well, how can you tell a twenty-something -year -old aspiring writer that you don't want to hear the story about where their family came from. I quickly realized I hadn't made any arrangements to get to their house tomorrow.

"Oh! My mom said they were expecting me at noon tomorrow," I wasn't exactly sure how to ask if it would be possible to borrow the fancy black Rambler and Panfilo to get there and was already just thinking of just paying about 10 CUC and taking a little Coco. Before I could answer, his squinty eyes and almost-bare eyebrows lifted , and he opened his thin - lipped mouth to interrupt me.

"That's perfect, cariña! We would like to come with you! We can take the car. I would love to meet your family!" He piped. My mouth fell open, but no words came out. I was at a loss for words for several reasons. One was a relief of having a ride there and back, another was a concern about what my elderly relatives would think when I arrived with two much older men, and the third was *'Awww, he cares about me as a human and wants to meet my relatives?!'*

"REALLY?!" I finally blurted, "That would be AMAZING! I mean, I have to warn you, where they live is in a very poor neighborhood, not glamorous at all, but,"

"Not to worry cariña, I too grew up in a very poor town in Haiti." He divulged with a half -smile as if he were exposing a secret that he was now proud to tell. "Shall we bring them something?"

With this new information and interest, I instructed him to wait in the living room while I ran to my room and re-appeared hauling the heavy bag of medicine and toiletries. I told him the whole story about how all of my family members in Miami met me before the flight to give me things to bring and how my second cousin, her son, had to flee Cuba more than a decade ago and hasn't seen his mom since. The story seemed to touch him, and he even asked to see my grandma's journal. After reading it, the tears in his eyes told me I'd definitely be getting more freedom to explore Cuba on my own. And I was definitely getting my own personal essay to write in the magazine.

Waking up at 6 am every morning was not necessary or required at all , but my lovely regular lucid dreaming and sleep paralysis thought otherwise, per usual. It didn't help that my room looked like something straight out of a horror movie. I feel bad even saying that but it's true; the one window has bars over it, and there's often a cat fighting outside or people arguing in the room below, then of course, the broken-record of a rooster who cock-a-doodle-do's no matter what time it is.

The full -sized bed with a rock -hard mattress is covered by an old, thin, scratchy quilt and faces a yellow wall with nothing on it besides a small wooden cross and the dresser mirror that of course reminds me of Bloody Mary. To the left of the bed are two large wooden armoires; one that's locked shut, and one that I hung some of my clothes in, which pops open randomly at any given time. I'm not so much afraid of it while I'm awake, but again, having sleep paralysis makes it extremely scary. I mean, imagine thinking you're awake in that room, then a shadow person starts to creep out of the corner or the closet, and you realize you can't move your arms or scream for help. Welcome to almost every night of my life. Thank God I've learned to control it over the years. And to think, some people actually *try* to have lucid dreaming.

This morning though, I was perfectly fine with the early morning intrusions that interrupted my sleep. I wanted to make sure I had all of my things ready to go and a rough outline of what I would film and even what I wanted to say to my long-lost-cousin. I knew she didn't speak a word of English, so I wanted to make sure my Spanish was perfect so she could easily understand me.

It took all of about ten minutes to get ready with the usual; heavy mascara on the top lashes, eyebrow liner, a thin layer of Mac Studio Fix, and a glob of NYX Butter Gloss. My hair went up in a top knot per usual, and I chose the nicest, most conservative dress I had. It was an aqua -crocheted thick-tank dress that went down to my shins, which to me was conservative, but the tightness and dipping neckline might have people saying otherwise.

I made sure my action camera was charged along with a spare battery, and I placed it along with the attached pink selfie stick in my black seatbelt bag. Next, I carefully extracted some items in my suitcase that I had hidden in my underwear bag, just in case my bag was searched or manhandled. First, it was my grandmother's delicate green cloth-covered journal, then the envelope of US cash that I was to give to my relative. Last but not least, I took out my daily budget of 20 CUCs from another hidden pouch and shoved it in the travel-sized tampon box in my purse that I used to hide my money. *No thief is going to want to look inside a tampon box.*

Checking my phone for the time once again, I re-calculated how much time I had until The Editor woke up. It was probably another hour at least, and then we had three hours until it was even time to go. After debating with myself for five minutes, I finally made the executive decision to leave a note saying I had woken up early and walked to the Presidente Hotel to use the Wi-Fi to do research on the best places to go in Havana. It was technically true , and also technically true that I wanted to finally send Nate that selfie from the Nacional. I added my Macbook Air to my bag and as quietly as I could possibly manage with the squeaky floorboards and heavy door, tip-toed out to the hallway. There was a credenza outside The Editor's room that looked like a good place for my note, so I placed it there, then sleuth-slid down the hallway and out the massive door.

"Una hora de Wi-Fi por favor?" I chirped to the morning front desk clerk at the Presidente as she eyed me suspiciously.

"Necesitas comprar..." She trilled matter-of-factly as if I was some drifter coming in for free Wi-Fi without the intention to buy something. *And I thought I looked rather nice today! Geez!*

"Si, si, yo se, compra comida tambien." I interrupted her as she pointed a gaudy red manicured finger at the sign I had been pointed to the day before, stating you must order something in order to use the Wi-Fi. She raised an eyebrow and made a face that looked like she was thinking '*Whatever gringa'* and handed me the little slip of paper with the daily code for an hour of Wi-Fi. "Solamente UNA hora, comprende?" She added on as if I needed to be reminded of the time limit when the Wi-Fi kicks you off after an hour anyway.

Surprisingly, there were a couple of people already having breakfast at eight in the morning, which I remembered, was normal for most people excluding me. It was definitely too early for a Cuba Libre (*or was it?*), so I asked the bartender for a hot tea and guava pastry. When I was little, guava paste on Cuban crackers was my absolute favorite snack. Whenever we'd go visit my grandparents in Hialeah, they would always have it waiting for me, along with freshly chopped sugar cane that my grandpa grew outside that he knew I loved to chew on. Depending on the time of year, they'd also always have not only fresh mangos sliced and ready to eat, but every possible thing you can make with mangos since their massive tree outside left them in abundance.

Ping, ping, pin-pin-pin-piiinngggg! My computer exploded with notifications again as soon as the Wi-Fi code went through. Like yesterday, there were notifications from my mom and Nate (*which made me smile like a tween with a severe crush*), but also a number I didn't recognize aside from the L.A. area code. Obviously, I checked Nate's first. To my surprise, there were quite a few messages, including two more selfies and the last one saying, '*Well, I know what Wi-Fi is like there, so assuming you don't have any, send me a pic tomorrow.*'

Fascinating. I thought slyly, realizing how my lack of communication prompted him to communicate more. I examined the two photos he sent; there was another at the bar, but this time with a friend, and the two of them were holding up beers. The second, sent after a few messages, was just of him...clearly laying in bed. I wasn't entirely sure how to take that. It definitely wasn't anywhere near the level I thought we were on, but I supposed it made sense. Young, cute, aspiring blogger, obviously very into the fact that he travels the world, why *wouldn't* he try to flirt? I wondered how many other female travelers had reached out to him and how many others he'd flirted with and probably hooked up with. But what if he actually did like me? We could be a travel power couple and work remotely while going on adventures together and live happily ever after! *Yes, that is really the way my brain thinks.*

I Air-dropped the photo I had taken at the Nacional yesterday, after heavily editing it of course, onto my laptop, then dragged it over to his chatbox. *'You were right. They DO have the best mojitos! And also yes, the Wi-Fi situation sucks.'* I decided to keep it short, as much as I was dying to tell him about my solo adventure on the bus and then the Coco. Maybe I'd add that I was going to visit my family today before my hour was up, so it didn't look like I was sending another message too soon.

My mom's messages said the usual, *'Hope you're alive and not in jail!'* and *'Tell your cousins we send our love! I'm so excited for you!'* I had started typing her the details of my adventure to the Nacional when I got another ping, then another. Nate had responded already! In my opinion, that was extremely rare; most guys wait hours, even days, to respond, which I assumed was to get the upper hand. *Or maybe I was just too used to the flakey guys in L.A.* But Nate wasn't from L.A., he was from Seattle, and he was also a traveler, so maybe things were different. I finished writing to my mom before even thinking about opening the new messages from Nate, forcing myself not to be too eager. But, remembering I had sent a selfie had me immediately clicking over to his tab.

'Nice pic! You should take more like that, it could be your thing!' He had said first, and I actually thought about this from a business standpoint. The selfie was half of my face, just my eye, half smile, a hat, and behind me was the glorious back of the Nacional. My "thing" was still not showing my face at all, so maybe he was trying to say...he liked my face? Or *calm down;* maybe he was actually just giving me business advice.

'Told ya! We should meet up somewhere and get a mojito when we're both back in the States.' The second message said. Definitely not a piece of business advice.

'For sure! Let me know if you're ever in LA!' I immediately responded, way too soon. Obviously, I instantly regretted it and wondered if it sounded desperate, like I was inviting him over or something. Or maybe it sounded amateur that I was asking him to come to me instead of offering to go to him. Or maybe, *ding!* He responded already!

'*I actually have a work thing in Vegas when I get back. That's close to you . Wanna meet me out there?*' Right then and there, my mind blew up, and my heart exploded with excitement. This guy was *the* most eligible bachelor for a girl who travels, and he wanted to meet up with *me!* I couldn't believe it , but again, I didn't want to get too excited. For all I know, he could just want me to do another interview about his business or something. In Vegas.

'*Yeah, I could probably drive there! I'll see if I can find any hotels that might want to collaborate*'. In reality, I was thinking, *How the F am I going to afford getting to Vegas AND getting a hotel.* That trip alone would cost all the money I'd make from writing my Cuba articles for the magazine. Secretly I hoped he'd say he had some hotel connections that he'd reach out to and *ping!*

'*I actually have a really nice two -bedroom timeshare there. You can just take the second bedroom if you want.*' My mind was extra blown. Not only did he kind-of read my mind, but now was making it clear there may be more than just business that he's interested in. But again, I didn't want to seem too eager.

Instead of responding immediately, I spent the remaining thirty minutes responding to emails, updating social media, and quickly uploading a blog draft I wrote the night before with my tips so far for traveling solo in Havana. I ignored the three new pings and promised not to look at them until just before my time was up.

With five minutes left on the Wi-Fi-time, I clicked over to my messages expecting all three pings to be from Nate. But there was only one, it said, '*Or I can probably see if I can get you a comped hotel from one of the properties we work with, but my place here is really nice.*' I couldn't decide what I wanted more; a nice hotel that I could also blog about, or to stay with Nate, the increasingly biggest crush of my current life.

'*I have a couple of hotel contacts I can reach out to,*' I lied, trying to seem like I didn't need him to help me and that I also was considering this a professional meeting, '*but thanks! I'll let you know if they don't work out! Heading to meet my family now, so excited! Will let ya know how it goes!'* Sweet yet professional , but where were those other messages from?

I remembered the number I had seen earlier that wasn't stored in my contacts. The tab for it now had a total of five new messages. Who on Earth could that be? I clicked it open and carefully read;

'Hey Alyssa! It's Antonio! Ashley's old boss!' Antonio? Why would he be texting me? We'd only met twice at a couple of his parties that Ashley had begged me to go to. He was only about five years older than us but extremely successful in the tech world, which gave us little in common aside from enjoying socializing in LA. And by "in common," I mean, "I'm successful at knowing how to use a laptop to make money."

'She told me you're going to be in Havana this week! I'm here too with a few friends!' Little in common or not, my eyes and attention immediately perked up upon reading that there might potentially be someone I know who speaks English in Havana!

'Let me know if you want to meet up . We're staying at the Saratoga Hotel in Havana Vieja!' The name sounded familiar, and I thought I remembered seeing it on a very fancy hotel from the tour bus yesterday. Which would make sense since I knew Antonio was loaded. My god, how nice it would be to actually have money to spend here? *Thought the girl who years later would throw a fabulous rooftop birthday party for herself with the artists and influencers of Havana.*

'Hey Alyssa! I'm guessing you don't have great Wi-Fi, but I just saw you posted a pic on IG, so I wanted to try to get a hold of you again!'

'Text me if you get this and want to meet up!' The rest of his text messages made it clear that he also had abundant Wi-Fi, something I almost forgot existed in real life. My fingers flew to the keyboard in a rampage, praying I had enough time before getting booted off.

'YES!' I immediately sent, *'About to lose Wi-Fi! Will try to text you later!'* I saw the *"typing"* dots on both Nate and Antonio's messages, indicating they were both responding to

my last texts, and just before either of them could hit send, my Wi-Fi shut off.

***

"Let me tell you about my hometown . Cuba is the island on the map that look like an alligator. Is in the Caribbean, 90 millas from Key West, FLA. The name of the town where I was born is "Santiago de Las Vegas," 12 millas from Havana, the Capital of Cuba. My town is only 1 millas long for 1 millas wide, 2 movies, 3 schools."

I looked up from the aged pages of the green, cloth-covered journal and out at the dusty, old, little town of Santiago de Las Vegas. I could hear my grandmother's thick Spanish accent as I read the words, and for a moment, it almost felt like she was there with me, in her hometown in Cuba, showing me where she grew up.

Never in a million years would she have ever thought I'd get to go to Cuba, or for that matter, that I'd actually want to see her hometown. I also don't think she would have expected me to move to LA and become a travel writer who gets sent to Cuba on a writing assignment that's based on her life growing up there. But I know she would have been proud. She might have fainted from shock and lectured me on safety, but she would definitely be proud.

"Izquierda, aqui," I instructed our driver, holding up the hand -drawn map to show where my mom had drawn an arrow to the left.

"She's been in Cuba one day, and it's like she knows the place!" The Editor remarked from the backseat at my innate sense of direction in the town I had never been to before. But in a sense, I had been, because I had read about and pictured it so many times in my grandmother's journal. To be fair, my mother had also drawn me a pretty solid stick-figure map of where everything was in regards to the park in the middle, which was strangely accurate and easy to follow.

I didn't even need to look for the house number of my cousin Ovia's house because as soon as we turned onto the rocky, unkempt road lined with pale-colored block houses, I

110

could see my other cousin Vinita waiting in the doorway. She looked like she had been standing there waiting all day, and I watched her face as she realized it was me pulling up in the "fancy" black car.

My heart sped up with excitement as I fumbled to gather my things and get out of the car. I handed the editor's boyfriend my action camera to video us meeting for the first time and dashed over to my short, stout, *prima,* who was clasping her open mouth with one hand, and her heart with the other.

There were no words, and they still aren't any to describe the formerly-unimaginable miracle of that moment. Tears involuntarily poured from both of our eyes, and we hugged for what seemed like an eternity. She leaned back with wide, blue eyes that were magnified behind thick glasses to examine the girl she had only seen in photos for the past twenty-seven years, shaking her head and gasping in disbelief. I choked out a laugh, nodding slowly in affirmation, and we hugged again, confirming that the moment was real.

All I could think was, 'I made it.' Because up until that very moment, I didn't believe I ever would. *And I certainly didn't believe I'd be back several more times.*

She ushered us inside the old, narrow house that stretched far back and ended with a small, tree-covered yard. Ovia came from one of the rooms, walking slowly with a slight limp and open arms. I could barely make out the fast Spanish words that came flying excitedly out of her mouth, but the same bewildered look and smile on her face was enough of a translation to know how she felt.

A thin, younger woman named Lizzy appeared in the open doorway and came to hug me as well. She was a friend of my cousins', who helped them with food shopping and cooking, and knew I was coming to visit them that day. She immediately disappeared into the back of the house to make us Cuban coffee, a hospitable trait typical to most Cuban people.

We all sat in the simple living room, on the same cane furniture that used to be at my great grandmother's house down the road, trying our best to converse for the first time with extreme excitement and the slight language barrier. I looked around at all of the photos of my second cousin, Ovia's son, who lives in Miami, and his family, that made up the majority of the décor in the small living room, aside from an old photo of me and my siblings that I was somewhat shocked to see. Like the rest of my family, my second cousin had been immensely excited, shocked, and happy that I was going to Cuba, and especially to the town he grew up in.

I had asked if there was anything I could bring them before I left and remembered the two cards he had given me with gifts for them. I handed them to my cousins along with the only other thing he asked me to give them, "A big hug and kiss from him and his family."

There was silence as they read the cards, and I could feel the heartache in their souls as they longed for the person they loved the most. Ovia put the card down and ushered me towards the back of the house where there were several rooms separated by stone wall dividers. She explained how the front of the house is newer, which is why it has tiles, and the rest of the house is made of stone and was built in 1863. She showed me her room which she was also born in, and my second cousin's room that still had teenage paraphernalia in it from when he lived there decades ago.

Next, they showed me the kitchen and explained how before the Revolucion, they had nicer appliances, but they were taken and replaced with basic ones in order for "everyone to be equal." They showed me the backyard that's abundant with fruits and vegetables, just like my grandma had written about at her home growing up.

I tried to translate that part of my grandma's journal the best I could, but the language barrier was a bit tough. Then suddenly, Lizzy seemed to have an idea and pulled out her tiny Nokia phone, hit one button, and held it up to her ear. After talking rapidly for about seven seconds, she hung up and said in careful English, "My son Julian, he speaks English, he will come here!"

Son? Cuban son? Named Julian? Jesus, I really needed to stop being so boy-crazy. It's like a telenovela is constantly playing in my head, and I am the star of it. Lizzy ushered me back towards the living room as she and my cousins spoke so fast that there was no way I could even attempt to understand it. "Ovia is going to wait here because her legs aren't so good, and we will take you to the places you want to see in your grandma's journal."

I followed Lizzy outside as she and Vinita chatted rapidly, and the editor and his partner examined the nostalgic atmosphere of the neighborhood. Then, as if there was radar programmed in my head to know exactly when a cute guy is approaching, I saw Julian strolling casually up the street in my peripheral vision. My head seemed to turn in slow motion, a soft gasp escaping my lips and is that an Enrique Iglesias song I hear playing in the background?

He wore crisp white shorts that cut off just above his tan, toned knees, and a black fitted T-shirt clearly showed his pecs and abs. *Oh my god, did I really just start looking from the bottom, up?* Anyway, the third thing I noticed was his full, pouty lips, strong jawline flecked with black scruff, and brown eyes adorned with thick black lashes. His equally thick black hair was cut coolly on the sides but tumbled freely on the top. I knew he was younger than me but DAMN, he was the embodiment of what I envisioned as a "Cuban lover." But alas, I was here on a mission to discover my roots, not create new ones.

"*HE should be one of our models! Get his info!*" The Editor whispered to me with a nudge, eyeing him up and down even more aggressively. *Well, if it's my job to get the hot guy's number, I guess I have to do it, right?*

I introduced myself and the editor in Spanish to Julian and showed him the notebook and my mom's makeshift map of the places I wanted to see.

"That's so cool." He said, revealing the most delicious dimples and a set of gorgeous teeth.

The six of us shuffled slowly down the rocky road as Julian translated to me what Lizzy and Vinita were explaining about the town. Any time there was a step, crack, or slightly larger rock in the road, they would all grab my arms protectively to make sure I didn't fall and literally stood in front of me whenever we crossed a road. There weren't many cars, maybe a few of the old 1950's run-down classics, and a horse and buggy here and there , but for the most part, everyone was just walking.

People stared as I passed, seeming like they had never seen a visitor from the U.S. before, and I didn't blame them since Santiago de Las Vegas isn't exactly a tourist attraction in Cuba. Life is simple there. It's as if it's still exactly the same as it was before the Revolution in 1958. And I loved everything about that, except the crumbling state of many of the homes that had no funds to be fixed and the lack of goods that were available to the people.

As we continued walking, Vinita proudly announced to all of her friends and neighbors that we passed, that I was her cousin visiting from the U.S., and the looks of bewilderment came at me again. Some people looked a little skeptical, but some were excited and kept up with us to chat a bit more about it.

"Mira! Alla!" Vinita said suddenly, pulling my arm towards a long, plain building that had completely crumbled in one corner. It was the first stop on the time travel tour of my grandmother's past, the elementary school she had gone to in the 1920's.

'I remember when we have time off at school for 10 minutes, all the girls get together and talk or if we have something to eat, we do it at that time, almost all the time I only have a piece of bread with guava jelly. We were so envious to see the other girls, not all, a few of them, they have an apple, sometimes they have grapes, oh, nobody knows how we would like to take it from them.'

It made me sad knowing that my grandmother hardly had any food to eat growing up. Especially since I was the world's pickiest eater when I was young. That was why the next location meant so much to me; the house she grew up in and the backyard filled with fruit trees that made her feel like they were the richest people in the world.

'[We] Believe that we were the most richest people in the world, we have 3 dogs, about 10 cats, chickens, rabbit, all that plus, mango, orange, avocado, guava trees, when we were too hungry, we always can climb a tree an get some fruits.'

Everyone kept warning me that the house was not the same as it was when she lived there. Since then, it had been completely rebuilt, with a new family living in it . However, the backyard was still somewhat the same. It was a bit far, so we let Vinita take the Rambler while we walked, which she said made her feel like a movie star.

On the way there, Julian and Lizzy told me about the old homes and how some of them got rebuilt by the government if they got really bad or if they had a family that sends them money from the U.S. The ones that don't remain the same as they were originally constructed, and sadly, the families have no other choice but to live in the crumbling remains.

The whole time I just kept thinking about how I was walking the same streets as my grandmother once had, and I wondered what her everyday life might have been like. I distinctly remember her once telling me that her mother got beaten by a scorpion and had to walk ten miles to the hospital in Cuba in an attempt to scare me into putting my shoes on when I went outside when I was little. I didn't believe her back then and would never put my shoes on, but seeing the area in real life made me want to apologize for ever doubting her.

She had also always told me and also written in the journal that when she was growing up, they used to smash charcoal until it was powder, put it in a box, then take a piece of cloth wrapped around their finger and use it to clean their teeth. The first toothbrush she used was when she was 12 years old. For deodorant, they would use carbonate of soda, and for face powder, they would take the shell of an egg, make a powder, and use it on their face.

If they were sick, their mother would give them natural remedies like lemon, fish liver oil, olive oil, and tea. If they had a cut, she would go to the back yard, take some leaves from the gumbo tree, and wrap it around the cut, or cover it with sugar to stop the bleeding. Hearing all these stories made it make sense why no one ever thought it was strange when I used to insist on living in a tree house when I was little or wanted a lizard or a chicken as a pet.

When we finally arrived at the house my grandmother grew up in, Vinita was already inside chatting with the woman who now lives there. She graciously welcomed us in, but I still felt slightly angered that the government had just taken my grandmother's house and given it away to someone else. But I knew the three little girls playing quietly on the small bed in one of the rooms needed the space much more than just one person did.

Light seemed like it was shining at the end of a dark tunnel, and I felt like I was being drawn towards it with involuntary hypnosis. I could faintly hear all of my grandmother's memories about the house, her stories about the backyard, and the secrets of her life that were written on the pages of the green, cloth-covered journal that was clutched tightly in my hands.

My grandmother had written about this place in a journal because she thought we would never get to see it, and I physically brought her memories back to the place where they were created. I could feel my eyes fixate on the light coming from the backyard and knew that the brightness and anticipation were causing my eyes to start welling up with salty tears. For a second, I even considered the possibility that I'd pass out or have a heart attack, but I kept walking towards the backyard anyway.

I couldn't hear anything anyone was explaining to me about the backyard. All I could hear was my grandmother's memories, flooding into mine like she was there, quasi-lecturing me about only having fruit to eat and explaining why she always grew so many trees and plants in her backyard in Hialeah.

Nostalgia swept over me as the yard came into focus — even though I had never been to this seemingly familiar place in my life. I could never have pictured her as a little girl before I read her journal, and still, her stories about catching lizards are hard to believe since I only knew her later on. She had always yelled at my grandfather for teaching me how to catch

116

lizards with a piece of string or trap random animals in a metal cage, but I knew now that it was because of her own consequences as a child, because she had been adventurous and gotten in trouble, just like me.

That was the point of her journal, to explain her life growing up and why it made her the way she was with us. It was to show that maybe she was or wasn't just like us growing up, and I would have never known she was, had I not found that journal. But her childhood was only the beginning. The time -traveling machine was just warming up.

A half-hairless dog with mange was barking at me as I gazed up at the massive avocado tree in the backyard. I felt like my brain was typing subtitles out in front of me as my cousin explained apologetically in Spanish that the only thing that still remained the same about the entire property was that tree that was now almost one hundred years old. That would mean that my grandmother probably climbed it when it was still a seedling, and for that, I was grateful for the giant tree.

I couldn't understand why they kept making me look at the bathroom that was attached to the outside of the house, but later I realized it was because her family had built it when my aunt was young and too afraid to use the outhouse that my grandmother had to use growing up. It was another part of the house that was still original from when she lived there, and it definitely showed when I peeked in to see rusted amenities.

I took a photo of it, mostly to make everyone stop trying to get me to go inside of it, then tried to steady myself as I took everything in. All of the memories, thoughts, images, and emotions of my grandmother's life, mixed with the commotion of conversations and explanations from everyone in the small, tattered yard, made my head spin. For some reason, as much as I wanted to stay, I felt an overwhelming sense to leave.

The dog wouldn't stop barking at me even though it was wagging its tail, which offended me since I consider myself an animal whisperer. There was a grungy-looking, orange and white kitten in the doorway, which I subconsciously cooed, *"aw, gatico"* at, but consciously refrained from petting it after being yelled at earlier to not touch the stray animals. The wind blew hard suddenly, making the underwear that was hung on the clotheslines sway, and I felt a pang of embarrassment for seeing a stranger's private clothing in public. No one seemed bothered about any of it though, except for me and the weather.

I didn't want to make eye contact with anyone, and I couldn't anyway; my pride and poise would not let me show the strong emotions and energy I was feeling from that yard. I looked back up to the rustling branches of the towering avocado tree, trying to figure out what exactly it was that I was feeling, but there were no words. The dog was still barking, the kitten was still sitting in the doorway, and the sounds of Spanish banter were still drowned out in the background like white noise.

Suddenly, out of nowhere, dark, pillowing clouds came tumbling over us, and I could feel the reflection of their grey color absorb into my eyes. The sudden contrast made everything in the backyard seem even more detailed and surreal as it had been in the bright sunlight, and for a moment, I felt like it was either a warning or an acknowledgment that I was there.

Chills ran up my arms, and the thought of a torrential downpour worried me for the sake of my cousins' and colleagues' well-being. The dog finally stopped barking, and I pet the little cat anyway on my way back inside, which was shortly followed by a plea for me to wash my hands. Still, I kept walking back towards the front of the house, eager to take a picture in front of it before it was too dark, and before I was too embarrassed to use my "selfie-stick" in an area where cellphones hardly exist.

When I got there, a little girl was at the front porch door, her name was Isabelle, and she had hazel-yellow eyes with a tan skin tone that matched her hair. She was too pretty to look so shy when she asked to come in, but I smiled at her quietly and held the door open for her to run to her friends in the small bedroom inside. I probably would have acted the same way when I was her age and wondered if my grandmother would have as well.

I waited out front for everyone to exit the house, feeling as though I was in the Twilight Zone in between two time periods and not entirely sure of which generation era I was actually in. I think everyone could tell the emotional toll it was taking on me even though I tried to hide it since they mingled by the front door while I attempted to suppress tears of happiness for a photo in front of the house my grandmother grew up in.

Finally, after a few attempted photos in the front yard, I fixed my top knot, and hid my messed-up make-up with my oversized black glasses and prepared myself for the next important part of my grandmother's life legacy: The park where my grandmother and her friends went to "meet boys" when they were in their teens in the 1930's.

I remember my grandmother briefly reminiscing about her teenage years when I was younger and always telling me to never settle. I always thought she was just teasing me but never really knew the entire story about why she said that until I read about it in the journal.

We walked to the park that we had passed when we first drove into the small yet bustling town. It seemed like there wasn't much to do besides hang out and talk to each other, so it made sense for the park to be rather populated. The park itself is a square, concrete area with a smaller square in the middle that has four steps that lead up to a prominent statue. My cousin insisted I take a photo with the statue because apparently, it's one of my grandmother's cousins who was a war chief and hero in the 1800's named Juan Delgado Gonzalez.

On the perimeter of the park are palm trees, bushes, and a few park benches on each side. That is where my grandmother would have probably sat with her friends to talk about the boys in the park -like she describes it in her journal. The only boys I saw were a group of about six little boys who looked at me like I was a robot alien from the future, which made me question again which time era I was actually in.

They asked to take a picture, but for some reason, they were extremely shy and standoffish when I sat down next to them. They didn't smile for the photo . They just kept staring at me, each of them with a different shade of skin tone, although they were all from the same place.

My grandmother met my grandfather around this time in the early 1930's . His family had just moved to Santiago de Las Vegas and was even poorer than hers. She wrote that he was so skinny that she only saw him as a boy and as her best friend's brother, plus the fact that she was an entire year older than him made him unsuitable for a suitor. It broke my heart more than anything to hear about my grandfather being hungry when he was younger. And it breaks my heart when he gets so upset that I'm so skinny now, but that's because of a different reason.

Instead, my grandmother and her friends would walk in the park; the girls would go one way, the boys the other, then the girls would sit on the benches, and the boys would come over. She wrote that that was how they would find out if he was good -looking and clean, and if he wasn't, they would make an excuse to get up and go around the park again. Kind of like an ancient version of Tinder where instead of just swiping your finger, you have to physically walk to the left.

Another square perimeter makes the road that goes around the park, and facing it is my grandmother's school, a church, several shanty homes, and little market shops. My favorite shop was a "bookstore" I stopped at on the way in, whose walls were piled high with old, dusty books that only cost about five cents to buy. I ended up buying more than I could carry because the adorably hunched old man who works there kept shuffling back and forth with different titles saying, *"Mira, mira, en Ingles!"* when he realized I was looking for books written in English.

At sixteen years old, in 1936, my grandmother started working and made seventy -five cents a week and also had her first boyfriend.

She worked for a dressmaker and said the lady had a maid who knew how hungry she was and would secretly save her scraps from dinner. My grandmother would give her mother 50 cents and keep 25 cents for herself, which she used to buy her first real toothbrush, ice cream, and even some perfume.

She wrote in her journal that she ate her first apple when she was 16, *"it costed 5 cents, which was considered a lot in that time, especially with so little money"*.

She also had her first boyfriend, and she wrote about how his family came to meet hers, which was what usually led to marriage. Many of her friends were getting married at that time, but she got scared because she didn't love him and asked her mother if she could go stay with her sister in the then-thriving city of Havana. That was how she broke off the relationship.

Although the war was starting, things in Havana couldn't have been better. In my grandmother's journal, she writes about how the "yankees" came to build an air force base, and she started working at it making $40 a week, which made her feel like a "rich girl".

Things changed for her in 1944 . She had money to spend and could finally afford to buy nice clothes and other small luxuries. She wrote that she met a couple of nice guys and would go out dancing every weekend or go on a tour around Cuba and that it was all good clean fun.

She hung out on the Malécon often, which is the long, winding stone wall that separates the city of Havana from the daunting ocean waters below it. It's where friends, family, and lovers have gathered for decades to enjoy a beautiful sunset, drinks, and time together, laughing and chatting. I immediately understood the appeal of the Malécon when I went there for sunset the day before . Although I had no one to share it with, I felt enough love from the warm Havana atmosphere to enjoy it regardless.

I can tell that my grandmother loved that year. I could imagine her at one of the discotecas, dancing innocently and laughing more than she ever had in her life. I imagine her being cautious and well-aware of her surroundings, not afraid to turn her nose up at an unwelcome solicitor or snap at someone for getting fresh.

Soon though, my grandmother started to realize that things over in Europe weren't going so well with the war. She wrote that she was too young to worry because everyone was working in Cuba, and it was the best year for her country. Money was flowing in like water from the U.S., and new places were opening, like movie theaters and restaurants. There was electricity and radio, water, and good things to eat, but they never put their minds to the fact that hundreds of people were dying in France, England, and all over Europe.

"In 1945, things started getting bad, young people started going to war, your grandfather went to the U.S., enlisted in the army, and went to the war in Germany."

The radio had started announcing men from Cuba that were either killed in action or prisoners of war and suddenly, my grandmother became worried. She was close with my grandfather's family, and his sister, Olga, was her best friend.

She was 24 at the time and said it was when she started changing. Things weren't looking too good for the U.S , but there was nothing anyone could do in Cuba to help the situation. She kept working in Havana so that her mother, who was then widowed, could have money and groceries for herself and the younger siblings. But she kept listening every day on the radio for the names of the Cuban soldiers who were missing in action.

She kept listening for one name that she didn't want to hear. Until one day, she heard it. My grandfather, Plinio F. Muñoz, was a prisoner of war, captured in Normandy. He was starved, tortured, and forced to walk across entire countries in the freezing cold, as fellow soldiers were dropping dead around him. I was never able to get him to tell me many details about his time at war or as a prisoner.

The most he would tell me is that when he was finally freed, he fled and hid in a cave with other soldiers, and all they had to drink for a few days was whiskey, then finally a US troops tank drove by and they ran out to get on it. His PTSD of being starved was also always very evident and is why he would always sit next to me at meals when I was little. He'd eat everything I'd leave off my plate, most famously, the tiny bit of meat in the tail of a shrimp. A few times, he also joked that I looked as skinny as he did after being a prisoner of war. But we all know there's nothing funny about that. And I knew the severity of his trauma from the tiniest things, like the fact that he still had German language records (yes, like vinyl records) in his house and that my middle name is German. Once when I was younger, he even told me to never tell anyone I'm Cuban, and to say that I'm German. I can't help but wonder if he manifested my blue eyes and light hair.

Anyway, the next stop in her journal was 1945 and resumed back in Santiago de Las Vegas, in the very park that I was standing in.

My grandfather returned to the tiny town of Santiago de Las Vegas after being a prisoner of war for ten months. My grandmother returned too, and the town threw a big party for him and honored him as a hero. He was also a hero in the eyes of my grandmother, who no longer saw him as a boy, but as a man that she was very much in love with.

They enjoyed the good life for a bit in Cuba after the war. They got to go out dancing and to shows like the Tropicana, which was the very same show I would watch in the very same place in Havana almost seventy years later. But my grandfather, a very smart man, knew there was more money to be made in the U.S. He had dual citizenship, so he went back to find a job in America. He would send letters back and forth, begging my grandmother to come to the U.S. because there was something very important that he wanted them to do there.

Finally, she went, and in 1946, they got married in a courthouse in New York City where the only witnesses were another couple who were getting married after them. But they had each other and the hopes and dreams of building a life in the United States.

The time travel timeline of my grandmother's life in Cuba pauses at this point because the next two years were spent scrambling to make money and raise a baby in the U.S. It wasn't nearly as easy as they thought it would be. Times were bad, jobs were scarce, and the entire nation was reeling from the war.

Since my grandmother married my grandfather as a U.S. citizen and had her two children in the States, the whole family had U.S. passports and could travel freely to and from Cuba as they pleased. Although they went to Cuba often in the late 1950's, my grandmother wrote hardly anything of it in her journal. I assume because it was a bit of a sad time for them.

This was around the time when Havana was notorious for being considered the "Las Vegas of the Caribbean." Although it was a flourishing era for the wealthy people of the U.S. who'd visit and the workers benefiting from the income, the rest of the country was suffering because of the corrupt relationships of the Cuban leader, Batista, and the majority of the mafia, mob, gangster, and government leaders in the U.S.

In fact, the last stop on the time travel treasure map of Santiago de Las Vegas in my grandmother's journal is at the old church that faces the park she walked in as a teenager and where my mother was baptized as an infant around 1955.

It was good Friday, so there were many people inside the church . They were sitting on the wooden pews and peeking out from behind their prayer hands at me as I quietly made my way to the various statues and displays.

I had seen all of the places that my grandmother wrote about in her journal from 1921 to 1958, and still, it all seemed so surreal, like there was so much more to see and stories to hear. She ends her journal with a brief introduction of my mother's younger years, noting that the rest of her life is for her to tell me, but doesn't talk about her last three years in Cuba or anything after the 1960's. And I think I know why.

My grandmother may have omitted the facts from her journal, but luckily my mother recalls her last memory in Cuba as clear as day.

"It was January ▣st, 1958 . We were sleeping at my Grandmother's house — your great-grandmother — when she came to my mom in the middle of the night and said, 'You have to get up. Get your girls, get your things, and get to the airport . You have to leave Cuba right now.' We were on one of the first flights out of Cuba the next morning."

As my mother, aunt, and grandmother took off in the early hours out of Havana, Fidel Castro, Che, and the

124

Revolutionaries took the power of the government and marched into the very same area they had just left.

I had already been to my grandmother's very last time travel stop in Cuba in 1958 because it was the same airport I had flown into a few days earlier.

The time travel tour of Cuba through my grandmother's past ends there because after that, she wasn't able to go back, and it was very painful for her. She was separated from her family, just like the Revolution separated an entire island full of families and left them with lives torn in half. She was heartbroken when she got the news that her mother had died seven years later and that she hadn't been able to see her before.

Then she got news shortly after that her only brother was dying, and she spent almost a month in the Bahamas trying to gain clearance to go see him before he died, but by the time she did, it was already too late.

I knew there were many Cuban and Cuban-American families who experienced the same pain she did because of the harsh consequences of communism, and it was for them too that I wanted to time travel through my grandmother's past, to show what so many went through.

As I made my way back out to the middle of the park, I squinted around, taking in the history and reliving the legacy of my grandmother's past. My mind was filled with more wonder than it was before I read her journal, and I felt pain and regret for not asking her questions sooner before she left. Still, I was grateful for the conversations we had and the memories I had found and grateful for the curious person I had become that led me to seek out what she had wanted us to know.

She wrote about an era in Cuba that is intriguing yet difficult to understand and what she wanted us to know about her and her life.

It was for that reason that I was standing there in 2015, in her tiny little hometown of Santiago de las Vegas, Cuba, holding back tears behind big glasses as I twirled the little diamond of her wedding ring around my finger and clutched onto the green, cloth-covered journal of my grandmother's past.

"Oh wow! It's already almost four o'clock!" The Editor suddenly announced, sending me spiraling out of my moment just in time to prevent the tears from rolling in again. I was as shocked as he was that four hours had flown by and also that I had just relived my grandmother's past in that amount of time.

We all walked back to Vinita's house, where we made plans to come back over the weekend for a proper meal. She insisted on cooking even though we knew their ration cards did not offer enough food for guests, and also a bigger problem; they didn't include fish, only chicken, which I don't eat. I tried to convince them that I would be fine eating salad and black beans and rice, but apparently, that was unacceptable, and I had to have protein. She would have to find someone to trade ration cards with in order to get the fish.

Saying goodbye and driving away was similar to how we do it in Hialeah as well. The entire family walks out to the street and stands there waving until your car is out of sight. Then they put their arms around each other and head back inside, filled with love and heartache all at once.

Once back on the road, The Editor and his partner were back to business, talking about the next steps for the photoshoot. I was actually glad that they didn't want to talk because I was still soaking in everything that had just happened and manifesting that my grandma could somehow know what I had done in her memory.

"What do you think, cariña?" The Editor said loudly. I had completely zoned them out and only realized they were talking to me because he had leaned forward into the front seat.

"Sorry, what? I was, um, looking at the footage." I held up the action camera that was sitting ready in my hand in case we passed something worth filming and swiped the screen to show the previews of videos.

"Always working! I love it! We were just saying that maybe when you go out tomorrow, you can start scouting some locations for the photoshoots? Maybe something grungy in

Havana Media and something more modern and chic in Havana Vieja? Maybe you can find out if we can shoot at the Nacional or if we need yet another permit..." He said, not knowing that he had just produced music to my ears.

"Yes! For sure! I can definitely do that! I already saw a bunch of cool buildings in Havana Media, and I actually know some people staying at one of the fanciest hotels in Havana Vieja!" I thought that last bit would impress him, but I realized as soon as I said it that it might also raise some questions.

"Oh? You know people here? In Cuba?" He sounded very surprised but not as skeptical as I expected.

"Yeah," I said, trying to sound as if that were casual, "some friends from L.A., they messaged me this morning saying they saw my Instagram post and asked if I was here." *Dammit! Make it sound more businessey than that!* "They're with some friends from Panama who are looking for a hotel property to invest in . They'd definitely be good people for you to meet in case they're interested in the magazine!" I added, knowing fully well that The Editor had been trying to find new investors for his luxe lifestyle-turned-passion-project.

"Would love to meet them! Why don't you go see them tomorrow and see if they'd like to have dinner somewhere in town this weekend? We could use a nice night out, right darling?" he said sweetly to his partner.

Talk about manifest destiny! I couldn't believe my luck and secretly thanked my grandma's spirit for having something to do with it. Granted, I wasn't entirely sure how a young successful tech guy from LA would perceive me being in Cuba with two older men conducting a full -on editorial photoshoot. I would make sure to casually boast about being there on assignment and, oh, mention they're gay.

The Editor and his partner had the driver drop them off at the audition location, where there were already several young guys and girls lined up waiting for them. I had to admit, this was probably one of the most glamorous things to happen to them in their lives, and I really hoped they saw it that way rather than being cattle-called by a couple of Americans.

With the car left to myself to get home, I asked for a slight detour to the Presidente Hotel to use the internet.

After going back and forth with the front desk woman about paying extra for Wi-Fi since it was later in the day, I finally got my code (for a whopping 7 CUCs) and planted myself at my typical pool-facing table. I set my 4 CUCs that I knew would get me my Cuba Libre and meatless-Cuban sandwich in a little pile on the table and opened my laptop, preparing to get as much done as my brain and fingers could manage in just one hour.

"Hola senorita! Dos veces en un dia! Quieres lo de siempre?" I was touched that the bartender not only remembered my typical order, but also noticed that I was there for the second time today.

"Si, esta es mi oficina!" I swept my open palm in front of my laptop to indicate that this was my office and handed him my stack of coins with a smile. He gave a little laugh and a nod that seemed to say, *'Not a bad office'* and returned behind the bar to place my order.

Once the annoyingly long Wi-Fi log-in process went through, the usual bombardment of *Ping! Ping! Pings!'* commenced. Although I could see that most of them were from Nate, my attention span had new motives; make plans with Antonio. Namely, so I can actually have some fun finally.

Unlike my calculated messages to Nate, I didn't care how much or how fast I wrote to Antonio. I wasn't trying to play it cool or flirt, I was trying to have friends to meet up with in Cuba, and this was too perfect of an opportunity not to seize it. I just hoped he had Wi-Fi right now as well in order to respond within my one hour.

'Hey Antonio! Just got back from my cousin's house! Such an amazing experience, can't wait to write the editorial about it! Anyway! My editor said I could go meet up with," I hit the backspace button immediately, he didn't need to know I needed permission to go off on my own, *'Would love to meet up with you guys tomorrow if you're free! I only have one hour of Wi-Fi at this hotel, so you'll have to give me a time and place*

to meet you, like in the old days, ha.' I laughed to myself but then immediately considered that he might be older than I thought, and might take that offensively. Too late to backtrack, and not enough time to worry about it.

Instead of wasting my precious fifty-three remaining minutes on Nate's multiple texts, I clicked open my email instead. Nothing that needed my immediate attention that anyone would get in time since it was already 5 pm. Forty - seven minutes left. I decided to upload some of the photos I took with my family earlier. Admittedly, I know how to "play the game" from being played so many times, and I knew that if Nate saw my posts before hearing from me, he'd know I saw his messages and chose social media over him. Which I should be doing. Since that's the job I'm trying to have and trying to attain it without any help, especially from him.

Ping! The noise both shocked and excited me. My eyes fluttered over to the iMessage box; it was from Antonio! Already!

'Hey Alyssa! Super cool to hear you saw your family! Can't wait to hear about it! Definitely meet up with us tomorrow ; I'll plan a whole day! Just meet us on the mezzanine level of the Saratoga around 11am. Oh, and if you can't find us, just log onto the Wi-Fi using my password: "Garcia210," I have the unlimited plan!'

My jaw hung open and for a second, I thought I might drool. Is someone else planning things for once? UNLIMITED WI-FI? I only hoped it wasn't too good to be true.

***

Walking into the Saratoga Hotel in Havana Vieja was nerve- wracking. It was much smaller than the Nacional but equally as fancy, if not more since it was also brand new. Unlike the Nacional's historic glamour, the Saratoga was sleek and chic, with enormous black chandeliers and checkered rugs.

Again, I had worn one of the nicer things I brought; a vertical black and white striped maxi dress that never fails to turn heads. Per usual, I put my hair up in a twisted top-knot, sported my oversized black Chanel sunglasses, linked my heavier-than-it-appears black seatbelt bag on my elbow, and rocked a confidence that shouted, "*Why yes, I am staying at this fancy hotel.*"

The doorman opened the gigantic glass door for me with a friendly greeting and no question as to whether I was checking in or not. I decided to pretend like I was staying there and find the mezzanine on my own rather than ask and give it away that I wasn't.

Now, THIS is more my style! I thought once again, realizing I had the same thought at the Presidente and Nacional hotels. The Saratoga was by far the nicest though. With it s cool air conditioning, sweet smell of fresh flowers, and glossy marble-everything. I remembered Antonio's parties back in LA and how immaculate they always were. It made sense that this was the hotel he chose to stay at. His parties were always over the top, with catering, servers, and fullon themes that everyone dressed up to.

As I ascended one of the flanked marble staircases to the mezzanine, my excitement grew. I hadn't thought much about what exactly he was going to plan, but if the Saratoga was any clue as to his level of capabilities, I was in for one hell of an epic day.

I heard them before I saw them; three guys laughing and talking loudly. Two had American accents, and one sounded like some sort of Spanish but not Cuban. I followed the voices, and when I spotted them, my heart skipped a beat.

What? No way! It can't be... It's impossible?! My eyes fixated on what I thought was a familiar face. Tall with broad shoulders, tan with dark hair and scruff, and wickedly handsome. *Mr. TDH?*

"Alyssa! Hey! Over here!" Antonio spotted me and yelled across the mezzanine, standing up and waving as if it weren't clear that I was staring directly at them. Well, at Mr. TDH. How the hell did he know Mr. TDH? He said his friend was from Panama, not Turkey...*Oh.* My heart stopped fluttering around frantically upon realizing that this wasn't the guy from Istanbul that I met and fell in love with after one week of volunteering together in South Africa. *Bummer.* But on the bright side, there was a tall, dark, and handsome man here who I was likely about to spend the entire day with.

I tried my best not to look at him as I floated over and gave Antonio a big hug. From his body language, I could easily tell he was the type of guy who knew he was hot and expected women to just throw themselves at him. Unlike the original Mr. TDH, this guy had his facial hair professionally manscaped, along with the thick black locks on the top of his head. They were carefully combed and styled to make a flip to one side, and he had a trendy line shaved at the base of the flip. I connected the dots to realize that *he* was Diego's friend from Panama who came to Havana to look at a new hotel to buy. Admittedly, that was hot. Young, attractive, *and* wealthy? *Nate who?* I shook the thought out of my mind . I knew all too well it was a recipe for disaster.

When I pulled back from Antonio's embrace, my eyes nearly bulged out of their sockets. There on the low mirrored coffee table next to us was what had to be every item on the bar menu. Considering I hadn't eaten much besides black beans and rice and Cuban bread with cheese in about a week now, this was like giving a stray dog a steak. There were platters of Mediterranean dips with veggies and pita chips, fruit salad, king crab legs, jumbo shrimp cocktails, *actual* cocktails, several tall glasses of beer; wait, wasn't it only eleven AM?

"We only have two days here, so we're going big." Diego explained as I eyed the table of delicacies, "What do you want to drink?" He asked, shoving the cocktail menu into my hands and picking up his own off the overcrowded table.

"Oh sorry! This is Drew, he's a finance investor from Connecticut," I almost hadn't noticed the tall, slender, blonde guy, but now that I was reaching for his hand, I noticed he too was attractive but in more of an Edward Cullen way.

"Hi! I'm Alyssa!" I said cheerfully, with the cheer one thousand percent being from the fact that I was about to hang out with hot guys in Havana all day.

"And this is Andrik, from Panama," he clearly knew he didn't need more of an introduction than that. Andrik looked less than interested, so I returned the vibe with a flimsy handshake and brief, "Hey." Ain't nobody got time for men who think they're hot shit.

After the introductions, Antonio ordered me a specialty cocktail after veto-ing my Cuba Libre request on account of it being "too basic." Then we all sat down and listened to his plan for the day.

First, we would sightsee around Havana Vieja, which he actually asked me to be in charge of. In fact, he had explained to the other two that I was a great travel blogger and that he had read my post from the other day and wanted to see a few of the places I mentioned. Edward Cullen was very sweet and seemed impressed, but Andrik couldn't care less. *Whatever.*

So, after I showed them the must-see places; the Floridita where Hemmingway allegedly dubbed the best daiquiri in the world, and the rooftop of Ambos Mundos for a Cubata (anejo and cola), we would then go on a cigar factory tour. Which, to be honest, I wasn't thrilled about, but Antonio was super into it.

What I *was* extremely thrilled about, however, was when Antonio nonchalantly announced the last event of the day, "And then we'll take one of the cool old classic cars and go see a show at the Tropicana! I already got you a ticket."

By the time six PM rolled around, we were all exhausted and tipsy, but the best part of the day was yet to come! The guys said they wanted to go back to the hotel to change before the Tropicana show, and my irrational, irresponsible mind opted to go with them.

I'm not sure if it was the booze and the fact that *both* cute guys had started competitively flirting with me all day, or the booze and me not being used to someone else telling me what to do. But for some reason, I decided it was a better idea to go back to the Saratoga to wait for them over going all the way back to my casa particularly to tell Ralph what the plan was. To be honest, I feared that he would say no to me going out with three guys at night, and I'd miss my opportunity to see one of my grandma's favorite shows since I couldn't afford a ticket on my own.

I'll just say they planned an entire dinner and show for me and that I couldn't get a hold of him to let him know. Irrational-Alyssa thought as we approached the Saratoga. *Better to ask for forgiveness than permission.*

"Go ahead and get something from the bar and put it in my room . We'll be down in ten minutes tops!" Antonio said, pointing to the mezzanine bar as the three guys headed towards the elevator.

"I'll be down in five to join you for a drink," Andrik added as the gold elevator doors shut and the other two snapped their heads sideways to look at him.

My cheeks flushed at the public claimage of me. Clearly, he was interested now, but whether it was because of my expert tour-guiding throughout the day, ability to hang with the boys, the fact that I had pretty much ignored him all day, or more realistically, the fact that I was the only girl going to a show with three men, I did not know.

Andrik was back downstairs, surprisingly, in exactly six minutes. He had re-greased his hair, doused himself in cologne, and changed into a yellow button-down shirt (of course unbuttoned halfway) with tight white jeans. *Yes, Ok, we get it, you're hot AF.*

He strutted over to me, ordered a drink, then sat down, putting his muscular legs on either side of my crossed chicken legs.

"You're not like other girls ; you know that?" He purred in his deep, sexy accent. *Yes, I do know that but go on,* I thought to myself slyly but obviously didn't make that known.

"I do," I said coyly, with a smirk and a big sip of my mojito.

"I'm intrigued. Usually, women are all the same to me, but you're different." He continued. As much as I wanted to believe him, the fact that we were about to go to a sultry dance show and there was competition for my attention made me continue believing he was more interested because I was the only girl.

133

"Am I? Or is it because I'm the only girl?" *Dammit! That wasn't supposed to come out!*

He laughed, exposing his big, perfectly straight, white teeth. I noticed when he smiled genuinely like that, he got dimples in his cheeks. *Ugh, stop being so hot.*

"That may be true , but even so, you are actually smart. And you are not so interested in money, I can tell." His drink came, and he motioned for the bartender to put both of our drinks on his tab.

"Oh, it's Ok, Antonio said," I interjected, not wanting him to pay for my drink after he had just noted that I'm not interested in money. He waved a big hand in my face and spoke quickly to the bartender in Spanish. Judging by his nod and disappearance, I guessed he insisted on paying for mine anyway. I dropped the hand I was waving onto the bar in defeat. To my surprise and shock, he gently took it in both of his hands and held it on his knee, forcing me to look down at the exposed six -pack that was peeking out of his shirt. When I looked up to meet his warm brown eyes, he smiled again, making me extremely shy and nervous.

"Will you be my date tonight?" He said finally. *What?* So many thoughts flooded my brain. Yes, he was extremely sexy, and this was the best -case scenario, spending a night dancing in Havana with a hot Latin guy I had just met , but also like, *we just met*, and it was through *my friend* who also *bought me my ticket.* Would that not be awkward AF if I suddenly just cozied up to his friend who again, *I just met*.

"I already told the other two I like you. And it was me who bought all of the tickets. So, you don't have to look so worried bella." He touched my face with the back of his fingertips and smiled, somehow knowing exactly what I was thinking. *Well, if you put it that way...*

When would I ever get another chance to have a foreign fling with a young, sexy, hotelier *in Havana?* Was this not one of my wildest dreams come true? Who cares what the others might think of me ? Think of what an epic memory and story this will make later!

"Ok." I said cooly, taking another big sip of my mojito, "I will be your date , but don't try anything funny ; we just met." This seemed to appease him, and he easily slid my stool closer to him, locking me in a strong embrace and kissing me hard on the cheek.

"Tonight, we dance at the Tropicana!" He announced, tinking glasses with mine as the other two guys approached.

I felt like we were in the movie 'Midnight in Paris' except, obviously in Havana, as we rolled up to the Tropicana in the red 1950's convertible Chevy. We had had quite a few mojitos at dinner, which made us late, and we had to argue with the staff outside to even allow us in. Nothing a one -hundred -dollar bill that Andrik slipped over couldn't fix. It took some effort to get us all through the door and to our seats in the dark, which apparently were upgraded thanks to whatever Andrik said to the man leading us, and another one -hundred -dollar bill.

Once we were settled in and Adrik was as close to me as the metal chairs would allow, the people around us stopped staring. It only took about seven minutes. There was already a bottle of Havana Club rum on the table, and a server in a white button-down and bow tie poured it neatly into our glasses, then asked if we wanted to order anything else to drink. *Because a cocktail in addition to a triple shot of rum is a good idea.*

Apparently, the boys thought so because they all ordered something additional, including Andrik who ordered something for me as well. The next server came with a box of cigars that he opened and handed to each one of us. I'd never smoked a cigar before, but when a Cohiba is offered to you at the Tropicana in Havana, Cuba, you try it.

"You sure you want to try that? They're disgusting!" Andrik whispered, laughing at me as I took tipsy selfies with the Cohiba in my mouth.

"I'm in Cuba, of course, I'm going to try it ," I mumbled with the thick tobacco roll in my mouth. The server reappeared at my side and lit my cigar for me first. It was basically like any movie I'd ever seen of someone trying to smoke a cigar for the first time. I inhaled the smoke into my cheeks, tasted and smelled the volatile aroma, and immediately spat it out and coughed incessantly.

"Maybe I'll just take it home." I choked, much to the amusement of the server and the boys. Drew opted to do the same, but Andrik and Antonio proceeded to smoke their Cohibas like pros. I assumed it obviously wasn't their first time smoking Cuban cigars.

"It's starting!" I hissed excitedly as the lights on the massive stage began to flicker.

"Biiieeennnvenidos mujeres y hombres! A la Trrrrrooppppicaaanaaa!" A deep voice roared from a tiny man in the middle of the stage, and suddenly there were flashes of movement coming from all directions.

What must have been over one hundred women, all with perfect bodies and beautiful faces, clad in just a few strings and feathers with giant headpieces, glided and shimmied in unison towards the stage. About thirty of them passed right by our table, wearing nothing but a few strings of clear gems and giant chandeliers *on their heads*.

I would have felt extremely self-conscious about all their nakedness, but the rum and Andrik's smothering grip around my entire body made quite the blanket of reassurance. I imagined these must be the type of women he was used to just getting then disposing of. Beautiful, young, fit women who men see as sex objects or trophies. I knew that's how it was because that's how I was treated by men the majority of my life. They'd fall for me so hard because of my looks, but it would always end quickly because either they couldn't see something serious with someone who's stereotypically "hot" (not bragging, I have literally been told this), or the fact that I was also smart would intimidate them. Oh, not to mention independent and a feminist. I've always been a guy's dream until I open my mouth.

Whatever, it wasn't like I was expecting anything from Mr. Macho Trust Fund, which is probably why he was trying so hard.

The show was absolutely spectacular even though my vision was a little fuzzy. From what I could gather, the history of Cuba was depicted through a series of scenes and dances. With each one, the stage kept expanding and expanding until there were three different levels on the main stage, plus several additional stages up in the trees on either side of the main stage.

It was much shorter than I expected, and I was a bit shocked when the short stumpy man on stage started calling everyone up to dance.

"Oooohhhh, let's go on stage and dance!" I wailed. It was definitely the rum talking. Andrik immediately said no, but once I got up and started dancing by myself, and a random man immediately joined me, he cut in. The four of us made our way to the main stage, where Antonio and Drew were immediately accompanied by two half-naked dancers and happily whisked away.

I turned to Andrik and was about to start busting out my salsa moves, but he pulled me so close against him that *everything* was touching. His right hand was firm against the middle of my back, and his left held mine delicately against his shoulder. He bent his head down so the sides of his lips were pressed against my forehead and then started making small steps to the beat of the music, which his hips easily followed. He had such a controlled grip of my entire body that it involuntarily moved with whatever his was doing, like I was a blow-up doll or something. What about my cool dance moves? Was he going to do any fun spins? Did other people think we were about to fornicate right there on the stage of the Tropicana?

It was a little too sensual for my liking, so I wiggled away from his embrace, spun myself with his hand, and took a step back to do my own salsa moves.

"You're supposed to follow my lead!" He laughed, even though I knew he was totally serious! *Yeah, I bet you'd like that, wouldn't you, Mr. Macho Man.*

"But you're not dancing! Dance like this!" I retorted, doing a little side-step-cha-cha-cha.

He rolled his eyes so hard that his head rolled with them. Then in one movement, he grabbed my hand, my waist, and cha-cha-ed so smooth that when we finally ended with a low to the ground, I was convinced I may actually be in love with him.

"Better?" He purred, clearly soaked with self- satisfaction as I hyperventilated and looked at him like I wanted to jump on him.

"You kids ready to go?" Antonio interrupted the moment, thank God, I wasn't sure what my hormones were about to do in public.

Andrik lifted me back up on my feet and into reality, where once again, I was washed in the happiness of realizing I was really in Havana, Cuba. And not just there. I was dancing the night away with a sexy Latin man who didn't even so much as look at any of the near-naked dancers. For a split second, I started to think about how The Editor would have loved to be there. *Oh crap! The Editor!*

"What time is it?! My editor is probably freaking out!" I gasped suddenly, realizing it was probably getting late and I had not checked in or even told them what time to expect me home. I felt like the Cuban version of Cinderella.

"It's late. You're going to be in trouble either way . You might as well stay out." Antonio said casually, making me feel like a child with a curfew who was trying to hang out with the older cool kids. "Plus, it's dangerous to try and take a taxi alone right now. You might as well just come with us and just say it wasn't safe for you to go back by yourself." He added, and I couldn't tell if he was genuinely concerned or wanting to help his friend out.

"It's true. You can call him from the hotel when we get back, and if he wants you to come back that bad, we'll arrange a car from there, but not this area." Andrik boomed in that sexy Spanish accent. He brushed my cheek with the back of his fingers and bit his thick lower lip. *Yeah, I bet that's what you really want me to do when we go back to the hotel.*

It was technically true. It wasn't safe getting in a taxi at night, especially alone, and with the additional fact that I didn't have a working phone, I'd most likely get lost as well. Guilt stabbed at me in every direction, but I didn't have much of a choice. I guess I'd just have to continue living the most epic possible night in Havana.

When we finally found our hired car through the masses of people also outside looking for theirs, it was such a relief to be heading back. After a full day of sightseeing, well, sightseeing-while-drinking, then drinking more and dancing, I was beyond exhausted.

"Oye amigo, queremos ir a la Casa de la Musica." Antonio instructed our driver, slipping him a twenty -dollar bill that was probably equal to what his regular salary was for the month.

"Wait, what? Casa de la Musica? That's the nightclub!" I piped from the backseat, elbowing Andrik in the ribs in order to release myself from his embrace and intervene in the conversation in the front seat.

"Mmhmm, sounded cool when you mentioned it earlier. Like I said, it's already late, and you're going to be in trouble anyway." He said casually again, clearly with no concern for my growing anxiety. "And if they kick you out, Andrik will get you a hotel room." He added with a smirk.

"I'm mostly worried about losing my paid writing job!" I squealed, trying to battle the devil on my shoulder.

"Not a problem. My hotel will pay you to write about it when you come to visit me in Panama." Andrik purred, pulling me back by the shoulder and tucking me under his arm. "By the way, do you want to come to Panama next week?"

Antonio gave me a big smile, and a double eyebrow raise from the front seat before spinning around and saying, "Adelante!" to the driver.

Was this real life? Was I really going to just dance the sultry Havana night away with a hot ass guy who just invited me to go see him in Panama next week? And not just to see him, to write about his hotel as well? He mentioned paying me to write about it, but was that too close to prostitution, or was he really just trying to help me out? I decided if I did go, I wouldn't take any money. I would treat it like any of my other writing collaborations that offer free stays for free publicity. Except this one happened to have a really sexy client. *Uh, YOLO?*

Casa de la Musica was a sweaty blur. The club was set up in an old theater, and a live band replaced where the shows used to perform. It was loud, dark, and moist from the amount of perspiration in the air. The crowd was mostly locals, and they were dancing provocatively like Andrik had attempted with me on stage at the Tropicana. Of course, that only made him try it again. This time I allowed it, giving in to the temptation of his seductive moves that were only enhanced by the vibrations of the music coming from the guitar and saxophone.

Antonio and Drew somehow managed to find an empty table, albeit covered in used plastic cups and had already somehow obtained a bottle of Havana Club rum. *How in the actual hell were they still drinking?*

It must have been because of their lack of available female options. Because not even ten minutes later, they wanted to leave, insisting we could stay, but I further insisted that was a hard pass.

Apparently, the Casa de la Musica was on the outskirts of Havana because it took about forty -five minutes to get back to the Saratoga Hotel in Havana Vieja. We were all gross from sweating and dancing, but I felt extra gross coming into the nice hotel late at night with three guys.

"See you guys in the morning!" Antonio announced as if it were already understood that I was to go with Andrik. Suddenly I felt uncomfortable. I hoped he wasn't expecting me to sleep with him, but like, let's be serious. That's definitely what he was expecting.

"I'm going to try to call my editor." I blurted, pointing to the phone on the reception desk. He smiled and took the hand I was holding up in his.

"You can use the phone in my room." *Of course.* "Don't worry . I'm not going to try to have sex with you. Unless you want to of course." He whispered with a wink. I tried to listen

140

to my gut, but it was so full of rum that it made it hard. My argument was basically to take advantage of getting to sleep in a five -star hotel next to a hot man or try to get home to my haunted casa particular, where I'd likely wake up the entire house trying to get in. There! That was it! My justification for staying! Even if I tried to go back right now, I wouldn't be able to get the key to get in because everyone was probably asleep.

His room was like something straight out of a luxury travel magazine, but I could tell he was used to it judging by the way the pillows and blankets were just strewn haphazardly about. *Little did I know that in just a few years, I would be the one used to being in luxury hotels.*

"Sorry about the mess . I wasn't expecting company. I'm going to shower . Feel free to use the phone." He said, or I think he said, I was too distracted by what was being revealed when he unbuttoned his sweat-drenched yellow shirt. As I suspected from what I could feel when we were dancing, he had chiseled pecs and a perfect six -pack. Maybe even an eight pack. I swallowed hard, trying not to make it obvious that I was staring, and beelined for the phone on the nightstand.

The number on the piece of paper the abuelita gave me worked, but no one answered. I called three times, so at least I tried. Hopefully, that meant that they were sleeping and not waiting up for me. A million thoughts rushed through my mind and started to make me dizzy. I decided to put my head down on the pillow for just a second, but as soon as I felt the cloud-like plushness, I was out cold.

When I woke up finally, Andrik was already dressed to the nines and ready to go. He noticed me stirring and came to sit on the bed next to me.

"Buenos dias Sleeping Beauty," he purred, stroking my face. I was mortified at the fact that I had utterly just passed out in his bed and probably looked like a disheveled zombie.

"Oh my god! I'm so sorry!" I started, but he put his finger to my lips to shut me up.

"Stay as long as you want. I have to go to a meeting with a potential new hotel , but I've made reservations for the dinner show at the Nacional for us later. Eight PM. Just the two of us."

Yup. I was Cinderella de Havana, and this was my Latin Prince Charming. But wait! What about my "evil stepmother" who doesn't let me out of the house? He kissed me on the forehead, then left the room. As soon as I heard the door click, I attacked the phone. I dialed the number again and waited, not entirely sure what I was going to say.

"Buenos?" The abuelita answered finally on the second try.

"Señora! Soy la chica que se queda en tu casa!" I blurted, "Necessito hablar con el hombro que se queda alli tambien!" There was a very audible gasp on the other side of the phone as the abuelita realized it was me who was calling, followed by, "Ay dios mio chica!" and a very fast, long rant that was hard to understand, but I definitely caught the gist of it as, 'Are you crazy? The man was worried for a while, but now he has gone back to work. He left a note saying he wants to see a draft by tonight.' At least that's what I thought she said.

"Lo siento, estaba con mis amigos," I stammered, not entirely sure why I felt the need to apologize and explain my whereabouts as if it were my mom asking. At twenty -seven years old, I hadn't had to explain to anyone where I was for a while, which suddenly made me irritated and wish I could have come to Havana alone. That was one of the many reasons I loved traveling solo so much; not having to ask or tell anyone what you're doing. The abuelita continued to rant, and I continued to try and figure out what she was saying while mentally noting to never agree to share an accommodation with someone I'm working for ever again.

"Entonces, para verificar, el hombre no estara en casa hasta mas tarde esta noche?" I spoke slowly and clearly to get a verbal verification from her that she had said they would not be back until much later at night. That way, I could have time to both delay potentially getting yelled at and also have time to explore more on my own. She confirmed, and I asked her to leave a note in case he returned sooner, saying I was sorry and that I tried to call last night and will have both drafts ready by tonight.

Since I was no longer in a rush to get back and explain myself to The Editor and definitely in zero rush to get yelled at in person by the abuelita, I decided to enjoy the luxury of the hotel room while I had it to myself.

With Andrik gone, I was finally comfortable enough to undress and took my time in the hot shower with actual water pressure. Noticing there were luxury toiletries and an actual hairdryer, I took the opportunity to finally wash my gross sweat and dust -coated hair. I hadn't done so at the casa particular because the water would always get cold before I even had a chance to open the shampoo bottle, and I didn't bring a hairdryer under the privileged assumption that all accommodations had them. *Not in Cuba.*

As the strong aroma of roses and jasmines whirled through the thick steam I was creating from the shower, I closed my eyes and imagined that this was always the way I traveled. Getting to stay in luxury hotels rather than haunted guest rooms where I'm watched more closely than I ever was as a teenager. *One day. One day.*

Once I was thoroughly washed, and my hair was blown out the best I could do using Andriks man-comb, I put my dress from the night before back on and used what little makeup I had in my purse to *not* look like I had just shacked at a random guy's hotel room. Just as I was about to head out, I had a massive *DUH* moment, realizing I could have been using his free Wi-Fi this entire time! Then a second thought flickered to the forefront of my mind; *Nate.*

It had been a full twenty -four hours since I messaged him . Would he assume I went home with someone? Would he even care if I did? I quickly took my seatbelt bag off my shoulder and yanked both my laptop and my phone out of it, simultaneously logging on to the Wi-Fi. The pings came through on my phone first, so I abandoned my laptop and gave my phone my full attention. Five messages from Nate.

'How's your day going over there?'

'So pissed I'm still stuck on this island.'

Then after a few hours' gap, there was yet another selfie of him at the bar with a beer in hand.

'Was going to invest in a property here, but the weather is making me change my mind.'

'Guessing you don't have Wi-Fi, that sucks.'

'Sleep emoji'

Nothing substantial enough to make me feel guilty. And not that I should even care, considering we aren't even dating. His lack of flirtation compared to Andrik's over-flirtation was a turnoff, so much so that I didn't even bother writing back. Why waste time texting a guy who talks to me because he's bored on an island (that I would *die* to be able to go to) when there was one making plans to wine and dine me in Havana? Not to mention when I was in Havana in general.

Surprisingly my mom hadn't texted me, but I sent her a quick message anyway, hinting at a juicy story to tell her, along with a photo of me trying to smoke a cigar at the Tropicana. She'd get a good laugh at that.

Next, I checked my email but realized it was Saturday, so no one was working or bothering me to work. Well, except The Editor, who I remembered gave me a sudden deadline for my article draft. No big deal, I've written full books for people in a week, so writing a one thousand word article about a dope destination would be a breeze. I just needed a bit more content and a nice inspiring place to write it.

I started wracking my brain for places to explore today. I'd already covered all the different neighborhoods of Havana but hadn't been to a beach yet, and wondered if there were any nearby. From what all of the general tourist websites said, the closest tourist beach was Varadero, but that was several hours away. Suddenly I remembered something *not* from a tourist website.

Sometimes, doing your research really pays off. While brushing up on my extremely rusty history of the Revolucion and gawking at photos of Che on the flight to Cuba, something stuck out to me that no one had mentioned while recommending places to see while I was there.

'*Villa Terara, the only gated community in Cuba, where Che spent months recovering and where he wrote 'Guerilla Warfare. Ernest Hemmingway also had a vacation home there where he wrote his famous novels.*" My eyes had bulged out as I imagined a scruffy, long-haired Che relaxing on the porch of a beachfront house in Cuba, writing one of the most infamous books in Cuban history, potentially with Hemmingway as his neighbor, sipping a mojito. Maybe that was where Hemmingway had written his Pulitzer *and* Nobel Prize -winning book, *The Old Man and the Sea. A book that reminded me of my grandfather and which several years later, I'd splurge a couple of grand on the first edition of it.*

I had made a mental note to try to find the beach where the community was but completely forgot about it until right now. That was *definitely* where I should be writing my articles. I just needed to figure out how to get there.

Suddenly another overlooked thought flashed in my mind; I remembered seeing the name but had questioned if it was the same place. Now I was sure that I saw Terara on the route of one of the more local tourist buses that takes you outside of Havana. It would make sense since the last stop is Playa de Santa Maria, which I knew was further than Terara.

How epic! I would have a beach hopping and writing day! Then late, I would come back and meet Andrik at the Nacional. And hopefully, buy a new dress somewhere along the way.

The tourist buses were parked in the city square just outside the Saratoga, which was extremely convenient since if I was coming from my own place, it would have taken 10 CUCs and about forty -five minutes to get there. A five -minute free walk was way more convenient and made me dream once again about the day when I'd start getting higher -end collaborations. I spotted the older white bus next to the sign that I'd seen the route for the beaches on and strolled overconfidently.

"Hola señor! Es este el autobus que va a Terara?" I asked the driver, just to make sure I wasn't getting on a one -way bus to Varadero or something.

"Terara?" He said, apparently surprised, "Si, si, te puedo llevar ahi." He seemed to consider it before confirming he could take me there, which made me wonder if it was a rare request to make. "Cuesta cinco CUCs para ir y volver." He added, tapping the clear box of currency on the dashboard of the bus.

For only 5 CUC, I could take this tour bus to and from Cuba's "only gated community" and see the private beach where Che and Hemingway both used to write their novels! Plus, if I had time, I could check out the more popular Santa Maria beach. Today was going to be the best day ever! I took an empty seat near the very front of the bus both to avoid all the people in the rows behind it who were staring at me and in hopes that the driver would tell me when to get off.

It only took about twenty -five minutes to get to Tarará from Havana Vieja, which makes it one of the closest accessible beaches to get to. When we pulled up, I saw the supposed "gated community," which consisted of a metal pole-gate that a guard had to hand lift. The community wasn't entirely what I expected — it looked like houses built mostly in the 1970's, similar to ones you'd see in Hialeah, but spaced out more with land surrounding each of them.

Since the Revolucion made it so that everyone is equal in pay, housing, food, etc., the prestige of the neighborhood before 1958 was probably way higher, but now it just seemed like a ghost town. I got off anyway and was the only one on the bus of tourists to do so. I assumed they *hadn't* done their research on what made the town so unique. Or more likely, they didn't care and preferred the nicer atmosphere at Playa de Santa Maria.

As I stepped out into the hot, dry air, my ears perked up towards salsa music that I heard coming from behind a large building with a sign on it that said "Casa Club ." I followed it around the structure while an enormous smile crept across my face like I had just found sunken treasure.

Off in the distance ahead of the Casa Club was the distinct palate of shimmering hues of blue that went from crystal clear to indigo, starting at the white sand shore and stretching off into the horizon.

Before making a mad dash for my found paradise, I decided to sneak up into this Casa Club, where I knew I'd be able to find a Cuba Libre. What better way to celebrate my find than by having a rum and coke on the beach? It turns out this Casa Club is some sort of community center, but it looks like a four -star resort's pool. There seemed to be many Hispanic people there, no Americans or Europeans, so I wondered if they lived in the area or were renting rooms in the neighborhood.

Anyway, I got my Cuba Libre for a mere one CUC and headed out to the beach. *Oh wow!* The beach was nearly deserted; only a few young locals hung near a bench, and a woman lounged on a single chair near the shore. Surprisingly, there was someone kite-surfing, but other than that, the beach was empty. I wondered if living on an island made pools more desirable.

Immediately I hiked my dress up to my thighs and ran into the water. I splashed around for a bit like a child before noticing that all five people on the beach were staring at me. I didn't care, and I even took out my selfie stick from my purse, connected my action camera to my phone, and clicked several photos of the glorious tropical beach.

Per usual, my selfie-stick act caused a few giggles, so I walked farther down the beach away from the too-cool chicos and found a nice stretch of beach to set up my beach-office. Since I didn't have a towel, I sat straight in the sand and used my purse as a lap table for my computer.

Where to even start? I knew Ralph would want the article to be "sexy ," but how could I do that without exploiting the Cuban people? *I know.* I'll exploit myself. I started writing about my sultry Havana night, but of course, as a fictional Cuban woman who's merely having a typical night out with her husband who she's been promised to since birth, but she still dresses up to the nines for him every single day. She prays for her family every morning and night at the Catholic altar in her home, where she still lives with three generations of family members. They don't have much money, but their love makes them the richest people in the world. *Wait, wasn't that last part something my grandma wrote in her journal?* I felt a pang of pride, turning the story that my grandma waited so long to tell us into a whimsical fairy tale.

It only took about an hour to write the fifteen-hundred - word article. That's what happens when you integrate your real life into your work. Well, and when you are determined to go explore but know you need to get your work done first. Suddenly, I felt another body pang, but this one was sharp in my stomach, followed by a dizzy feeling in my head. *Oh shit. I forgot to eat today again.*

I'd gotten so used to my morning meatless-Cuban sandwiches that I didn't even realize I had skipped breakfast and was now going into lunchtime on an empty stomach. My fast metabolism never has any problem with reminding me of when I'm supposed to eat. I just hoped this wasn't one of the times where the nausea was going to be so bad that I barfed , especially since I wasn't exactly sure where to get food.

Farther down the beach, I could see a lot more people. It must be Playa de Santa Maria. The bus wasn't supposed to come by where I was for another half hour or so, and who knows how late it would be, considering everyone in Cuba is on permanent island time. I decided my best bet was to walk down the beach to where the crowds were. It would probably take less time and would distract the hangry monster.

There were a couple of houses close to the beach along the way, and I wondered if one of them may have been Hemmingway's or Che's. They were worn down now, but I could tell there were still people living in them. I decided to do what I do best when I'm alone with no Wi-Fi; daydream of what it was like decades ago. From what I read, Hemmingway seemed a lot like my grandpa, so I imagined hanging out with him and his many cats on his patio while we both wrote stories on typewriters. Then I imagined a young, hot version of Che walking along the beach talking about his crazy ideas to instill equality through Socialism and Communism, and me telling him there's definitely a better way to do it. *Yes, these are actual things I think about.*

When I finally approached the crowds of people, it was like night and day. There were actual sun chairs and umbrellas set up, music playing, and even a couple of beach shack restaurants... *THANK GOD!*

"Hola señora! Quieres comer? Algo para beber?" A deeply tanned guy in a t-shirt, boardshorts, and mirrored sunglasses came running towards me, waving a paper menu. In the corner of my eye, I could see a similar guy coming towards me. I realized the restaurants were probably in an intense competition. I was so hungry though that I didn't care what was on the menu ; I just cared about who could get me food first.

"Si! Gracias!" I said, taking the weathered paper from him.

"Ven, ven, sientate aqui!" He said, gesturing with one open palm towards a plastic white lawn chair with a little plastic table in front of it, and his other hand gently pushing me towards it. "Tenemos el mejor comida! Tenemos pollo, ensalada mixto, cerveza, mojito, que te queire?"

He seemed to be determined to get my order before someone else did, so I quickly scanned the menu for something I could actually eat. There wasn't much. It was mostly chicken. So I went with the safest option; side dishes.

"Puedo pedir una ensalada, y plantanos? Y para beber, un mojito!" Salad, plantains, and a mojito. Sounds like paradise, even though I was warned *not to* eat salad, and I don't like it anyway. Whatever, it was all only four CUCs and it was better than feeling like I was going to pass out or vomit.

"De donde eres señora?" He replied, asking where I was from rather than repeating my order. *Shit.* Was this a test? Americans weren't supposed to be allowed to do touristic activities without a guide . Would he tell on me if I told him the truth?

"Uh, soy de America, pero tengo familia aqui!" I mumbled, hoping that saying I have family here would translate to *I'm allowed to be here without a guide.*

"Es verdad?! Wowwww! Que bueno! Te ves como una estrella de cine!" He announced dramatically, clutching his heart with both hands. *Well shit!* If I had known people in Cuba were going to react to me being American by telling me I look like a movie star, I would have been saying it more often! Or maybe not. I don't want to get kicked out of the country just yet. I giggled and profusely thanked him for the compliment as he backed up towards the food shack with the biggest smile on his face and hands still clutching his heart. *That would have never happened if I was here with a guy!* I thought to myself, mentally listing yet another reason why I loved traveling solo.

The food wasn't great, but the mojito was strong, and the view was unbeatable. I even bought a handmade kite from a kid who had colored the Cuban flag on it with markers. Somehow it was already three o'clock, so I decided to order one more mojito to-go and walk down the beach before catching the supposed three-thirty bus back to Havana.

In my head, walking down the beach with a mojito was going to be much more enjoyable than it was. I'm not sure if I'm paranoid or self-conscious, but it seemed like everyone was staring at me and talking. Maybe it was because I was wearing a maxi dress? Or maybe it was because I was the only person not in a swimsuit? I was about to opt to head up through some dunes towards the street when I saw a blondehaired, pale - skinned guy approaching me.

"Hola! Hola!" He said in a clearly European accent.

"Um, hola. Are you from Europe?" I responded automatically in English. This seemed to shock him. After revealing that I was actually American and a travel writer on assignment to write an article for a magazine about Havana, he revealed something even more surprising. He said he thought I was one of the Cuban women who walk along the beach looking for paid sex deals. After he apologized profusely following my harsh reaction and backed away as bright as a tomato (since now I clearly knew he was looking for sex), I added a tick mark to my mental list of the downsides of traveling solo as a woman. Suddenly, I couldn't wait to be back in Havana and getting ready for my date with Andrik.

It took an hour to get back to Havana Vieja, then forty-five minutes to take the Coco back to my haunted house in Vedado. There was no possible way to sneak inside my room since you had to verbally call for someone to throw you down the key to get in. My heart was pounding out of my chest as I reached the third floor and turned the key to open the heavy door. I had been rehearsing what to say to The Editor over and over again in hopes I could somehow write off my bad behavior as necessary and impress him with the story I had written.

When I stepped inside, he was nowhere in sight. That was a relief, but I still felt the wrath of the abuelita coming.

"Hola chica!" She said with a mischievous smile, approaching me from the living room. I handed her back the key and apologized again, but she waved her hand in my face and cut me off.

"No es mi asunto. Se fueron a pasar la noche, diviertete mientras puedas." She whispered with a wink, handing me a piece of paper with a note from The Editor confirming what she had said about them going out for the night and having fun, doing whatever I wanted. I couldn't believe it. She wasn't mad. The Editor wasn't mad. Well, from what I could tell. It would probably be another story when I actually saw him , but she had told me to go have fun while I can, so I guess I had to listen, right?

The cold shower didn't faze me in the slightest, probably because I had been roasting in the Havana sun all day, and my skin felt like it was on fire. I scrubbed the sand out of places I didn't even know you can get sand and double washed my armpits and the area under my boobs that, for some reason, always has a worse sweat-odor than my pits.

I was paranoid that The Editor would come back early and forbid me from going on my date, so I moved at lightning speed to get ready. I gave up on my attempted blow-out and twisted my hair back into a top-knot, and applied my usual minimal makeup, except with the addition of a top eyeliner wing —my classic wannabe-Audrey-Hepburn look, blonde edition. I chose my teal crocheted dress once again and opened my black seatbelt bag on the bed to pack. This time instead of my laptop, I rolled a thin black cotton maxi and a pair of extra underwear up and shoved it into the bottom of the bag , along with my toothbrush, powder compact, mascara, and extra cash.

Since there was no Wi-Fi and no time to run down to the Presidente, I made the bold move of leaving my laptop with the article draft on the credenza outside of The Editor's room. I wasn't sure how serious he was about having the draft to him by tonight, but as irresponsible as I am with my moral decisions, I'm chronically on point with my business deadlines. I told the abuelita why I was leaving the laptop there and vaguely mentioned that I was going to see the dinner show at the Nacional. This made her swoon and reminisced about her younger years, which apparently excited her so much that she practically pushed me out the door.

It was getting dark, and I felt a bit nervous walking the ten blocks to the Presidente Hotel to get a taxi. Tonight, I definitely looked nice and like I had money, but would anyone really go as far as to rob a tourist? The answer was no.

I got to the Presidente at six forty -two, which was just enough time to use the internet for a bit because *priorities.* After my usual transaction with the front desk clerk and bartender, I was logged on with my phone and went through the usual routine of checking iMessages, social media, then emails.

In chronological order, they went:

'Hellooooo? Starting to get worried about ya! Let me know if you're Ok! And if you still wanna meet me in Vegas next week!' From Nate.

'Hola mi amorr, can't wait to see you tonight, hope you had a great day! Don't forget to look at flights to Panama for next weekend.' From Andrik

Then moving on to social media, I nearly fell out of my chair. My posts on Instagram from earlier this morning had over five hundred likes! More than twice as many as I usually get! I quickly scrolled through the comments. Of course, Nate had commented, but nothing telling, just a bland, "Loved that place!" likely to let everyone know that he'd been here before. I liked his comment but didn't respond. And decided to wait until I got back to the Saratoga to make another post. I had just enough time to check emails before I had to go, and the one third from the top immediately caught my eye:

'Hello Alyssa! Thank you so much for reaching out to Keflavik Inn! We have received your proposal for collaboration and are very impressed with your blog and social media! We would like to offer you five nights at our hotel in Keflavik in exchange for the blog post and social media posts you mentioned. Please let us know when you plan on coming, and we will book your room accordingly!"

"WHAT? YEEEEAASSSSSS!" I shot up out of my aluminum chair with both arms raised over my head, instantly drawing the attention of everyone on the entire pool deck and bar area. I turned from side to side, hands still raised over my head, smiling like an idiot who was looking for someone, anyone, to tell the good news. The only person I obviously recognized was the bartender, so I yelled, "I'm going to Iceland!" to which he tilted his head with a very confused look.

"Voy a Icelandia!" I translated, to which he and multiple people around me responded with a smile and applause.

I couldn't believe it. Getting a hotel collaboration in another country had been something I only dreamed of and had worked on getting for so long before I left for Cuba. Screw traveling to meet up with guys, I had my own business deal, where I would travel by myself, work for myself, and not have to worry about anyone else.

And this was just the beginning.

Chapter Six

Don't Date a Guy Who Travels

In case anyone is wondering how dinner went with Andrik that last night in Havana, I'd give it a *'WTF.'*

I'm not sure if he had been drinking all day with clients and was cranky or if my lack of smothering attention was annoying him, but he was a straight -up man-child during the whole performance. He acted less than interested in the show, complained about all of the food dishes, and downed his Cuba Libres so fast that the bottle of rum was gone before the end of the meal.

He promised we would have a better time in Panama, where he was from and had connections and friends, and assured me his behavior resulted from a long business day. Thank God he was so drunk that he passed out at the hotel that night and had to wake up extremely early for his flight home.

In case anyone is wondering again, yes, I went to Panama. And it was one of the worst decisions I've made, right up there with getting convinced to go to Dublin with my ex a few years ago, who ended up holding me hostage for three days. *HOW do I not learn from my mistakes?!*

Turns out Andrik is an extremely privileged, entitled, trust-fund baby who treats everyone like shit. And that's straight out of the mouths of his friends that he introduced me to. They had told me in secrecy that they were surprised such a nice, smart girl was hanging out with him because he's such an asshole.

Sadly, I found out that was true the hard way.

For the first time in over a year since my last abusive relationship, I found myself screaming and crying on the floor, begging a man to just leave me alone. Don't worry, nothing physical happened, thank God. But he did literally say to me that I should at least have sex with him since he got me a hotel room.

My pride and ego were shattered, and I felt absolutely disgusting. How stupid and naive had I been to actually believe he was interested in my work as a travel blogger? Not to mention, I actually thought he was interested in me as a partner, not just a sex object.

I had thrown my cash and credit cards at him, screaming to take all of my money for the room and just leave me alone. That finally got him.

He had texted me non-stop afterwards, insisting that I stay and even offering to set up a private tour of Panama City, but I wanted nothing to do with it. I immediately found an affordable hotel nearby and left, blocking him from any form of contact. I found solace in texting with Nate during the whole debacle. Of course, he had no idea what was going on besides that I was "doing a hotel collaboration in Panama," but it was nice to have someone to talk to at any time of the day or night. It was actually a bit strange that he would always reply no matter when, but I wrote it off as a traveler thing.

Somehow, I pulled myself together and made the best of my time in Panama, taking a tour of the Panama Canal and learning its morbid history yet essential purpose. I was too distraught to remember much and found myself once again desperately wanting to just go home.

When I got back to L.A. a couple of days later, I had a new ferocious attitude that was focused solely on my *own* collaborations. I'd used the accepted proposal with Keflavik Inn to further enhance my pitches to other companies in Iceland . I had succeeded in landing deals with Silfra Snorkeling, Icelandic Horse Treks, and even a prominent car rental company.

My two articles for The Editor's magazine got published, and I re-published my family story on my blog, which got a lot of attention. I even got offered a grant to write the story in more detail for another publication.

In addition to the five thousand word story, I had also written about ten blog posts about Cuba, but none about Panama because I was so scarred by the experience. It felt good to be focused on my own work again and not distracted by toads dressed as Prince Charming. In fact, I purposely never mentioned Vegas again to Nate in fear of falling for yet another frog prince.

But just a week after I got home from Panama, he brought it up again. He made it seem like it was just a meeting of two travel enthusiasts, with the potential for me to meet new connections in Vegas that could potentially help with my career. Not that I really wanted to be working on posts about Vegas since I was trying to get away from the party scene, but as a newbie blogger, I assumed any connections were better than none.

The day before I was due to drive to Vegas from LA to meet Nate, I was having lunch with a British friend who owns one of those soft-porn magazines similar to Maxim. We were having our typical banter about how I would never pose for his magazine because I had more integrity than to just wanting to be famous for showing my body (no offense to anyone, it's always been my mindset), and per usual, he applauded me for it and treated me to lunch anyway.

But my lunch was suddenly disrupted and turned completely upside-down with a text from another travel-world friend who I had texted earlier to tell her about my plans to meet Nate in Vegas.

"Ummm chica, I love you, but he has a long-term girlfriend. Like I'm pretty sure they live together..." The message was like a dagger to the heart and a punch to the stomach. Even though there had been no talk of a date or anything romantic happening in Vegas, the truth was that Nate had been non-stop texting me for over a month now and had made plans to meet me in Vegas.

There were only two ways to take it. The first was to say nothing and treat it as if it were one hundred percent a total business meeting. Be professional, only talk about travel and how to monetize it, and do not respond to any sort of flirtation. If he did have a girlfriend, then it would be fine because I would convince myself we are completely platonic anyway.

The second option was to risk sounding like a crazy girl with a growing crush and just ask him for the truth.

As you can probably imagine, I opted for option number two. I excused myself from the table, walked around the corner so that I was out of sight, caught my breath, and immediately texted Nate:

'Hey! So, I don't mean to be dramatic bc I know nothing is going on between us.' That was a lie, *' but someone just told me you have a long-time girlfriend and I really don't want to impose on that, so I'm not sure it would be a good idea to meet you in Vegas.'*

I pushed send before I could convince myself that I was overreacting or sounding like a psycho girl who assumed he was trying to be more than business colleague. Nausea rose up in my stomach and didn't mix well with the bubbles I had drank at lunch. I pressed my fingertips to my forehead, begging my brain to stop saying all the things I *really* wanted to say to him and trying to breathe to slow my heart rate before returning to lunch. I assumed the shock of the message would result in Nate either ignoring me indefinitely or at least make him wait a while to come up with a good excuse. Or maybe he would simply tell me it was true and that he had no intention of being anything more than acquaintances...in Vegas.

After one more deep breath, I took a step forward when *Ping! Ping!* Two new text messages came hurling across the technological gap between us. Obviously, I couldn't help but to immediately read them;

'No, we aren't together. We have been on and off again for a really long time, but we're not on good terms right now. I haven't even spoken to her in over six months.'

'I like you, Alyssa, I don't know how that isn't obvious, but I promise you I do not have a girlfriend.'

What in the actual fuck just happened? I stared at my phone dumbfounded, not knowing what to believe or think. Should I be happy that he says he doesn't have a girlfriend and likes me? Should I be smart and consider the fact that he's probably lying? But why would he text me every day, all day, if he were lying? What would my travel friend think if I went anyway after she told me he has a girlfriend?

I decided to do what any logical woman would do and screenshotted the conversation with Nate to send to my friend for her opinion.

'Idk chica, I'm like 90% sure he has a secret gf. A lot of guys that travel for business do. I'm sure he likes you ; you're totally hot! But I'm also pretty sure he has a gf.' She said, throwing me into an even worse mood. First of all, did she think the only reason guys like me is because I'm "hot"? What if Nate liked my determination to be a travel writer? What if he thought I was cool? He did constantly tell me he was my biggest fan. Anyway, my second train of thought was that maybe she was jealous. Nate was the ultimate catch, especially for a girl who loves to travel, and I didn't exactly know her well enough to be giving me honest dating advice. But that was such a typical girl-move; believing a guy's potential lies over another woman's truth. I had no idea who to believe.

Frozen in place on the sidewalk of Sunset Boulevard, I just stared at my phone as if I was willing to tell me the truth.

'Listen, I'm telling you that I'm not with her and that I want to see you. I hope you'll still drive out tomorrow, I just got here.'

....no pressure.

'*For the last time, STOP texting me. You're a jerk, and I'm not interested.*' Nate was still texting me non-stop since I up and left Vegas without telling him a week ago. His game was obvious, and I honestly wanted nothing to do with it, but I can't deny that his begging to make it up to me wasn't enticing.

Essentially what had happened was (*famous last words*) I drove the four hours from LA to Vegas to meet Nate. He somehow convinced me that staying in the second bedroom of his timeshare condo was completely normal, so I met him there, and as I'm sure he was anticipating, I was instantly impressed. The condo had high ceilings and those massive glass windows that take up the entire walls. It was clearly furnished by a professional interior designer and maintained by a staff who apparently expected guests all the time because the bar was fully stocked, and the wine cabinet wall had expensive bottles in each slot.

Much to my liking, Nate had offered me a glass of white wine as soon as I got there and poured himself a glass of red. Our conversation was natural like it was meant to be, and before we knew it, we had been talking for three hours and finished both bottles of wine. During that time frame, he had forgotten to mention that we were both supposed to go meet some of his business clients, the GM and social media director of one of the big hotels he had helped develop a renovation for, for dinner.

As you can probably imagine, getting told you're going to a business dinner in one hour after downing a bottle of wine is absolutely terrifying. Unlike Nate, who had business meetings and dinners almost every day, I was yet to start having them. I didn't want to pass up the opportunity, but I also didn't want to mess it up.

Long story short, it was incredibly awkward. The GM was a woman, and it was beyond obvious that she was interested in Nate and not happy at all that he had brought me. Especially a *drunk*-me that tends to talk too much and isn't shy about voicing opposing opinions. Whatever the true reason was, it made her decide to tell him that he couldn't bring me as his plus one to an activity they had planned for him the next day, but he didn't tell me this until much later. So let's back up to before that conversation.

I'm not going to lie . The way he treated me the whole day before the fiasco was on point, and I had no idea if he really was the perfect guy or if it was all an act to sleep with me. We spent the day lounging by the pool with a bottle of wine on ice. It was mostly because we were both extremely hungover, and I very much appreciated that he was on my level. We had a nice early dinner, and as soon as we got back to his place, it was like a magnetic bomb went off and we were immediately engulfed and intertwined with each other. It was the type of chemistry you'd pray to have with someone, the kind you know will never fizzle out. And it was also the first moment that I knew I was going to fall in love with him for a very long time. It was obvious we both badly wanted to go farther but somehow, a smart little birdie in my brain told me that I'd probably regret it. So, I pulled myself away from his strong arms, apologized, and said I didn't think it was a good idea since we had just met the day before and all. He settled for a passionate make-out sesh instead, which, of course, is just translated to you still being potentially DTF. When we finally got to the point of not being able to resist each other any longer, I suggested that we probably should just go to sleep. Assuming that would mean in the same bed. But nope.

He straight up left the guest bedroom and went to the master. I was literally shocked and even asked why he was going to sleep in the other room after he just tried to have sex with me. He said it was a thing he did ; he has to sleep in his own room. Where he didn't invite me to sleep either, yet had no problem trying to hook up with me in the guest room. That's what made me start to really question things.

In the morning, I had woken up to a note on the counter that said he had gone to yet another business meeting and would be back around 11 am. So, like a lovesick puppy, I waited. And waited. And waited. By 2 pm, I started to get irritated. He had just left me in his condo after I drove all the way to Vegas

160

to see him and was now three hours late. Realizing I was in the party capital of the United States, I started to wonder if maybe this meeting was more like a pool party or something.

I checked his Instagram and Stories for the twentieth time, but still, no posts. No, he's smarter than that. He knows I'd be looking, but then my inner spy slash stalker had a thought; if he was with someone, they would probably post about it and tag him.

Sure enough, as soon as I tapped on the icon for Photos Tagged of You, there he was, flying in a little three-person fighter jet that I knew was a new tourist attraction in Vegas. And of course, the second passenger sitting in front of him was a girl. My heart dropped, and my stomach twisted. How could he leave me in his condo while he went and took another girl to his "business meeting"? It got worse. When I scrolled down to see who the girl was, it was none other than my travel friend who had been the one who warned me that Nate had a girlfriend in the first place. That stung. A lot. It was my first of many backstabs in the travel industry. And it was a double-dagger since I knew both people involved.

So many emotions exploded through me. Part of me wanted to wait for Nate to get back to give him a piece of my mind, but the majority of me just wanted to get the hell out of there, get back to LA, and get back to work while swearing off men for a while. *I'll show him. I'll show everyone.*

Two hours into the drive back to LA, Nate started texting me, asking where I had gone. That meant he had finally just gotten back and would have left me in the condo until 4 pm without so much as an update. My heart was pounding with fury and pain. I wanted to rip him a new asshole so badly that I literally screamed in the car. I was so pissed that I actually had to pull over, mostly because I needed two hands to type the hate text.

By the time I had slowed down from going eighty-five miles per hour to zero, my heart rate had slowed down a bit too. The novel-length text I had been constructing in my head watered down as well as the world stopped rushing past me. *Remember, you're not even dating, don't be crazy.* I reminded myself of this teeny fact but also wondered why it felt like we had been married for years.

With the car fully stopped on the side of the road, I took a couple of deep breaths and finally picked up my phone. He had written three more texts, apologizing for being so late and saying he wanted to take me to a nice dinner. *HA!* Sure, take another girl with you on a fun activity all day, after trying to have sex with me, then expect me to just want to go to dinner with you, not to mention stay with you? *What a dick.*

The phone rang as I was still deciphering his excuses. I immediately clicked ignore, and he immediately responded with a text asking again where I was.

There was so much I wanted to say, but I decided to go for the dramatics. I screen-shot the photo of the three of them in the jet and sent it to him with a simple message. "You're a dick. By the way, that's who told me you had a girlfriend and to stay away from you."

My phone rang again, and immediately I hit Ignore. And again, and again. I solved the problem by turning off my phone, turning up the radio, and taking my time getting back home.

A week later, after pointing out that if I really wanted him to leave me alone, I would have blocked him, I started to wonder if I should give him a second chance. I mean, he was trying *really* hard. And I really couldn't deny that I was *really* into him. Or at least the idea of him. He texted me from the moment I woke up to the last minute before I fell asleep. I was stand-offish, and he could tell, but he kept trying anyway. He even asked if he could meet me in Iceland, which I immediately declined, explaining a little too harshly that after getting left in a condo in Vegas, there was no way in hell I was letting him just come on my hard-earned trip to Iceland. Even though, secretly *all* I wanted was to travel together. But the trust was gone.

'I know you don't trust me, but let me make it up to you, please! Come meet me in Napa next week . I have a business meeting with a hotel I helped develop there and it's near

wineries...' Damn him! He knew how to get to me! Travel and wine!

Chapter Seven

Escape to Iceland

"Zone three. Now boarding zone three." As soon as the airline clerk started saying the word ' zone,' the remaining people waiting to board made a bee-line for the check-in desk, except for me.

As excited as I was that the day had finally come for my first ever self-attained sponsored and completely solo trip to Iceland, I still clung to the last remaining minutes I had to use my phone. Like an idiot, I wanted to see what Nate had to say for himself this time.

'I swear, it's not what you think! I just need some time, I want to be with YOU!'

Let me re-cap what our latest blow out was about. I ended up agreeing to meet him in Napa Valley like an idiot. The hotel he was working at was gorgeous; a stone cabin with a glistening pool nestled in the middle of the vineyard. We had enjoyed two blissful days together there, doing wine tastings, and he even helped me take some photos for my blog and social media! That's the real way to a female travel blogger's heart. Then on the third day, as we were lounging by the pool, he got a phone call. He answered it right in front of me with a shaky voice, and I immediately heard a woman yelling at him. *Guess that answers if he really does have a girlfriend...*

It may have been partially my fault that she found out because I posted a photo from Napa and she clearly knew he was also in Napa. At least that's what Nate said when I asked, along with mentioning she sometimes looks at who he's following and then checks their accounts. I didn't blame her at all, especially now realizing how easy it was for him to cheat on her without either girl knowing the other exists. I also didn't want to hurt her at all, whoever *she* was. And felt extremely bad and gross now knowing that I was "the other woman."

For some reason, despite now being officially in love with him, I was extremely calm when it all went down. He was caught. There was nothing he could do or say to deny what I had just heard. I immediately told myself it was over and to just enjoy the remaining time I had there. It was for the best anyway. Not only had I started to realize all of the red flags from him keeping me a complete secret, but now there was the blatant fact that he was a cheater, which meant that even if we did ever have a relationship, he would likely cheat on me as well. When he returned to the pool, he looked like he had seen a ghost.

"So that's her, I take it." I had said, as he looked from the floor to my face with the ultimate look of, *'I am so fucked.'*

'Alyssa, I swear, we aren't together, she just flipped because she saw your picture and because she wasn't expecting me to be with someone so soon because,' he started trying to explain some blabber of bullshit but I raised my hand to cut him off.

'Because you really are still with her? And she just saw you're on a trip with another girl? Yeah, I'd be pissed too. Good thing *we* aren't together. But I feel *really* bad for her. How can you do this to people?" I snapped, then slid into the pool and under the water so he could let that soak in for a sec. We still had dinner and a long drive the next morning, so I decided to just completely shut off. I got white-girl-wasted at dinner, as

165

one does when they're on a trip with a guy and his girlfriend slash non-girlfriend calls. Then slept most of the drive and acted like he didn't exist for the time I was awake. *Mature, I know.*

When we got to the airport in San Francisco, he asked for a hug, but I gave him an eye roll instead and walked towards my gate for Los Angeles, leaving him to head to his and back to Seattle, where he may or may not have been going home to the woman on the phone. Even if they truly weren't together at the time, the way she sounded on the phone made it clear they would likely be getting back together. It was a ballsy move, and I was proud that I didn't give in, but I won't deny that it stung like hell. Mostly because I secretly didn't *always* want to be solo, and I really thought we could conjoin travel lives, but that's just not how the universe made it for me. *In fact, I almost won't deny that Nate's constant let-downs for several years in the future is what kept me as a solo traveler and ultimately led to my success as one.*

My dreams of finding a cute, successful, fun guy who also travels for a living and who could be the other half to the vision I had of a power couple was shattered. Not to mention, my heart. Who knew how long it would be before I found another rare gem like that. Someone who knew all of my aspirations to be a successful travel blogger and see the world and didn't think it was the least bit silly, strange, or unattainable. Someone who told me regularly that he was my biggest fan. Nate made me feel like he actually believed in me and like it was only a matter of time until I made it. Of course, he hadn't helped me with any connections or anything, even though he easily could have with how many hotels he had done business with. But I wanted to prove to him that I didn't need it and that we could be together and I could become successful, all on my own. Of course, that idea was blown to hell the second I walked away. Or at least, so I thought.

Nate didn't try to text me for three whole days after the Napa incident. I was sure he was either being closely monitored or completely scared away by my dramatic reaction. He had finally asked what I was up to as if nothing had happened on the fourth day. Naturally, I waited three hours to respond, then merely mentioned how excited I was for my trip to Iceland in two days.

Of course, his response to that was offering to meet me there, of course after mentioning he was looking at apartments in L.A. to move there. You know, where I live. Just like that, the hopeless romantic in me swooned at the thought of the perfect travel couple adventuring around the globe together again, and it was just so easy to see because I *knew* he was capable of booking a flight for something with a day's notice. I'd told him that if he happened to be there, we could potentially hang out *as friends*, but I needed some solid verification that he was not in a relationship. That seemed to scare him off, and he stopped bringing up the trip for the next two days   until of course, the mere minutes before my flight.

All it took was him saying, '*Have an amazing time in Iceland! Wish I could go back with ya, that place is amazing!*' to fire me off. I'd gone on full-on Oh-she's-hot-but-a-psycho-mode and let him have it about all the reasons why he *could* have been coming with me but chose not to, likely because he had a freaking girlfriend! That's what his latest response was about. He's quote '*not with her, just needs to figure out some legal things for some things they share.*' Might as well tell me he's waiting for the divorce papers to be signed. *Wait...was he?*

'*Well, I don't want you to come anyway. You're unreliable, sketchy, and you keep getting my hopes up only to let me down. I'm over it. Don't text me while I'm in Iceland.*'

It wasn't fully true or at all what I wanted, but it had to be done. My heart hurt, and my stomach was in a triple knot. Worst of all, I could feel hot tears welling up in my eyes when I should have been crying of happiness. The check-in line was down to the last seven fellow budget-travelers, so I dropped my phone in my Harvey's seatbelt bag, pulled out my passport and boarding pass, and joined the queue (as they say in Europe).

"Thank you, Miss Ramos! Enjoy your trip to Iceland!" The Barbie-doll counter clerk said to me with a brilliant smile. And just like that, the glittery wanderlust filled my veins, and my brain went right back on its one-track mind of seeing the world, even if it meant doing it solo. Who needs a guy to share the experience with anyway? He'd probably just piss me off the entire time and ruin it for me. I kept repeating those thoughts as I squeezed down the narrow aisle of the hot-pink furnished airplane, ignoring my phone buzzing like crazy in my purse.

If you haven't been on an infamous budget-airline before, let me enlighten you about how awful they can be. First, they get your hopes up worse than Nate does to me about traveling together by offering insanely cheap "base" flight prices. For example, my one way flight on WOW! Airlines was advertised as only $99 from LAX to Reykjavik. But then they get you with the add-on fees, which is basically everything other than the recycled air you breathe. Luckily I was only taking one carry-on, so I only had to pay $45 extra for that, then another $30 to pick my seat so I wouldn't get stuck in an aisle on an overnight flight, but I mean, come on! The bag and seat are almost as much as the ticket! Of course, food and drinks are also extra, and since only one of those was in the budget, I opted for the wine so at least I could go to sleep and get the flight over with quicker.

Another thing about budget airlines is that the plane is usually so crappy that you wonder if it will even fly. I'll fully admit that since the entire plane was literally covered outside and inside in hot pink ; it distracted me from how tiny the actual seats were. But after a few hours of watching the poor 6'2" guy in the aisle across from me try to maneuver fitting his legs under the seat, I realized these seats were a lot smaller than regular name brand airline's. It should come as no shock that this airline went out of business shortly after my trip. Luckily for my tiny self, I was able to curl up against the window like a cat and passed out for a few hours until we got there.

'Wow!' I gasped as I stepped foot into the small Icelandic terminal. And I was not talking about the airline.

So many things caught my attention; the cold air, the cozy furnishings, and my favorite, the giant sign that said, "*Welcome to Iceland !*" It wasn't crowded or hectic like the airports I was used to in the U.S., and interestingly, everyone seemed...happy!

I pulled my overstuffed carry-on towards the doors with the sign for 'Rental Cars' over it. The words were written both in English and what I assumed was Icelandic but looked more like alien hieroglyphics to me. There was a little coffee shop just before the doors, which reminded me both that I hadn't eaten and that what I was about to attempt was a bit extreme, so I should probably get something to go.

Si nce it was my only free day without any planned collaborations, and my flight landed at six AM, but I couldn't check into my sponsored hotel until three PM, I thought it would be a great idea to immediately drive five hours across the south coast of Iceland to get to a cool looking Glacier Lagoon I had researched...and then back. I figured that since I used to make six -hour drives from my hometown to my college in Florida, it would be kind of the same. Granted, I'd be driving on the opposite side of the car and road for the first time, but that wasn't such a big deal, right?

So overall, the plan was to drive straight to Jökulsárlón glacier lagoon, find the glacier beach near it that someone had posted a photo of but didn't give any information *(inspo to do the opposite with my blog)*, maybe stop at a waterfall if I was good on time, then drive back to hopefully get to the hotel by eight PM . Again, I had no idea what to expect with the driving conditions and destination that looked like I was on another planet.

After purchasing the biggest size hot tea they had and a couple of different cheap pastry-looking things, I set off again for the doors that led outside. When they flung open, an arctic blast nearly toppled me over, and I bursted out laughing. I couldn't remember the last time I felt air that cold! I mean, it was cold in Australia, but this was like ice-cold! Immediately I prayed that it would snow and that I could say my first time seeing snow fall was in Iceland!

My excitement temporarily shielded me from the actual coldness that was making my body go numb, but that suddenly sank in . I had to prop my tea and snacks on top of my carry-on

169

to add the two extra coats I had been carrying *(to avoid extra luggage fees)*. My shoes crunched over the ice on the gravel, making me smile stupidly, assuming that meant it might snow, as I headed for the big orange sign that said Sixt.

"Hello! You must be Elisa?" A young, jovial guy in what looked like a gray Christmas sweater chirped as I approached the check -in desk.

"Alyssa, yes! I have a collaboration," I started, pulling out the screenshot of the email from the manager confirming my rental.

"Yes yes! We are expecting you! We love your blog! We just started getting travel bloggers here in Iceland ; it is very exciting!" He looked as excited as he sounded, which made me blush. I didn't think my blog was *that* great yet, and I certainly hadn't gotten comfortable with claiming out loud that I was a travel blogger. '*Fake it till you make it*' I reminded myself and carried on an equally excited conversation with him all the way to the car.

It was a dark gray, four -door, something I can't pronounce, that looked brand new and more importantly, safe. Nothing like my Ford Mustangs that I've been speeding around in since I was sixteen. I made a mental note to remember this was not a Mustang and that I should attempt not speeding. He showed me how all the levers work, how the radio was pre-set to Iceland's best stations, even though there were only three, and most importantly, how the GPS works. This was crucial since I didn't have service on my phone unless I turned on the international roaming, which I had already learned the hard way costs a shit ton of money. That was fine though, it was motivation to not be on my phone and to soak in the sights, and , of course, to not even try to talk to Nate.

After signing off that the car had no damage, I did a cute little goodbye with the rental guy and started off for the open road in Iceland!

As soon as I exited the airport and caught my first glimpse of the snow-capped mountains in the distance, the black lava rocks covered in bright green moss, and the long stretch of road in front of me and *only* me, I did something I've never done before. I screamed. At the top of my lungs, in my rental car, by damn self, I screamed.

'*WOOOOOOOOO AAHHHHHHHHH WOOOOOOO!! I DID IT!!!!*' I screamed over and over again as the hot tears rolled down my perked up cheeks and into the corners of my wide smile. This time, they were the happy kind and the only kind I ever wanted to have. My heart was full, and for the first time in my entire twenty -seven years of living, I felt truly proud of something I had accomplished completely on my own. It was my first time renting a car in another country, nonetheless, first time going on a road trip by myself in another country, and even more importantly, doing it in a destination that I never thought in a million years I'd be able to get to. I felt like I was in one of my nightly lucid dreams. There was no way this was real. It was all too perfect.

I hadn't been driving for more than ten minutes, but I couldn't help myself. I pulled over on the side of the road, grabbed my action camera and selfie stick, and walked towards what I recognized as "Troll Grass" as if I were under a spell.

'*Ow fuck!*' I instantly realized why they call it Troll Grass and the myth behind it. What I thought was fluffy patches of lime green grass turned out to be a slippery layer of deceivingly thick moss atop jagged, porous lava rocks. Like an idiot, I hadn't thought to change out of my Tom's slippers and into my pleather boots before going gallivanting onto unknown lands, and my foot immediately slipped through the Troll Grass, into a crevice, and sent my leg sideways, which both twisted my ankle *and* cut my leg on the sharp edge of the rock. '*Dammit! Really ? REALLY !*'

Naturally, I looked around suspiciously, as if a troll were going to pop out and say, '*That's what you get for trespassing bitch!*' But the fact that there was not a soul in sight made me even more scared. But not scared enough to *not* quickly take a photo, even with my foot still stuck in the rock. After carefully pulling It out and examining the bloody slice in my ankle, I eyed the death-traps closely as I tip-toed back to the car. I only twisted my ankle two more times before I got to it, then immediately changed into my boots.

Once back on the road, I set the GPS for Jökulsárlón, which was not easy to do at all. Apparently, you need to know the exact spelling...in Icelandic. Luckily there is only one road around the entire country slash island though, but unluckily, all the signs at the roundabouts are also in Icelandic. It took me two trips around the first round-about to exit off the correct one, but from there, everything else was straight -forward. Like literally, there was only one two-lane road, and it just went straight forward, forever. Or so it seemed.

The ridiculous smile never once left my face as I drank in the other-worldly views of landscapes I'd never seen before and never imagined in my wildest dreams I'd see in real life. It started with thick, rolling hills covered in brilliant green grass (*real grass, not Troll Grass)* that was flecked with furry sheep of all shades from black to white. Then it was flat lands of black gravel that seemed to stretch all the way to what looked like the ocean, which was another bizarre concept to grasp. An ocean in the arctic. I'd never thought about what that would look like before. But the reminder that I was actually in the Arctic made me smile even bigger.

'Is that ? Oh my god already ? Is that a ! 'WOOOOOOOOOOOOOOOOOO!!!' I started screaming like I had just won the lottery. I wasn't expecting to see anything on my self-made itinerary for another hour or so ; was that really it ?

'WOOOOOOOO!!! AHHHHHHHH! OH MY GOD!!!! I FUCKING DID IT!!!' The first waterfall I've ever seen in my life was straight ahead on the left-hand side of the road. I wasn't expecting it to be so easy to get to, which is why I doubted if that's what I was seeing, but the cars ahead of me, turning towards the stream of water in the distance, confirmed it. It had to be Seljalandsfoss.

I followed the other cars and watched with pure awe and true love as the waterfall grew bigger and bigger with proximity. It was every bit like any fairytale I could ever imagine.

When I got to the gravel parking lot where the other cars were going, the fairytale got a little intense.

It had looked so small when I first saw it in the distance, but now even from the parking lot, it looked like it was about six stories high and as powerful as a hurricane. Judging by the mist pelting against my windshield. I got that giddy-anxious feeling like if I didn't get out and go see it immediately, everyone else was going to get to it before me, or it was going to turn off or something.

Assuming I would probably get wet, I looked around for the most water-resistant thing I had , which was nothing. I opted for the closest thing to it; the cheap faux-leather jacket that my mom had given me from one of her donation drives for the homeless center she works at. She had insisted that no one in South Florida would need a jacket that warm and that I couldn't afford one anyway, so embarrassingly, I took it. And thank God, because I really did not own anything warm enough that could have helped me in Iceland.

I zipped up the size two jacket, which fit perfectly, grabbed my selfie stick a nd action camera, and zipped the rental car key into one of the pockets. Eyeing my iPhone in the cup holder, I considered taking it as well for an in-the-moment Instagram Story but retracted the thought in favor of not breaking my phone the first day I'm in Iceland.

Ok, ready, one, two, threee!' I pushed the suddenly heavy door open against the strong wind that was generated from the beast of a waterfall. Within seconds I was soaked and freezing and I hadn't even left the parking lot yet!

What do I do? What do I do? Do I go back to the car? Or just go? Just go, you idiot! Fighting the urge to retreat back to the heater in the car, I walked as fast as my numb legs would go in order to get to the path that led behind the enormous waterfall. It felt like one of those lucid dreams where you know you need to be running, but conveniently, your legs just don't work.

Every other second I considered turning back, but the one thing that motivated me to keep going was seeing all of the other tourists continuing to climb the metal steps up to the waterfall. I literally could see them holding on to the railings, trying to keep the hoods of their red or yellow raincoats on, and continuing to go forward even though the waterfall mist was blowing them backwards. *And I thought waterfalls were cute and dainty, pfft.*

My feet were officially numb and likely had frostbite *(not that I'd ever had it before)*, my clothes and shoes were soaked, as was my hair. I assumed I would get pneumonia in a few hours, but I kept going. It was like I was under a spell in some sort of Nordic fairytale. The glacier water pounded down into a shallow black lagoon, but the rocky land surrounding it was covered in the same lush, vibrant greenery as the fields of sheep. You couldn't make this shit up in a Disney movie if you tried. It was just too perfect to see and so intense to *feel.*

As I reached the second tier of the metal steps, it was as if my eyes were seeing a life-sized glossy page from National Geographic magazine. It was too breathtaking not to stop. The arch of the waterfall as it blasted out over the cliff above, then slanted to fall straight down, was almost as alluring as the cloud of smoke that formed at its meeting point with the placid stream below. There was the jet-black, mysterious cave that stretched behind the entire waterfall, shining like onyx and tempting me to walk through it.

Naturally, although my entire body was violently shaking, I held the button down to turn on the time-lapse photo setting on my camera and stuck my arm as far as I could in an attempt to blindly photograph the entire scene. *One of those fifty should work.*

Did I dare continue attempting the entire path? I was already soaked and freezing, if I turned back now, it would take maybe ten minutes to reach the car, but if I kept going, it would be more like twenty to twenty-five. I couldn't remember any other time in my life when I was that cold and wet, but I also couldn't remember ever seeing something so stunning.

'Mmmmnnnmmmmm.' I grumbled pathetically, shoved the pink selfie stick back inside my jacket, wrapped my arms tightly against myself, and kept going, head down in an attempt to

avoid the piercing sheets of mist blasting from the falls. I didn't even want to know what my eyes looked like, judging by the thick black smear of mascara that came off on my hand when I wiped them.

It was so slippery and ominous in the half-cave behind Seljalandsfoss that it almost made waterfalls seem scarier than magical for a second. Literally, all I could think was that if I slipped and fell into that water right now, I would one hundred percent die, and no one would probably save me because it's so cold. It was beyond relieving to finally get to the metal steps at the other side, which meant now I was only fifteen minutes from the car.

But as I climbed up to the viewing platform, my rush for warmth was replaced by awe again. This platform was higher than the one on the other side and got sprayed much less. The view offered a more expansive scene of the glorious waterfall, and I could actually see it clearly since the mist wasn't stabbing me in the eyeballs. My mouth was wide again with a smile, even though my teeth were violently slamming together. Though I now couldn't feel my hands, I couldn't help but take the camera out and shoot photos from three different angles. It was so glorious that I briefly forgot I was even freezing.

It was, however, in fact, freezing. It made the battery of my camera die, which reminded me just how cold it must be, so I shoved it back inside my jacket and started to descend down the metal steps. Stopping every five steps or so to turn around and see Seljalandsfoss from a different perspective.

Reluctantly but necessarily, I started walking back across the black gravel of the parking lot. Somehow it was even colder there than it had been right next to the waterfall and made it seem like the walk would never end. I fumbled for the key in the jacket pocket, and when I took it out with numb fingers, I noticed it was soaked. *Shit!* Did I really just ruin the automatic lock within a couple of hours of having the car?!

Beep beep! The car chirped, giving me a huge relief. I immediately jumped in, not registering the fact that I was soaked, and turned the heat up to full blast. If that was just the first adventure I had in Iceland, I couldn't wait to see what I'd get myself into during the next week!

I'd spent almost an hour at Seljalandsfoss, which was way longer than I anticipated. But I calculated if I drove straight to Skaftafell National Park, I could still fit seeing that in before heading to Jökulsárlón and making it back at a reasonable time. Thankfully the car heater worked extremely well and it was hot in a matter of minutes, but I also looked like a hot mess. Well, or a cold mess. At least I had about three and a half hours to dry off. I carefully drove across the narrow gravel road and back onto the never-ending road.

'*WHAT IS THAT?*' I gasped out loud to myself as the view of an even bigger waterfall rounded the corner. It looked twice as wide and twice as tall as Seljalandsfoss, which meant it had to be the notorious, Skógafoss.

'*Eeeeeeeee do I stop? Or do I see it on the way back?*' I asked myself, having a legitimate conversation alone in the car. '*Fuck it.*' Before I could remind myself that I was coming back to see Skógafoss in two days, my hands turned the wheel and off I went towards the enormous waterfall.

Luckily the lot was a lot closer than the one at Seljalandsfoss, and it looked like you could just walk right up to the monstrous falls. I turned the camera on to see if the heat had made the battery come back to life; it did, forty percent. I got it ready on video mode, turned off the car, and prepared myself for the cold once again. There was only one way I was going to be able to handle it again *and* have enough time to get all the way to Jökulsárlón; run.

'*Eeeeeeeeeeeeee!*' I squealed as I ran haphazardly straight towards the one-hundred-eighty foot tall waterfall. I kept my arm stretched out behind me as stable as I could in order to record a video at the same time, which made onlookers look at me strangely, but I didn't care. I ran as far forward as I could before the sheets of mist were too strong to battle against, '*WOOOOOOHOOOOOOOO!*' I screamed from pure adrenaline. I was even more soaked than I was before, this time with my hair sopping wet and my boots heavy from the water soaked in my socks inside them.

It had been a while since I felt like a child. Just purely happy and excited with something you found incredible in nature. I wanted to live in that moment forever *but* it was painfully freezing, and I had a time constraint, so in slow motion, I jogged back towards the car, suddenly noticing all of the other spectators were wearing raincoats. *Face palm.*

This time I at least learned from the last waterfall and parked the car sideways, so the driver's door was facing away from the mist blasts. That way, I could open the door and sit on the edge of the car to take off my wet jacket, boots, and socks before getting inside and soaking the rest of the car. I literally could not feel my feet as I peeled off the thick thermal socks and placed them on the dashboard to hopefully dry by the next destination.

It was extremely difficult and took a lot of self-restraint, but I managed to only stop one other time before reaching Skaftafell National Park. It was because I was just so mesmerized by the six -foot tall purple and blue lupin flowers that flooded either side of the road that I couldn't *not* stop to see if they were actually taller than I was. Turns out they were, and it was actually a little terrifying stepping into them and immediately getting surrounded by stems. Mostly because it reminded me of the trolls, and I was honestly still a little spooked by them after their Troll Grass attacked me earlier.

The giant violet flowers added a stunning visual effect to the drive that was otherwise jet-black, grey, or vibrant green. I passed plenty of fields with furry sheep, but the real treat was when I could spot smaller waterfalls trickling down in the distance. Far ahead of me, I had an endless view of something even more magical; a volcano topped by glaciers. I assumed that's why Iceland has the nickname "Land of Fire and Ice ." For me, everything about Iceland so far was like the land of fairytales.

Finally, I reached Skaftafell National Park, and although I was a little loopy from the long drive and lack of food, I decided to attempt it anyway. The weather had warmed up with the rising afternoon sun, so I felt confident that I could get away with just my zip-up gray hoodie over my two layers of long sleeves. My thick socks had surprisingly completely dried, so I pulled them on over my toasty toes and almost-dry leggings, followed by unfortunately still-soaked boots. I did a quick check in the mirror to make sure I didn't look like a raccoon, and to my surprise, my hair actually looked, *dare I say,* good! The mist from the waterfall must have had some fairy magic powers because my normally dry-damaged hair was shiny and bouncing with soft waves! I wondered for a second if it would be possible to take a small bottle of water to use back home. I could just see it now, '*Your hair looks great! What do you use? Water from a glorious waterfall in Iceland.*'

My face, on the other hand, was a bit of a mess; as I expected, my mascara was everywhere, and no matter how hard I tried to get it off, it still looked like I had smokey eye makeup on. I didn't exactly have time to waste on what my face looked like though, so I zipped up, grabbed my pink selfie stick, and headed off towards the trailhead. According to the very confusing map, I could take a harder but shorter trail to get to the main attraction; Svartifoss, the waterfall surrounded by black basalt rock that's seen in several Hollywood movies like Batman.

So off I went, excited for my third waterfall of the day. The hike up wasn't too hard for me, but I noticed most people coming down were struggling and wondered what I had gotten myself into. When I started to pay more attention to the people coming down, I noticed a few more things.

One was that they were all decked out in token hiking gear; loose cargo pants, thermal vests, rubber-grip soled shoes, and some even with walking sticks. Two was that they were *all* looking me up and down, and a few of them were whispering about what *I* was wearing.

'*She's hiking in that?!*' I heard one woman whisper as she passed. The sting it caused came as a shock, and suddenly I felt extremely self-conscious. I re-examined my attire, which is what I basically wore every day; black leggings, long-sleeve black shirt, grey jacket, and boots. What was so wrong with that? At first, I thought it had to be my boots. With the short heel and trendy lace-up to my ankles, they were definitely far from hiking boots, but they were all I could afford. They were also quite comfortable, so I never felt inclined to get "real hiking boots." Then I realized it was probably the fact that my clothes were tight, my hair was down, I had makeup on, and I was alone.

My final consensus proved true after continuing to listen to whispers from tourists I passed in both directions. It was almost laughable that the ones I passed ahead of in the same direction, who were struggling with the hike even in their name-brand hiking clothes, made comments about what I was wearing when I wasn't struggling at all. The feisty Cuban in me finally didn't feel like taking it anymore, and I whipped my head around to dramatically look at the family of three who were giggling in their matching khaki pants and bright red raincoats which stopped them dead in their tracks.

"Do you need some help? I noticed you were struggling with the hike?" I said sweetly, cocking my head to the side and batting my eyelashes. This made the teenage daughter blush hard and hide behind her short, plump father, and the frazzled mother gasped and immediately put an arm around him as if my glare were meant to seduce him. *Please.*

"No? Ok! Enjoy!" I added and literally skipped along the path, purposely emphasizing how easy it was for me, even in my non-official hiking gear. Sure, it was a bitchy move, but I was sick of people judging me when I *just* wanted to go see a damn waterfall. Plus, not only could I not afford professional hiking clothes, but I personally would not be caught dead wearing them. Lara Croft was more my style than Dora the Explora.

The stares and comments continued right up to the viewpoint of Svartifoss. It was actually so bad that I decided to climb the rocks below the viewing platform to get closer to the waterfall. To my surprise, there was a cute Asian couple on the rocks closer to the waterfall as well, taking photos just like I was except her selfie stick was her boyfriend. But she was dressed in non-hiking clothes like I was and looked fabulous. I wondered if the pro-hiker tourists gave her shit as well, or if it was acceptable because she was accompanied by a guy. I noticed them trying to take a photo together, so I offered to take it for them. They didn't speak English but smiled excitedly and handed me their chic, fancy camera. They were the nicest people I had encountered all day, and we didn't even speak the same language ; go figure. They seemed to be very happy with my multiple angle photoshoot (*complete with directions on where they should stand, look, and pose*), which then led to the unthinkable; they gestured to my camera and the waterfall, offering to take my photo for me! I couldn't believe my luck!

I looked up at the viewing platform of tourists and hoped all the ones who had judged me for being alone were watching as I made friends and *didn't* have to take a selfie. Just to be for good measure though, I still stretched my arm out behind me and took some photos once the couple had climbed back up the rocks. When I turned back around, almost all of the tourists were following the pathway I took to get a similar photo. *Oh, now they want to copy the poor solo traveler girl with shitty boots.*

Hardly any of them so much as looked in my direction as I easily jumped back up the rocks, passing them on their way down. There was only one who smiled and asked if it was a good view and another who said "be careful," and something about my shoes, to which I sweetly replied, "You too!"

I made it back to the car feeling empowered, both because of the strength in my muscles from the physical hike and my mental strength that fought back against the judgements. It really didn't occur to me that what I chose to wear hiking would be such a big deal, but now that I knew what the response was like, it had me wanting to stay as far away from tourists as possible.

Part of me desperately wanted to turn the pricey international roaming on my phone to complain to Nate about what had just happened but I couldn't do that. I couldn't let him see that I was already struggling, not to mention running back to him *again*. I shook my head and scoffed, thinking about how none of those people would have given *him* or probably any man for that matter any sort of negative judgement for what they wore hiking. If he had been doing that hike alone, it would have been considered completely normal, even adventurous and commendable, but when I did it, dressed the way I was, it was just downright ridiculous. *Whatever.*

Re-setting the GPS to Jökulsárlón, I pulled out of the gravel lot and back onto the never -ending Ring Road. The scenery had changed drastically the closer I got to the east side of the island. Instead of rolling green hills and lupin fields, there was now dramatic, jagged mountains, most of which were likely volcanoes as well. It even felt colder over here, like bone-chilling cold, and the sky had turned smokey gray, which seemed to be a threat for rain. Or if I was lucky, my first snow fall!

The mountain ahead of me grew bigger and bigger, and I started getting that feeling of *am-I-allowed-to-even-be-here?* Everything just looked dangerous, and since I was alone, what would happen if I needed help? What if suddenly I started sliding on the non-existent ice on the road? What if my brand new tires popped? What if a troll ran out in the middle of the road and turned my car into a pumpkin?

Finally, my GPS pointed me to yet another gravel lot, and beyond it, I could see a body of water which I assumed was the glacier lagoon. I could also clearly see that it was extremely windy, and the few people who were walking around outside were visibly shivering. I reached around to the back seat and flung open my carryon, pulling out the other two long-sleeved shirts I had brought, plus a crocheted white sweater and my only other pair of warm socks. Wiggling around uncomfortably in the front seat, I got it all on, then zipped my damp jacket over it all, shoved my camera and selfie stick inside, and braced myself for the frozen tundra.

"OH SHIT!" The wind was so strong that it slammed the car door back on me! That's not good ; what if the wind also pushed me into the icy glacier lagoon? I made a mental note not to go too close to it. Maybe.

Using my shoulder, I shoved the door open, jumped out, and let the wind slam it back shut. It slammed so hard that the whole car shook as I stumbled sideways. The icy air was piercing, and instantaneously my feet, hands, and face went numb. Going back inside the car sounded like an ideal choice, but I hadn't just driven over five hours across the entire country of Iceland to sit in a damn heated car and just look at the lagoon.

As I walked forward and fiercely battled against the arctic blasts, I squinted to see through the tears in my eyes, which I wasn't sure if they were from the brutal wind or the actual pain I was in. I was leaning so hard against the wind that if it were to suddenly stop, I would have fallen on my ass. Finally, I reached the hill that I saw the other onlookers perched on top of and began to climb it as if I were summiting Mt. Everest. *So close, just keep going.*

When I reached the top, it was like the wind had suddenly just stopped. Or maybe I was just in awe. No, it was definitely less bad up there and got even calmer as I involuntarily descended down the other side towards the glacier lagoon that I had just sworn I wouldn't get too close to. Before I knew it, my boots were soaked as I stood on the shore, hypnotized by the massive ice chunks that were somehow floating on the placid surface.

They were so beautiful and so *foreign* to me. I'd only ever seen icebergs on movies like Titanic before, but here in real life, they were much more majestic. *Little did I know I'd be seeing them in Antarctica...three times.*

Crrraaaaaaaackk POP! The sudden soul-crushing sound sent me toppling backwards onto my ass, soaking my leggings on the wet black pebble shore. My eyes darted around, trying to find the source of noise as if something were going to collapse on my head, and somehow I saw the action happen *after* hearing it. A massive chunk of one of the icebergs had broken off and went dunking straight down into the glacial water.

Before my body could catch up with my brain, which was yelling, '*Move your ass! A wave is coming!'* the tumbling ripples of dark freezing water came right for me. For some reason, I envisioned the lochness monster coming to attack me or something and tried to shuffle to my feet, but it was too late. By the time I got halfway up, I was soaked from the ass down. The adrenaline from thinking a lagoon monster was about to

182

come out and eat me, along with the shock of the cold water, eradicated the frozen feeling I had originally. Now I was pretty sure I was in hypothermic shock. Oh, and the burning humiliation from the multiple onlookers staring and gasping warmed up my insides as well, and not in a good way. Naturally, I decided to try and appear like a badass and simply brushed the pebbles off my soaked leggings and continued to nonchalantly pull out my camera for at least one photo.

Within minutes, the entire glacier lagoon had gone back to being completely flat and serene. As if it had purposely soaked me, then turned the other way and pretended like it didn't. The chunk of ice that calved off of the bigger iceberg had bobbed to the surface and immediately started drifting out towards what I knew was the ocean. It made me instantly think, '*That's global warming for ya.*'

"GAAHH!" I barked suddenly, nearly falling to my knees as my feet involuntarily jumped away from the shore. My peripheral vision mistook the sea lion that had popped up out of the water just ten feet away as the Lochness monster, or maybe even Jaws, and sent me scrambling back up the hill. Who knew glacier lagoons could be so exciting?

Back at the top of the hill, I stood and watched from a safe distance the phenomenal masterpiece that nature had created. I squinted hard to see the actual massive glacier in the distance, which according to my research, gets pushed forward little by little at a constant rate as the glacier "grows ," and once it reaches the lagoon, it breaks off and forms the icebergs. Of course, I also did thorough research on how global warming affects this process. Essentially it melts the glacier a lot faster than it's supposed to, which of course causes an increase in the levels of water, which can eventually put coastal areas underwater. I keep telling this to my mom in Florida, hoping she'll move from my dreaded childhood home in the middle of nowhere, but she says she'll wait until the waves are knocking on her door.

After the twenty-eighth photo or so, I realized my hands were burning again from the cold. Such a strange oxymoron of a feeling , being so cold that it actually feels like you're burning.

I realized my toes were past the point of burning and just straight up numb, likely turning black from frostbite and would need to be amputated. I shuffled my frozen feet back to the car, cranked the heater on full blast, and set off for the final stop of the adventure: Diamond Beach.

When I reached the main road, I looked around for any sort of sign directing me to the newly-famous beach that photos show has black sand with clear ice chunks. There were none. I looked at the map on my phone, which also had not even the slightest hint at where this Diamond Beach would be but assumed it couldn't be far, judging by the drift of the iceberg chunks out to the ocean. My instincts told me to go back west, remembering an un-marked turn-off I saw on the way to the glacier lagoon. If that was where the beach was, and there wasn't even a sign, it would be interesting to see how quickly the government puts one up to accommodate the growing influx of American tourists thanks to social media and, well, people like me. I made a note in my phone about the whereabouts to add to the lengthy blog post I was planning on writing from my warm hotel later.

Carefully, I turned onto the rocky turnoff, which was literally just a gravel road flanked by endless land. In the distance though, I could see the ocean, but not a beach. Up ahead, I could also see two cars parked in yet another make-shift parking lot, so I knew this had to be the right place. As I drove closer and closer though, I still saw no proclaimed-to-be-glorious Diamond Beach. Finally, I reached the other two cars and realized the lot was atop a large hill. I looked down, and sure as shit, there it was! A black sand beach adorned with massive glistening chunks of ice and even more bobbing at the surface of the shore, waiting to get washed up. My usual *'must get there before it disappears'* anxiety slash excitement took over once again, and within minutes I was parked, packed, bundled up the best I could be, and bounding for the epic scenery.

Almost as fast as I walked to the beach, the freezing air completely took over my body. I was convinced that this was the coldest place I'd been to all day and wondered if it was like

L.A. where it's always colder at the beach. It was so cold that I was already considering turning around before reaching the actual shore. But again, I scorned myself for not coming all this way to just turn around.

Finally, my soggy boots crunched down on the peculiar black "sand," and I couldn't help but drop down and scoop a handful of it up to examine. It was bigger than regular sand grains and a lot smoother. It looked wet, but it was dry and just shiny. When I looked even closer, it looked more like tiny pebbles of onyx, but I knew it was broken pieces of lava rock, buffed and shined by the rolling tides of the ocean. It was fascinating and so beautiful, and naturally, I wanted to keep it. I looked around to see if anyone from the other two cars were nearby or watching me, but they were far down the beach. First, I wondered *how* they got so far without freezing, then I nonchalantly dumped the handful of black sand into my boot as a souvenir. What exactly I was going to do with a handful of tiny lava pebbles back home, I did not know. Maybe I would get a fish tank and put a sign in it that said Jökulsárlón and find a fish that looks like that damn sea lion that scared the crap out of me.

As I looked back down to the "sand ," I saw something even more peculiar; tiny bright red, eight-legged creatures that looked like mini versions of the typical brown sand crabs you normally see. So instead of white sand, it was black, and instead of brown crabs, they were red. Oh, and instead of beige and gray rocks and boulders, there were crystal clear chunks of ice. Right then and there, I decided that Iceland was officially a parallel universe.

As much as I wanted to capture one of the little red lava crabs, I convinced myself that A) There's a good chance they might be poisonous, and B) My hands were way too cold to even attempt such a feat. I willed my shaky legs to rise up, despite it being much colder at standing height and crunched over to see one of the glacier rocks before I couldn't bear the cold any longer.

It was hypnotizing. I reached out and ran my fingers over the top of one of the once-jagged and now smooth points of an ice chunk that came up to my ribs. It was like frozen silk and completely see-through, likely having just gone through the tumbling and shining process in the ocean like gemstones do in labs.

It was extremely tempting to lick it, but that one scene in Dumb and Dumber, where the guy licks ice on a ski lift and gets his tongue stuck to it, immediately came to mind. What in the actual hell would I do if I got my tongue stuck to a glacier rock while alone on a near-empty, frozen beach in iceland? I let my fingertips dance along its smooth surface for a bit longer, like little tiny ice skaters on the most glorious rink on the planet. When my hand was finally too numb to tolerate, I attempted taking a few photos that I knew would not turn out well because my hand was too shaky and retreated back up the hill to the car. I could feel the mound of black sand in my boot and smiled, thinking I was just oh-so-clever for *accidentally* taking some back with me. I wouldn't post about it on social media, knowing it would encourage others to do the same and likely also encourage a few people to call me out, but I would cherish it forever as a reminder of one of the most epic days of my entire life. *Thus far.*

"We were expecting you a lot earlier!" The middle-aged, cozy-dressed Icelandic woman trilled from behind the front desk of Keflavik Inn. Her son, a blonde-haired, fair -skinned guy about my age, who had a similar Nordic wool sweater and accent, had greeted me and was looking at me curiously.

"I know, I'm sorry, I tried to email you, today was my only free day, so I drove to Jokulsal-uh-laron? I don't know how to pronounce it," I said sheepishly, hoping she hadn't been waiting around for me.

"Jökulsárlón?!" She said with perfect pronunciation. Simultaneously she and her cute-viking son looked at each other with wide eyes. "The glacier lagoon?!"

"Yes! I really wanted to see it, so I drove there as soon as I landed at 6 am..."

"That's five hours away! You drove there and back *today?!*" She seemed shocked, and I couldn't tell if she was mad or impressed.

"Y-yes. I really wanted to see it and the black sand beach with the ice chunks on it!" I mumbled, hoping I didn't sound absolutely crazy. She stared at me with her wide warm brown eyes for a moment while her son's mouth crept into a wide grin.

"That's very impressive. Most tourists don't even make it to Jökulsárlón. It's a lovely place, I wish they would! Well, good for you! You're probably freezing though, let's get you to your room!" She wasn't exactly sweet, more like a nice businesswoman, and as a businesswoman myself, I thoroughly appreciated that. On the way to the room, she explained that what caught her attention about my pitch for a free stay was that I was a solo female traveler, and she admired that. And thank god, because no other hotels in the main area of Reykjavik even responded to me.

"It's not fancy or anything, but it does have a great view of the Midnight Sun." She announced modestly, opening the door to my home for the week.

"It's *perfect ,"* I whispered, drinking in the glorious scene of my first ever above-budget hotel collaboration. The queen bed was gloriously equipped with four fluffy pillows and traditional hotel-white sheets that were begging for me to bury myself in them. But the added touch of a traditional Icelandic wool blanket on top of it gave the room a cozier vibe. Best of all was the view. The entire back wall was glass, with a sliding door that opened to a roomy wooden deck overlooking a green walkway that ran alongside the dark, chilly water. In the distance, I could even see the boats that leave out of Reykjavik to take tourists whale watching.

"Just wait a few hours ; it gets better." She said with a proud smile, "The Midnight Sunsets just over the water there."

I checked the time on my phone, it was only eight PM, but as bright outside as it had been in the afternoon, and I was beyond exhausted. But I couldn't miss my first midnight sun! I could tell she noticed me checking the time, and I must have appeared to be worried.

"Don't worry, it happens every night. You should get some rest, you had a long day! The curtains are blackout curtains, I suggest closing them a few hours before you plan on going to bed as it helps convince your body and mind that it's time to sleep." She picked up a remote from the dark wooden desk and pushed a button which made the curtains start to close automatically. "You just push this one to close them and this one to open them." She gestured to the two buttons with her index finger then handed me the remote.

"Thank you! I'm going to try to get my first blog post done, so maybe I can see a little bit of it before I pass out." I insisted, pushing the button to open them back up.

"Hard working! Again, very impressive! Well, I hope you enjoy your stay ; please let me or my son know if you need anything at all!" She said, folding her arms in front of her and rocking back on her heels. "Oh! And we've never done this before; have a travel blogger stay with us, so we got you a small gift, I hope you like it!" She seemed as nervous as I was now . Apparently, it was both of our first times doing this sort of collaboration. I followed her nod to a gift basket on the small round wooden table outside. I absolutely could not believe it!

"Oh my god! You didn't have to -- thank you SO much! I'm going to start working on your posts right now!" I gushed, pressing my palm to my chest in appreciation.

"No rush at all ; enjoy your rest." She smiled and backed out of the room, leaving me in privacy to freak the fuck out over how epic everything in life was at that exact moment. My first instincts were of course, to jump on the bed and then throw open the sliding glass door to see what was in my welcome basket. *But*, I couldn't ignore the fact that I was wet, freezing, and had had to pee since the hike to Svartifoss over six hours ago.

Not wanting to ruin the perfectly set up room, I kicked my soggy boots off at the door and peeled off my now-musty smelling socks. Should be interesting trying to wash and dry those bad boys. Next, I wiggled out of my jacket and two layers of long-sleeves, followed by two layers of leggings, so I was just in my single base layer of thermals. Finally, I could pee, and what a glorious pee it was. You know, the kind that makes you feel several pounds lighter afterwards? I was sure I just peed out five pounds or more.

Knowing fully well that I'd probably pass out if I laid on the extremely comfortable looking bed, I decided to investigate my gift first, then get to work on the blog post. Grabbing my wet clothes off the ground first to hang to dry outside, I made my way to the sliding door, opened it, then slammed it shut. The warmth of the cozy room made me forget that it was still freezing outside.

The convenience-seeker in me immediately spotted the warm wool Icelandic blanket on the bed and yanked it off. I positioned the edge of it on top of my head, then wrapped it around me the best I could while simultaneously holding the pile of damp clothing. I opened the door again, and this time, I couldn't feel a damn thing! Those Icelandic people really know how to stay warm! Well, obviously. They do live on an Arctic island afterall.

Speaking of which, I quickly realized that the cold air probably wouldn't dry my clothes and definitely would be awful to put on cold in the morning, so I threw the pile back inside with the intention of spreading them out next to the heater. But first, I needed to see what was in this giant gift basket. I sat down in the sturdy slate-wood chair next to the table and pulled the ribbon-covered, dark brown straw basket towards me. There were multiple goodies packed thoughtfully inside it, making me not want to ruin the appearance by taking anything out. Naturally, I took several photos of it, which I had full intentions of posting online with a #humblebrag caption like *"Amazing welcome gift from my hotel sponsor in Iceland!"* Maybe I'd send it to Nate too, so he could see how professional I had become already. Or maybe I'd just let him see it online. I knew he was watching my every post anyway.

I started with the obvious, the dark purple bottle of wine that was placed at the back-middle of the basket. Normally I don't normally drink red wine because I prefer my wine chilled, but considering that the air was already chilled, and I didn't even think to stop and get white wine, the bottle of red would more than suffice. Taking my time to examine the label, I realized it was imported from Italy. I don't know why I was expecting a cool Viking or Icelandic label, since obviously grapes don't grow in the Arctic, but I also don't know why I was surprised to see it was from Italy.

The bottle was cold from being outside for what I assumed was all day, waiting for me while I was exploring the other side of the country, so I decided I should go ahead and have a glass and savor the moment for as long as possible. It's something I've always tended to do with gifts; open them as slowly as possible so the excitement lasts.

Inside the desk was a corkscrew and one wine glass. I wondered if that was on purpose. Usually, there's at least two glasses, but the hotel owner did point out that she knew I was a solo female traveler. It was actually quite thoughtful; otherwise, the two glasses would have reminded me that there are not two people in this room exploring Iceland together. It was just me and my camera. And I was totally fine with that. I popped open the cork and poured a giant, well -deserved glass. Since again, I'm not so into red wine, I decided to *not* smell it beforehand and went straight for a sip instead. If I had been blind -folded, and someone told me it was white wine, I probably would have believed it since it wasn't strong and tannin-ey at all.

Satisfied, I resumed my spot outside on the small balcony and began to pull each item out one by one. First was a fuzzy yet scratchy pair of wool socks, *thank god*. They were light gray with a band of white Icelandic designs around the top, similar to what I saw the hotel owner and her son wearing. Underneath it was a matching ear warmer headband! I couldn't believe my luck! These were the exact things I had seen at one of the gas station's gift shops earlier, but even there, they were way too expensive for my puny budget. These ones were way nicer, so I automatically assumed they were probably twice as much. I immediately put the warm headband on my head and replaced my thin thermal socks with the new ones. This moment definitely warranted a selfie, and I'd definitely be sending that one to Nate. Maybe.

The rest of the gifts were small packages of local Icelandic treats, or so I assumed. One was even a dried fish snack that although it did not sound appealing, I would probably eat just because I was hungry and trying to save money. Speaking of hungry, I was beyond starving. All I had ingested was those few pastries from the airport and some chips I grabbed from the grocery store. I walked back inside my toasty fortress to see if there was a hot water boiler for tea and coffee. There was perfect. My pre-anticipated idea to bring ramen noodles from home to eat in the hotel room in order to save money would work. Not to mention, hot, salty ramen noodles sounded damn good right now.

While the water was boiling, I jumped in the shower, staying in probably a little too long because the hot water was so soothing. My mind also meandered off in all directions a few times, re-playing the ups and downs of the day; the ups being the epic adventure and all the things I saw, the downs being the judgments from the tourists that for some reason still stung, and my lack of texts from Nate. I went back and forth feeling like I wanted someone to talk to but ultimately decided what I really wanted was to crawl into my cloud bed with my coffee mug of ramen noodles, big glass of wine, and laptop.

So I did just that and finished my first blog post for Iceland just before dozing off at eleven PM. I'd just missed the midnight sun, but I'd try again tomorrow night when I didn't have to wake up early AF to go exploring.

I woke up early AF because I forgot to fully close the blackout curtains. It was necessary anyway. I had so much exploring to do and so much to write about for my blog.

The most popular thing to do in Iceland besides the Blue Lagoon is The Golden Circle. There are tons of tours that offer it, but they're expensive, and none responded to my collaboration pitch, so I decided to DIY. Afterall, since the tour companies post the route on their website, it's not that hard to just follow it in a rental car. Plus, I could go whenever I wanted, which meant extra time to finish my blog post and skipping the morning rush of crowds from the tours.

After my research of the Golden Circle route, I wasn't entirely sure why it's called a circle because you technically just drive straight to the sites then straight back. Technically you could combine it with the South Coast to make it more of a loop, but according to most of the tours, that was an additional trip.

Since I had already done the South Coast and seen Seljalandsfoss, Skogafoss, and Reynisfjara black sand beach yesterday, I allotted myself more time to do the itinerary I had created for today with the Golden Circle, especially since it included snorkeling through the two continental plates in the Silfra fissure, and meeting up with a friend of a friend's later.

To be honest, I didn't really want to meet up with anyone. I knew I should be putting myself out there and meeting locals, but the truth was that I still am a bit shy about doing that alone and also not one hundred percent sure what I'd be getting myself into. The friend who had connected me was a notorious party girl in LA, so I could only assume that she knew similar people. Turns out that was true, and she told me that she met this Icelandic viking guy whose last name was literally Olafsson (like Olaf in Frozen!) at a music festival he was producing in LA. He hosts them in Iceland apparently, which shocked me because my whimsical fairytale vision of the country did not include raging festivals. He sounded nice when I spoke to him via Facebook Messenger though, so I scheduled to meet him at a hotel lobby bar at eight o'clock PM for a drink.

Now I just had to make sure I was able to fit everything on my agenda in by then. Hopefully, twelve hours was enough time to thoroughly explore the Golden Circle and the two -hour Silfra snorkeling. I also penciled in some wiggle room for lunch, the potential of getting lost, and the extra hour it took just to get out of Keflavik.

Thankfully my clothes had dried off overnight and were warm and well, a bit crunchy from sitting next to the heater. I layered on everything I had; three leggings, three long-sleeve shirts, my thin zip-up hoodie, then my crap jacket, and added my new Icelandic wool socks and head warmer. They made me look less Laura Croft and more trying-to-be-cute-tourist, but I couldn't resist. At least I would blend in with the hoards of other tourists, except for the fact that I'd probably be the only one there alone. Then something occurred to me; would it be awkward that I was doing the Silfra snorkeling by myself? Would I have to make small talk with couples and families?

I pushed the thought out of my mind and reminded myself that I should be proud to have gotten the snorkeling trip free as one of my collaborations. Boss lady Alyssa shoved insecure single Alyssa out of the room and started preparing for that particular part of the day. I grabbed an extra pair of underwear, assuming mine would get wet while snorkeling, and all of the three spare camera batteries I had left to charge overnight. My stomach grumbled ferociously, reminding me that I should probably eat something, so I grabbed the bag of what looked like trail mix from the gift basket, along with two Nature's Valley granola bars I had brought from home, and added everything to my black Harvey's seatbelt bag.

As I crept down the stairs towards the lobby, I half hoped I wouldn't run into the hotel owner or son and have to make small talk. I've never been great at it and wondered on more than one occasion how in the hell I've always managed to have so many friends my whole life.

To my relief, there wasn't a soul in sight downstairs. At first, I wondered if the business wasn't booming due to its far distance from everything, but then I wondered if maybe everyone had just left super early on tour. I hoped for the latter because that would mean they were finishing up as I was heading out, and it would be less crowded. My trusty little rental car was one of the few on the desolate street, which made me eager to get in and get going.

After a few tries with the GPS and the Icelandic names I did not know, I programmed it for the easiest destination I could find on its list of options: Thingvellir.

It's not only popular for its numerous natural phenomenons but also popular in history because of its cultural and geological significance. Thingvellir National Park is actually a double UNESCO World Heritage Site, which is extremely rare.

The first UNESCO site is the actual park because it's where the first parliament was held *in the world*. It was held by the first settlers, which were either vikings, trolls, or elves, I'm not really sure, but there's a tale that the daunting waterfall in the middle of the continental ridge is where nay-sayers would get executed via head-chopped-off. Hence its name, öxarárfoss.

Silfra, where I'd be going snorkeling, is the second UNESCO site and probably the coolest (and coldest) thing in the entire National Park. It's literally an underwater crack in the continental divide that separates the Eurasia and American continental plates.

The water is also one of the clearest waters in the world because it comes from a glacier thirty meters away that gets filtered through volcanic rock. It's also freezing, which adds to the clarity.

Seeing the Silfra Fissure underwater in Iceland was literally like some next level other planet liquid Nat Geo shit. Sure, I was a tad bit concerned about how freezing cold it was going to be to swim in glacier water while it's also freezing cold outside, but the tour company did a great job at preparing me for it both before I arrived and once I got there.

I'll admit, I was a little concerned when I failed to comply with getting the recommended thermal underwear and two pairs of wool socks that they recommended for wearing under the dry suit, but when the tour guides busted out the pre-sized, thick-ass thermal onesies for each of us, I felt a whole hell of a lot better! I put mine on and was all warm and snuggly before I even put the rest of the waterproof ensemble on!

The guides had also pre-selected the dry suits for each guest according to the measurements we gave when we signed up online. They were funny looking suits, with neoprene booties attached at the bottom and rubber suction bands at the wrists and neck that made sure no water got in. It was a little bit confusing and difficult to get on, but pretty hilarious to watch.

After the guides helped zip me up in my underwater astronaut suit, I was sure that there was no way I was going to freeze, but they took extra measures to ensure that absolutely no water leaked in whatsoever by taping anyone's wrist cuffs that seemed loose, and buckling a rubber band around our neoprene turtle-necks.

I had assumed my head wouldn't be covered and even seriously thought about how to wear my hair so it would look like I was a mermaid, but one minute in that icy Icelandic air had me seriously concerned about my head freezing off. Obviously, they weren't going to let that happen though. After our bodies were completely covered, the next steps were getting the head covers and mittens on, both of which were slightly awkward, uncomfortable, and embarrassing to get on but much appreciated as soon as you hit the water.

After we were completely freeze/water-proof in our alien scuba suits, we walked like robots over to the entry area of the Silfra fissure to get the rest of our gear on. We were all pretty excited to look down into the crystal clear water and see the iconic shades of blue on the rocky divide, but we still needed to get our fins and masks on before diving (AKA cautiously stepping) in. The guides helped each one of us get our fins on by having us hold onto a railing and lift our feet one by one as they slid them on for us since there was no way we'd be able to bend down to do it ourselves.

"Next comes the grossest thing you'll probably do all day," the female tour leader mumbled apologetically, "So, if you didn't already know, saliva is a natural defogger...which means I'm going to need you to spit in your masks, rub it around with your finger, then hand it to us so we can rinse it out!" She announced, obviously expecting the half confused, half disgusted faces in response.

"We're going to give you a number ; remember your number unless you want to become really close to your neighbor!" The icy-blue-eyed male guide added. She was right. It was the grossest part of my day. So alongside six other strangers, I tried my best not to see myself or them spit bubbly saliva into the mask and hand it to the instructors to dunk in the cold water. The numbers were so we knew which mask was ours after they rinsed them. When they handed mine back, they said I didn't spit in it enough and had to do it again. *Ugh.*

Obviously, my overly ambitious-adventurer self tried really hard to be the first one to go into the icy water, but the second spitting in the mask delayed me to third place. The people who were already in the water were bobbing up and down like they were trying to get used to the cold before plunging their faces in, but I was more eager to get that insanely clear view of the underwater continental divide and would have just jumped from the top if my previous cliff-jumping experiences weren't there to hold me back.

Instead, I carefully waddled my way down the metal steps in my fins like a bloated Puffin and began stepping in. But instead of gliding in gracefully like everyone else, I decided to launch myself face -first into the freezing water while attempting to hold my camera to film all of it. It felt like a million needles were pricking my face, but that was the only part of me that felt cold. The carefully-fitted dry suit, expert assistance, and immediate adrenaline rush will make you forget you even have a face at all, and if not, then the numbing water will as well.

Never in my life have I been snorkeling somewhere with water so clear! I mean, I know I like to brag about having LASIK eye surgery and all, but DAMN! This water made me feel like I saw even clearer than normal, even through the saliva-washed snorkeling mask! I could see all the way to the bottom, far ahead of me, and even up through the clear glassy surface, which I tried to avoid doing because any time I would turn my head, the painfully cold water would leak into my mask.

Aside from the sharpened details of the rocky edges that separate the two continents and the deep, mysterious caves and crevices below, there was also what seems like a field of neon green "troll hair" seaweed that is so perfectly situated that it almost looks fake!

There aren't any fish or fissure-creatures, at least none that I saw, which was somewhat comforting considering how creepy it would have been to see something jut out from under a random cave rock.

The guides had told us not to try to swim too much, which I began to understand almost immediately. Not only will you not *want* to swim too fast and pass up time with the gorgeous underwater views, but you won't even have to because the slight current and extremely buoyant snorkeling suits will allow you to just drift along like you're in outer space. The crew joked at the beginning that we could try to swim down if we wanted to, and to *"Please do because you'll probably end up just flapping your fins in the air and it's really amusing for us to watch,"* which, of course I attempted and proved true.

But regardless, I was pretty much having a field day trying to maneuver around in my extremely bouncy snorkeling suit to take in all of the epic views of the underwater cliffs and of course, to take some awesome pictures while I was at it, even though I could barely press the shutter button because my hands were so numb.

I can't float in real life, so being able to bob along the surface as the slight current pushed me along was also a real treat. It was also super fun when I discovered you can "stand" up right in the water because your suit will just hold you there, and you can bounce up and down like a child in a child seat?

There's only one turn they tell you to make before you set-snorkel, and if you miss it, you'll fail because the current picks up and you'll end up getting frozen in a glacier. *Just kidding.* One of the guides blocks the forward path, so there's really no way you can mess that one up. Hopefully.

Unlike most grand finales, the Silfra snorkeling one is at the beginning of the tour, not the end. This isn't to confuse you, throw you off, or prevent you from spending prolonged amounts of time in freezing water, but because it would be almost impossible to swim against the current and not anywhere near as fun.

Instead, you end your tectonic snorkeling adventure in a little lagoon area that still has crystal clear water, but instead of underwater cliffs, a sandy bottom with surprisingly non-black sand. It's also much shallower, and if you wave your hand around above the sand, you'll see that it swirls around and reveals the actual smooth rock surface below.

There's also a cute little neon green "troll hair" meadow...field?...patch?...I'm not really sure what you'd call it, but it's not scary or slimy like normal ocean seaweed, and it looks quite pretty against the bright blue and white background.

When it was finally time to get out of the lagoon, we were instructed to walk straight back to the area where we got ready to get the dry suits off. I was surprisingly warm, but I guess that's the point of the dry suit. I was also extremely annoyed because there were swarms of gnats that were for some reason, obsessed with wet walking humans.

I tried my hardest to get the damn dry suit off by myself, but between my numb hands and the attack of the gnats, I wasn't as successful as expected. Somehow, I managed to get the tape off from around my wrists, which was cutting off my circulation (or so it felt), and was able to unzipper the back of the suit, but there was no way in hell I could get the head and face mask off, or well, any other part of it. I started to whimper, trying to stay calm but really hating the feeling of being stuck in the suit while gnats attempted to enter my nose and eyeballs.

"Can you help me when you're done?" I finally whined to the female guide who was helping a large man who seemed twice as stuck as I was, specifically choosing her over the male guides for the sake of not knowing what my hair and face would look like after being squeezed in a seal suit.

"Oh goodness!" She chirped, examining the progress, or lack thereof that I had attempted on my own. I tried to pull the vacuum-sealed sleeves over my hands, but they were so tight that they got stuck, and now just my fingertips were showing. I also attempted to loosen the rubber around my face by pulling at it, which had resulted in some of my hair coming out and sticking to my forehead, further attracting the annoying little bugs.

"Jack! Can you help her? I'm working on someone!" She yelled to the ice blue -eyed Dutch guide. *Dammit.* Jack took one look at me and came running over. Did I really look that miserable? I mean, I definitely felt like a little kid who got stuck in an onesie that was three sizes too small for them, but their reactions made it seem worse.

"Here, let me help you ; the first part might hurt a little bit." *Great.* "I need you to put your head down, pull the sides of the facemask out, and then I'm going to pull it over your head, ready?" I held up my hands to show that just my fingertips were available for use, and he laughed, then rolled down the neoprene to free my hands. Following his instructions, I pulled the facemask as wide as I would, tilted my head down, and braced myself.

"One, two, thrreeeeeee!" He grunted as he did some maneuver I couldn't see to simultaneously stretch and pull the head mask from the back of my head over the entirety of it. It reminded me of that scene from *Ace Ventura: When Nature Calls*, when he gets stuck inside of the fake rhino robot and has to escape out of the rubber butt hole.

"Ahh! Freedom!" I gasped as my head felt the chill of the fresh air. I went to re-do my top knot and realized my hair was completely soaked. That should be fun to deal with the whole rest of the day.

Jack helped me out of the rest of the dry suit, which involved a very awkward position of him kneeling down, and me holding on to his shoulders as he battled to pull the pant portion of it down. I've never had a man struggle this hard to undress me before. It probably took a solid ten minutes!

They ended the tour with some much-appreciated hot chocolate, and some of the guides asked me about my blog. It was refreshing to hear that they had worked with other bloggers before, and even more so that they had checked mine out and liked it!

Since I drove myself to the park for the tour instead of using the included transportation to and from a hotel in Reykjavik, I was free to leave without waiting for everyone else to get birthed out of their space suits. One thing I absolutely cannot stand about tours is having to wait for every single person on it before you can leave.

I thanked the guides again and assured them that I'd have a photo posted later on social media, along with the blog post by morning, which they said they couldn't wait to see. That gave me extra motivation to get it done as soon as possible. By the time I had walked about seven minutes to the car, the cold had started to kick in again, especially since my hair was soaking wet. I realized then why they suggested wearing and bringing extra types of clothes. At least my clothes weren't wet, minus my socks, per usual. But those would hopefully dry by the time I got to the next destination on my DIY Golden Circle Tour: Geysir.

Geysir is, as the name implies, a geysir, and the second stop on the Golden Circle tours. This is a prime example of how awesomely strange Iceland is because you literally walk through a field of holes with boiling water from the hot magma below that explode every few minutes when they get too hot. But as they're exploding, you also see glaciers in the background, and then of course, it's also freezing outside. *Mind. Blown.*

The crowds were thick around a circular roped-off area, which I assumed was where Geysir was, but from what I could see through the thick layers of bodies, it was just a hole in the ground. It was very tempting to avoid the crowded area and go look at one of the smaller holes bubbling with boiling water instead, but judging by the intense focus that everyone had on the big hole, I could tell something was about to happen. I just wasn't sure if it was going to be worth waiting for.

Casually, I poked my head in between two tall shoulders to get a better view of the hole when suddenly, '*Glub glub glub',* the water in the middle of the hole began to get sucked into the Earth. *What in the actual hell?*

The crowd gasped and started buzzing like a red-ant hill that had just been kicked. Literally, everyone took out their phones and cameras, so naturally, I did too, putting it on Slow-Mo mode just in time.

200

The rumbling from the Earth and water rising up aggressively from where it had been sucked down into should have been an indication of what was to come, but there's no way I was expecting what I saw. The steaming water exploded from the ground with such force that it shot what seemed like a mile into the air in just a few seconds. And as fast as it had shot out, it had fallen back down as if nothing had happened. Thank god I got it on Slow-Mo because I was *very* confused as to what had just happened.

Most of the crowd stayed to watch it happen again for another seven minutes, but I was good with my Slow-Mo of it. Plus, I was already behind schedule. I still had Gulfoss waterfall to chase before needing to drive about two hours back to Reykjavik to meet up with Olaf on time.

Gulfoss is the most well-known waterfall in Iceland and also one of the most massive ones that's easy to see. It's so powerful that its power is harnessed and used to provide electricity to a nearby town! I walked all the way up to the dop of the viewing deck and per usual, immediately became entranced and drenched.

This had to be the wrong way. I'd been driving for nearly forty minutes, with nothing in sight but fields on either side of the road. I could have sworn I followed the right sign, but maybe not? I decided to pull over to try and play with the GPS because to be honest, I really wanted a Walter Mitty-esque photo in the middle of the road.

After a few minutes of messing with the car's GPS, I got stabbed with a sharp pang to my gut, the kind you get upon realizing you just drove forty minutes in the wrong direction. *Ouch.* Even more painful was the blow to my ego for somehow managing to mess up directions on the Golden Circle. If I turned around and made no stops at all, I could get to Reykjavic right on time to meet up with Olaf.

But I couldn't help but succumb to how beautiful the contrasting landscape was on the road ahead of me. It was identical to that scene in Walter Mitty and could very well have been the same location since that scene was filmed in Iceland. I got out to set up my selfie-stick-tripod, vowing to myself to only take a maximum of three photos. But then something even more magical happened.

Out of nowhere, on the field to my right, two Icelandic horses came trotting over. They must have been more than a half -mile away, but they saw the car and immediately came straight for it. *Holy shit, my life is literally like a movie!*

It was as if the Slow-Mo effect on my phone was happening in my eyes. It seriously seemed like these two magical creatures were running in slow motion, with long voluptuous manes and tales flying wildly in the Arctic wind. In a movie, I would have been the female protagonist who is so pure of heart that wild horses just run up to her, and she jumps on easily, then they ride off into the midnight sun. Except it was only six -thirty, so I had five and a half hours until that happened. *Oh shit! Six -thirty!*

Definitely running late, but I couldn't just *ignore* two *friendly* Icelandic horses! They had reached the wire fence separating the field from the road, and both of their heads were hanging over it, begging me to come pet them.

One had patches of black and white like a cow, and its mane was reminiscent of Cruella DeVille's hair from 101 Dalmations, except it was about four feet long. The other, I swear, looked like me as an Icelandic horse. Its coat was the color of butterscotch, and its mane might have matched once but it seemed like now the sun had bleached it to a beachy blonde just like mine. Also, like mine, it was wild, wavy, and all over the place, as if neither of us had ever had our hair brushed before. Alyssa-Horse's hair was also about four feet long, reaching just past its knees.

Cautiously, I reached my hands out for both of their noses at the same time. To my surprise, they nuzzled their faces against me in return! It was more magical than the waterfalls and geyser combined! Had I really just found friendly, beautiful horses in the middle of nowhere in Iceland?!

Remembering my ten-year -old self, when I used to have my own horse thanks to my dad (just before he left) doing everything my mom said not to do, I reached down and plucked two handfuls of lush grass out of the earth. It was a trick that made zero sense since the horses have plenty of grass on their side of the fence, but for some reason seem to think it's just way better if it comes from the other side of it. Maybe that's where the saying "the grass is always greener on the other side" comes from. They immediately took it from my hands, crunching eagerly and making it sound as though they were chewing a delicious, fresh salad. I bent down and plucked more, eager to befriend the beautiful creatures.

While waiting for them to finish their mouthfuls of earth-salad, I set up the tripod on my selfie stick to try and capture a photo of the magical moment. I clicked the camera setting to time lapse, aimed it at the horses, pressed the shutter button, and resumed my position next to them on the fence. Suddenly an icy wind blew mine and the horse's hair, and impulsively, I reached my lips towards its face and gave it a kiss on the nose. Again, it nuzzled me in response, making for the official most magical moment of my life.

Knowing fully well that I had spent way too much time with the horses, I tried to slowly back away from them, hoping they would realize I was leaving and run away. But just like my little dog Oscar, they stared at me with a look of "Why are you leaving me?" thoroughly making me feel bad as I forced myself back into the car. Then the unthinkable happened. As I turned around and started to drive back in the direction I came, they *followed* me. Cue the shattering sound of my heartbreaking.

I sped up, and so did they, galloping alongside the fence until finally, they reached the separator of the property next to them. My mouth curled downward into a pout as I watched them in my rearview mirror staring after the car, but not even five seconds later, they had made a U-Turn and started galloping back towards the other horses on the field. *Maybe they were just bored and this was the highlight of their day .* I tried to convince myself that it wasn't just my self-proclaimed connection with animals and ability to be an Animal Whisperer.

Glancing at the time, I realized that if I sped a little bit and made absolutely no more stops, I could get to the meeting spot exactly on time. This of course, sucked for my bladder, stomach, and brain because I had to pee really bad, hadn't eaten since the cookies after snorkeling, and the anxiety of running out of gas was ever-growing, but I didn't want to be flakey to locals, especially when I had no way of contacting them to say I'd be late.

After what seemed like an hour, but was only twenty -four minutes, I reached the sign that misled me to the horses. Now looking at it, it pointed right for Geysir and left for Thingvellir. I went left and before long, was finding the terrain familiar as I passed back the way I had come earlier in the morning. Once out of the national park, I had about forty minutes to the main area of Reykjavik, which as expected, would get me there right on time. I just hoped that last quarter tank of gas would also get me there, in general.

When I pulled into the city, everything changed, and it didn't even feel like I was in Iceland anymore. There were several brand new hotels, tons of restaurants, and even some sort of music festival happening in the city square. This of course, made it more difficult to find parking, but I finally found a spot on the outskirts, just a few blocks from where I was supposed to be meeting Olaf. I parked parallel with ease and checked my appearance in the mirror. I looked like I had just been blasted by a waterfall.

Quickly, I ran my fingers through my mystical-wavy hair and piled it up on top of my head in my usual topknot. I yanked the soggy jacket and sweater off over my head and replaced it with a gray long-sleeved shirt that had dried since getting wet from the snorkeling. My accessories were limited, and I didn't want to look like a tourist wearing my Icelandic gifts, so after much deliberation, I decided to just put the cheap black jacket back on, let my hair down, and glob on some lipgloss. I'd call it *adventure chic ."*

Even though I had gotten there on time, I was now four minutes late, thanks to my attempted makeshift makeover. I jumped out of the car, locked it, and speed-walked a couple of blocks to the hotel where I was supposed to meet him. For the twentieth time, I wondered if it was sketchy, or at least would look sketchy, meeting a random guy at a hotel. Why hadn't he opted for a bar or public area? Butterflies and nerves fluttered all throughout my body for multiple reasons. I was still shy about meeting new people and awkward about the idea of recognizing him. What if I said hi to the wrong person?

But it was too late to have second thoughts about meeting up ; before I knew it, I was standing in the lobby of a dark, modern hotel with purple chandeliers and black leather sofas. On them were six burly guys, all with trendy haircuts that had buzzed sides and long tops and then varying lengths of facial hair. One of them looked like a straight -up viking, with his long top hair braided down the back of his head and his goatee almost equally as long. They were all immaculately dressed, as if they were about to go out to a hot nightclub in LA, and had at least one cocktail in hand; some had two.

The main thing they all had in common was that they were *all* staring at me. *Not intimidating at all.* Olaf hadn't mentioned bringing friends, so I wasn't sure if these were his or if I was meant to figure out which viking was him out of a roomful of them. Should I smile and wave? What if they weren't his friends and just thought I was a random girl flirting with them?

"You must be Alyssa! I recognize you from your Facebook pictures!" The blond viking who was sitting on the armrest of one of the black sofas said as he rose up to full height. He had to be at least six foot two, maybe three, and double the width of me. Like the rest of them, the sides of his head were shaved, with the top long. His was dirty blond and strategically molded upwards then slicked back. He had a goatee as well, but it was neatly trimmed and had the same icy blue eyes as the receptionist from my hotel. His black jeans were tight at the ankles and tucked neatly into his enormous black boots, and he wore a light gray shirt under his expensive-looking leather jacket. What stuck out the most was the silver necklace he wore, with a charm that was clearly an Icelandic symbol.

"Yes! You must be Olaf!" I squeaked as he engulfed me in a powerful embrace. "Sorry I'm late, I took a wrong turn after I went to Geysir and ended up in a field with wild horses."

"It happens, no worries," he said with a gruff laugh, "Let me introduce you to everyone! They wanted to come meet the American!" He laughed again, gesturing to the group of guys with the hand that was holding his drink. It hadn't dawned on me that I'd be going out drinking with a bunch of viking-looking dudes, not to mention well-kempt, immaculately dressed ones. Suddenly I felt very underdressed and intimidated.

Olaf went down the line-up announcing Icelandic names that there was no way I'd ever remember. Then he introduced me as a travel blogger from LA, which both embarrassed me and boosted my ego in multiple ways. Would they think I was a joke like most of the guys did back home? Would they assume I had some mystery older man paying for my trip?

"Alyssa is a solo traveler and a well -known blogger! She's here on her own and doing a collaboration with some of the tour companies!" He suddenly announced, sending me into a fury of gratitude that led to me involuntarily giving him a squeeze and head nuzzle. This bit of information was responded with several "Oh wow's!'" and "That's awesome!" even a couple, "We can give you some tips for things to see!" I was more than humbled and very truly happy.

"Oy, finish your drinks so we can go to Skuli!" Olaf announced to the group. Then he turned to me and said, "My family owns this hotel and it's one of the easiest to find, which is why I said to meet here, but I want to take you to a true Icelandic bar!" My eyes widened both because of the mere mention of going to an authentic Icelandic bar and because his family owned the five star hotel. Would it be poor taste to try to pitch him a collaboration there?! I decided I'd wait a bit and maybe buy him a drink or two first.

They downed their one or two drinks within seconds and were up off the couches, ready to go, all towering over me like giants. There was a flurry of small talk with a few of them on the short walk to Skuli. From what I could gather, most of them came from important Icelandic families and now had some sort

206

of major role within the company. I smirked, considering the thought that I had just somehow managed to meet the country's most prestigious citizens.

When we finally reached the bar, I was slightly let down. It was the complete opposite of the opulence of the hotel lobby. Replacing the chic metals, shiny marble, and fancy cocktails was worn-down wood, dim lighting, massive mugs of beer, and loud drunk people.

It was so crowded that I had to hold on to the back of Olaf's jacket as he guided me through the thick forest of locals to get to a table in the corner he had automatically set out for. There was no way there would be an open table in this crowd, so I assumed he had reserved it, or perhaps even more viking men were saving it for him.

"Belinda! Helga! We're here! He bellowed, waving a massive arm overhead. *Oh right.* I forgot the obvious assumption that he was probably meeting up with girls. My stomach twisted a bit and I got nervous, knowing fully well that women tend to not always like me upon first meeting. And if these women were anything like the tourists hiking who judged me based on my lack of trekking attire, they definitely weren't going to be impressed with my hot-mess appearance.

We finally made our way to the opening where the table was and Olaf pushed me into the booth on the bench next to Belinda. She slid over and quickly but politely introduced herself before yelling at Olaf to order more beers before the server went away again. Two of the guys slid in across from me next to Helga, who was eyeing me and talking to them in Icelandic, making it very obvious she was asking who I was. Such a strange thing to feel immediate tension when meeting other women, but with guys, it's a completely normal thing. I wish I knew that later on in life, it's not always like that.

"Don't mind her ; she's a slight bitch." Belinda muttered, noticing my unease. "She's got a thing for that one, so she's giving him hell for not inviting her to 'drinks with the boys' when they showed up with a pretty American girl." She added. *Great way to make a good first impression.*

I tried to give Helga a half-hearted, shy smile, but she returned it with an eyeroll before shoving the two guys out of the booth so she could get out and go to the bar. They rolled their eyes as well and scooted back into the bench, joined by Olaf in the third seat.

"Let's get some brews then, shall we? And some shots." Olaf announced, smacking his paw-like palms together as if he were about to eat a delicious feast. I hadn't been a beer drinker or shot taker since my debaucherous days at Florida State University, but after that icy interaction, I was down to slam a few back.

After three shots and one mug of beer, I had successfully befriended all of the remaining people at the booth, less Helga and the guy who had apparently done something wrong by walking over in the group with me. It took me doing all three shots for Belinda to fully like me, and after ordering another beer on top of that, it was like we were best friends. She even invited me to come ride her Icelandic horses if I had time -- she had a stable of them because she teaches riding lessons to little kids.

As she was explaining this, a new face joined our table, one that was quite different from the rest and that I couldn't resist looking at. His name was Trigólfur, but he acknowledged that it was hard to pronounce and insisted that I just called him Triggy.

Triggy was just as tall as the other guys but much more slender and from what I could tell, very fit. Also, unlike the rest of them, his face was clean-shaved, and his hair was attractively tousled forward all over his head rather than shaved on the sides and slicked back. From what I gathered, he was the younger brother of one of the guys, and not exactly part of their clique, but also a good friend of Belinda's. When he sat next to me on the bench, I made sure to politely ask if she wanted me to switch spots with him so she could sit next to him, just in case they were a thing. But she had scoffed and declined, insisting that he was like a brother to her and informing me that sometimes he comes out to help with the kids. *Swoon.*

208

"So where are you heading tomorrow?" Triggy asked after answering his question on where I had been so far.

"I'm not sure, it's my last day, so I was thinking of maybe trying to see something new and heading up North ," I said, slightly tipsy but trying to still sound like I knew what I was doing.

"North eh?" Olaf boomed from a few feet away. Apparently, me not knowing what I was doing tomorrow had caught everyone at the table's attention. I hadn't thought they cared what I'd seen or what I should see until I said I was thinking of driving up North.

"My family is from Olaffson ; it's near Snæfellsjökull* you should go there." He added as he took two massive steps towards the table.

"Oh yes, I agree," Triggy added, "Say, do you have a map or something?" I totally did, but dare I pull it out in a bar of locals?

"Y-yeah, but don't make fun of me ," I murmured, digging through my disaster of a purse and extracting the torn and crumpled map that I had been making notes on throughout my roadtrips.

Triggy opened it up carefully and spread it out over the table, making sure to wipe down any wetness from the shots and beers first. He, Belinda, and Olaf all looked at it with shock.

"Wow, you've covered a lot in just two days!" Triggy said finally, as the other two examined the notes I had made. Apparently, my aggressive adventuring warranted my street cred because before I knew it, Olaf had shoved himself into the booth as well, and Triggy had magically acquired a pen.

They started throwing out names of places that I would never be able to pronounce or remember and excitedly circled and pointed to their favorite "secret locations," including towns where they were from or still had family living in. I felt like I was a treasure hunter who had just struck gold. Except, more realistically, I was a travel blogger who just got dope insider tips from locals. Same same but different.

Something started to rattle above me and I jumped sideways against Triggy. It was what seemed like a projector screen being lowered over the giant glass window that looked out onto the still-busy street.

"Oh, they lower a black out curtain and start playing movies at 11pm, so you know it's getting late." Triggy explained, "Since there's twenty -four hours of daylight, it's easy to forget what time it is and stay out all night." He continued, clearly seeing the look of confusion on my face. It took me a second to understand, thanks to the shots, but then I realized that if it doesn't look dark outside, you'll think it's still early and keep drinking. That was definitely true because the brightness outside had me thinking it was still only 8pm and ready for another beer.

"It's eleven!" I blurted, much to the amusement of the table. "That means it's almost time for the midnight sun! I haven't seen it yet!" All eyes widened and mouths either smirked or gaped.

"Hey, I have an idea!" Belinda said, taking the pen back from Triggy. "Why don't we go ride the horses now! Under the midnight sun!" She took a big chug of beer and started to circle on the map where her ranch was.

"YES! Let's do it!" Triggy exclaimed, squeezing my shoulder with the arm that I had just realized was around me. *Woah, was all of this really happening ?*

"You kids go ahead, we're going to head to Austur. Unless, Alyssa, you want to experience a real Icelandic nightclub?" Olaf asked as he slid out of the booth. I did not. At all. But I did feel bad abandoning my host to go have a romantic fairytale adventure with one of his friend's little brothers.

"Well, we still have some time ; the ranch isn't far," Belinda said, noting my hesitance, "I need to go pick up my boyfriend on the way home anyway. Triggy did you drive?" Triggy nodded and extracted a set of keys from his jacket pocket. It suddenly dawned on me that I was tipsy and would have to drive all the way back to Keflavik.

"Ohhh shit." I mumbled, "I drove too, and I'm staying in Keflavik."

"Ok, ok, so this will work out ," Olaf said after a moment of thinking. "Belinda, you and Triggy go get Gunnar, Alyssa ; you come with me and maybe just don't drink for half an hour, then you guys can all meet at your place." It sounded like a good enough plan to me. I'd fulfill my politeness by heading to the club with Olaf and then fulfill my dreams of riding Icelandic horses under the midnight sun with Triggy.

We all agreed and headed for the door, which apparently led to a parallel universe. The light outside at eleven PM was blinding, and people were walking around as if it were mid - afternoon. As I was trying to recover from the shock of going from the purposely darkened bar to the blaring bright street, Triggy had taken my phone out of my hand to save his number on Whatsapp, even though I told him I didn't have service unless there's Wi-Fi. *"In case you get lost."* He had said, apparently not comprehending what I meant. He gave it back along with a big hug and followed after Belinda.

"We're going this way!" Olaf said, already starting to walk in the other direction. My hopeless romantic instincts obviously wanted to follow after Triggy, but I also didn't want to risk coming off as rude to Olaf, especially since he was the one who introduced us.

The club was just a few blocks away. It looked like a typical seedy Hollywood club except even dodgier since it was underground. Sweat seemed to linger in the air, and a black mixture of spilled drinks and melted ice from boots coated the floor. It was exactly the club scene I had vowed to never be caught dead in again after years of drunken nights in college. At least in my twenties, I was frequenting the fancy VIP sections of top -notch nightclubs like LIV in Miami and later 1OAK and Greystone Manor in L.A. This place however was something straight out of my college days, except with dozens of drunk 30-something dudes instead of raging under 21-year olds.

It took me until that moment to realize that my friend who had put me in contact with Olaf was still very much into this scene, so he probably thought I was too. I also realized that all the drinking we had done for the last three hours was just the pre-game. But there was absolutely no way I could continue partying. Not only were those days behind me, but I had super important things to do. Li ke ride horses under the midnight sun with a gorgeous viking descendant whose real name I can't pronounce. I also needed to wake up early as fuck in order to drive all the way to Snæfellsjökull (please, try to pronounce that out loud), explore it, and get back to Keflavik in time for my collaboration with the Blue Lagoon.

"Hey!" I yelled over the thumping bass of the blaring house music, "I think -- I think I'm going to go! I'm so tired!" It was technically true, but the absolute truth was that the last place I wanted to be in Iceland was an underground club where the strobe-lights were very close to giving me a seizure, and my anxiety was close to a level ten, mostly because I kept thinking *'Why am I underground when the midnight sun is about to debut?!'*.

"Alright, no worries," Olaf shouted back, looking a little bummed but understanding. "Do ya know how to get back to your car?"

I nodded and gave him a big hug, thanking him profusely for inviting me out. At that moment, I never would have expected in a million years that I would see him again in just three years, when I came back to Iceland as one of the world's top travel bloggers and influencers, hosting a group trip with my followers.

When I reached the top of the concrete steps and pushed open the wide, black, metal door that separated the light of the outside world from the darkness of the nightclub, it was like a breath of fresh air. I was a world adventurer back on a mission again and beyond eager to attain it.

Remembering Olaf's easy instructions for getting back to the area where I parked, I turned left and then immediately right down the near- empty street on the outskirts of the main area. It was eleven -thirty, and just enough time to make the ten -minute drive to the ranch, jump on a horse and fulfill my current dream of riding under the midnight sun.

As I was power walking towards the general direction of my car, I started to get an uncomfortable feeling. I knew Reykjavik and Iceland in general was very safe, but my vigilance as a solo female traveler could not be ignored. Sure, it was late "at night ," but there were hardly any people on the streets, so why did I feel so weird?

'*Heyyyy*' One of two guys passing in the opposite direction of me said. *Oh.* That was why. After an evening of fun with new friends, I was back to being the questionable girl walking around alone. Did people honestly think I had come to Iceland to find men to have sex with?

"*Look look!*" I heard the accent of a Chinese man and whipped my head to the left to see what he was exclaiming to look at. When my eyes focused on him, I realized the man was shaking his wife's shoulder, pointing towards me, while she and their daughter giggled. "*Prostitute! In Iceland!*"

The words stung but the alcohol inside of me boiled my blood and ignited my temper.

"Look! Look! Tourists!" I shouted back, fake-laughing at them and gesturing with exaggeration as they were. The smiles on their faces were wiped off and they almost tripped over each other to scurry away. What the hell was it about me being alone that automatically pinned me as a woman looking for sex? Was it the fact that my hair wasn't perfectly done? Was it because I wore make-up? Was it because I chose to wear tight -fitting clothes out of comfort rather than baggy ones that hid my figure? *Probably all of the above.*

When I finally reached my car, I was outraged. What the hell was wrong with people? Why couldn't they just mind their own damn business? My mood went from euphoric to abysmal in a matter of seconds. As much as I hated to admit it, the last two random interactions put such negative self-doubt in my mind that I wondered if I should even go meet up with Triggy at all. Would they be right if I did? That I was just a girl looking for a man?

Nah, fuck that. I decided as I shifted the car into drive. I was in fucking Iceland, one of my top bucket list destinations and one of my first fully covered collaborations as a successful travel blogger. No way I was going to let some rando's get me down because of their stereotypes and pass up riding a majestic horse under the damn midnight sun. Nopety nope, nope, nope.

Carefully and ten kilometers below the speed limit, I drove to Belinda's ranch. I got there just on time at eleven fifty, and when I pulled up, she and her boyfriend were already mounted atop their horses of choice. Next to them was Triggy, standing in between two gorgeous horses whose heads nearly reached his, holding the reins for both.

"We thought you weren't going to come!" Belinda shouted, sideways glancing at a nervous and now relieved-Triggy.

"Oh, I wouldn't miss this for anything!" I yelled as I hopped from the car and bounded towards the white speckled horse to Triggy's left.

"I'm glad you came." He whispered with a smile, helping me up onto the horse's saddle.

As we galloped off across the empty field, four horses, four people, and one extremely rare phenomenon of nature, I embedded the memory into my brain in hopes of keeping it forever. The bright orange-red sun seemed like it was about the size of my fist, yet bigger than earth in outer space. The colorful palette of sunset hues across the sky at twelve in the morning. The fact that there was a gorgeous Icelandic guy chasing behind me on a horse. It was all just too perfect for words. And so I kept it that way. *Until now anyway.*

The next morning was a clusterfuck of thoughts and emotions. I woke up in my bed in Keflavik Inn but couldn't remember for the life of me what time I got back and didn't want to think about what time it was now. My car was definitely still at the ranch, which I only agreed to because the option to have some Icelandic wine and ride the horse home sounded way better than leaving early and driving.

I tugged at something snug around my neck and upon unwrapping it, remembered Triggy had let me use his wool

214

scarf for warmth as a barter to promise that he'd pick me up in the morning to take me back to my car. Now I realized that wasn't a barter at all, but more of a win-win situation for me where I got warmth *and* a ride back to my car in the morning.

Triggy had willingly ridden alongside me on horseback for what seemed like hours just so I could get back to my hotel, where I felt comfortable. They had all offered me a room numerous times, but for some reason, I refused to accept it. It was a mixture of not wanting the hotel owner to wonder why I didn't come home, of wanting to be responsible and wake up early for my last day in Iceland, and as much as I hate to say it -- to not fulfil the stereotypes of being a lone woman in search of a man. I hoped I wouldn't regret that last feeling in the future when I'm married to one person for the rest of my life, with no epic scandalous stories to tell. *Oh wait, already have plenty of those.*

Robotically I reached sideways for my phone. *Thank god.* It was on the charger and fully juiced up, ready to go. With one eye closed, I squinted with the other to check the list of incoming messages I had somehow acquired in what seemed like only a few hours of sleep. What time was it anyway? I squinted harder to see the time in the top left corner of my phone; fucking seven AM?! Damn twenty -four hours of sunlight! I had wanted to sleep in until at least nine, but even with the blackout curtains, the sun still flooded the room. I really should get an early start anyway since the area I was going to attempt was a whopping four -hour drive away.

Just as I was wondering if it would be rude to text Triggy so early for that ride he promised me ; an incoming Whatsapp message popped up on my screen from him.

'Good morning beautiful! Hope you got some sleep. Let me know when you'll be needing that ride and I'll come get you.' I went ahead and added that to my long list of telepathic moments. As I was about to reply, I noticed he had sent a photo before that message. I scrolled up to see not one but three whimsical photos he had taken without me knowing of me riding the horse under the midnight sun. Remembering how magical that moment was temporarily distracted me from the

pain and discomfort that was pulsing in my head. I couldn't tell if it was a hangover or my allergy to early mornings.

'*Morning! Thanks for those photos ; I love them so much!*' I sent it first, since that was the only thing currently on my mind and also so that I didn't seem like I was just using him for a ride. '*I just woke up, give me ten minutes and I'll be ready to go! Thank you!*' Ten minutes was ambitious, considering the extremely slow pace at which I was moving. It was definitely one of those mornings where your brain just straight up refuses to work and you find yourself fumbling around in circles trying to get your shit together.

At least I had been either smart enough or cold enough to sleep in my base thermal layers, so I was already one-third dressed. The rest of my layers were in a pile at the end of the bed and clearly stunk of horses. Not wanting to appear to Triggy as if I didn't have any other clothes and also as if I hadn't even changed, I quickly pulled the inner layer of leggings and shirts out from the outer ones I had worn yesterday. I shook off the old outer ones, creating a cloud of horse hair, and quickly ran to my carry-on to pull out my go -to travel hack for this exact situation: dryer sheets. I took one Tide sheet out of the box and rubbed it all over the horse-smelling layer of clothes, then pulled them on over my existing base layers.

'*Aaaahhh so fresh!*' I giggled to myself, inhaling deeply to make sure my trick had worked. Next, I chose the gray pair of leggings that I had been wearing under the black ones yesterday and put them on over the black ones. At least changing the order and color of my layers would make it seem like I changed my outfit. Next, I layered on my only cute top -- an off-white thick faux-lace long -sleeved shirt, which wouldn't keep me warm at all but would at least look nice. I shoved the other two cotton long sleeves in my seatbelt bag just in case though, along with a couple more dryer sheets since they definitely smelled like my B.O.

All of that movement exhausted me to the point of feeling dizzy, which again could have been the hangover. I dragged myself to the sink, remembering the golden advice from the hotel owner that tap water in Iceland is the highest quality you can get because it comes from glaciers and that if anyone ever tried to charge me for a glass of water, I should laugh in their face. I filled up the glass by the sink and chugged two cupfuls of delicious, sweet, liquid glaciers. Then I got really crazy and splashed the cold water on my face. That woke me right up! Should have done it in the first place! Now I was t-minus two minutes until Triggy was here.

I finished packing my seatbelt bag with my camera gear, the few snacks I had left, money, chargers, extra clothes, and the white one -piece bathing suit I had specifically brought for the Blue Lagoon. I chose it over a bikini because in my head, it was " warmer," and also because I knew the white color would look great in the pale blue, steamy lagoon. Going to the Blue Lagoon is, of course, one of the essential things you do in Iceland, and I was beyond excited about it. Especially because the marketing department had graciously accepted my collaboration pitch and offered me their VIP package, which included entry, a towel, two free drinks, and free Wi-Fi. Basically, my idea of heaven.

Ping! My phone announced an incoming Whatsapp message that I knew was probably Triggy. *Damn, no time to post a photo!* Thanks to my little social outings, it would now be a full twenty -four hours since I posted anything on social media. People might think I died or got kidnapped by a viking in Iceland! Or more realistically, only my mom would think that, and no one else would notice. I self-vowed to come straight back to the hotel after the Blue Lagoon tonight and work for at least three hours. Strategically, I asked the marketing manager when the least amount of people are at the Blue Lagoon so that I could take photos without people in them. She had told me it was just before they closed, at ten o'clock at night. At first I thought, *"Hell no! It'll be freezing at night!"* but then remembered the whole twenty -four hours of daylight thing, plus the unlikelihood of most people wanting to go that late, and graciously accepted my time slot. It would also give me plenty of time to get up to the North-West coast and back.

'I'm out front!' His message said, sending flashes of heat to my cheeks. Would he still think I was beautiful at seven in the

morning after all his alcohol wore off? Then another pang of nervousness hit me; what if the hotel owner or her son was already awake and downstairs? What would they think if they saw a local guy picking me up, or worse, what if they thought we were both leaving?

'Coming! Do you mind pulling forward a block? I don't want the hotel owner to think I had someone sleep over since this is a business deal and all ;)' Lame, but necessary.

And thank god, because as I trotted down the steps into the lobby, the owner *and* her son were at the front desk already.

"You're up early! I'm surprised! I didn't see you come in before midnight last night!" She trilled. *Awkward.* There was only one way to make it seem like I wasn't out all night with a cute guy I had just met.

"Yes! I really wanted to see the midnight sun, so a girl I made friends with here who has a ranch let me take one of her horses out at midnight last night ; it was so cool!" I blurted, making sure to emphasize that I was with a girl and not a guy. I even took out my phone, tapped open my photos, and showed her the one of me on the horse under the blazing orange sun.

"Oh wow! That is absolutely beautiful! You are really impressing me with how ambitious you are to see the country! Where are you off to now?" She said, sounding genuinely impressed. I wondered if she still would be if she happened to scroll to the left and see the numerous photos of us taking shots and drinking wine.

"Well, my friend in LA connected me with her friend who lives here, and he gave me all sorts of tips for a fjord area in the North-West, so I'm going to try to go see Snaefelufagus...er... I don't know how to say it,"

"Snæfellsjökulll !" She and her son said in unison, both equally as shocked.

"Yes! Snaef-fells-jo-kull," I repeated carefully, trying to imitate their pronunciation of the impossible word.

"No one ever goes there! Good for you! You won't be disappointed!" She said sweetly.

"Thank you! I'm excited! Oh and then I have a reservation at the Blue Lagoon at ten PM, so I'll probably be back around eleven." I added, for some reason feeling the need to sound a little more responsible.

"Sounds like a lovely day! Enjoy!" She said, waving after me as I said my goodbyes and backed out the front door. I prayed she didn't follow me out, especially since I could see Triggy standing outside of his car waving at me.

"Morning beautiful!" He said softly as he gave me a complete body embrace.

"Morning," I tried to reply but it was muffled since my face was pressed against his sweater. He seemed taller somehow but just as cute as I thought he was when I was tipsy. His car was similar to my rental except electric blue and a bit sportier looking. *Oh wait, just kidding.* I realized it definitely was not like my basic rental when I got inside and saw the five silver rings on the steering wheel branding it an Audi. *Hot viking, drives an Audi, calls me beautiful.* I wondered what it would be like if I just happened to move to Iceland.

"Thanks for picking me up so early ; I feel bad." I admitted sheepishly as I buckled my seatbelt.

"No, not at all, this is when I usually wake up for work anyway, and I wanted to make sure I saw you again in case you're busy later." *And sweet, and caring?* Screw Nate and his sketchiness ; there are near-perfect Icelandic men in the world!

"What do you do anyway? I don't think I asked yesterday, sorry." I said in an awkward attempt to dodge what seemed like an invitation to hang out later. The truth was that I wanted to ; *however*, I knew if I did, I wouldn't get any work done again. And no work means no travel. *But I do need epic experiences to write about.* I'd see how I felt about it later.

"I'm an agricultural engineer. My family owns a large majority of the farms you see when you're driving. You might think they're simply owned by poor farmers, but we actually employ them all, let them live on the land for free, and then we handle the business back end of it." He explained as if assuming I would think he was just a farmer or something. A farmer that drives an Audi. But my attention peaked the second he said engineer. Maybe I will hang out with him later. And see if he wanted to invite me back to live with him and get married and live happily ever after in Iceland.

"So that's how I know Belinda ; she rents the ranch from my family." He added, continuing to thoroughly impress me. *I'm moving to Iceland.*

He talked a bit more about what being an agricultural engineer entailed, and I did my best to understand him and keep the conversation going. What I really wanted to talk about was what our plans were going to be for later.

When we finally pulled up to the long dirt driveway, I got hit with another wave of embarrassment. Belinda and her boyfriend were already up and teaching a horseback riding class to a group of little kids right next to where my car was. *Great*, I thought, *she definitely is going to think we shacked.*

"Don't worry, I brought the horses back here last night, remember?" Triggy said sweetly, clearly reading my body language as I tried to sink down into the seat in an attempt to hide. *Oh right.*

Luckily Belinda was too engulfed in her class to come over for a conversation, and I was happy to simply exchange energetic waves. Triggy walked me to my rental car and opened the door for me, leaning his arm on it as I slid in and dumped my bag on the passenger seat.

"So I know you'll be out all day, but I work pretty late as well, let me know later if you want to grab a brew when you're done exploring?" Ah, there it was. The tentative plans I was secretly hoping he would make.

"Sounds good, yeah! I'll message you when I'm leaving the Blue Lagoon!" I chirped a little too enthusiastically. Or maybe not, because it caused him to swoop down and give me another hug, which was slightly awkward since I was already sitting in the car.

After about four more goodbye's, he shut the door and watched as I drove away on the road we had ridden side by side on horses just a few hours before. Yes, that was a story for the books, but now I needed some stories for the damn blog. It was time to continue the solo adventure.

It was my fourth solo road trip in Iceland, so I pretty much mastered the whole feeling comfortable stopping to look at things on my own, thing. But I wasn't entirely prepared for one impromptu stop at a troll grave cave, especially after my incident on the first day in the troll grass.

I was on my way to this lesser-known beach that Olaf recommended called Djúpalónsandur, when I saw a few cars parked on the side of the road and some people walking up to what looks like a giant crack in the side of a mountain.

"Waterfall?" I wondered aloud, trying to figure out what the fuss was about without crashing on the one -lane highway. But after careful examination of the sheer rock wall, I concluded that there were no waterfalls. I kept driving, mostly because I had to pee really badly, but couldn't stop wondering what the hell they were looking at.

"ICE CAVE?" Suddenly it occurs to me that it's freaking Iceland, and if people are going into a crack in a mountain, it's for a damn cool reason. Like seeing an ice cave.

I made the executive decision to turn around and head back to the random spot that wasn't on the map, park my little rental car, and start hiking up to the crack. I read the sign to figure out the name and learned that it's called Rauðfeldar Canyon and that there's a spooky story to it.

According to the little sign, Rauðfeldar Canyon is where an angry troll killed one of his two nephews by pushing him into the canyon because they pushed his "curvaceous" daughter into the water and she ended up drifting to Greenland on an iceberg (unharmed of course). The angry troll was so pissed that he then "climbed into the glacier" and never came back out.

AKA Rauðfeldar Canyon is where one troll died and where an angry one still "lives ." Sounds like a great place to venture solo in, right?

For some reason, I was compelled to still go inside of this "troll grave ," so I started hiking up to its base where people were going in. It looked really pretty from the outside; there was green mossy grass growing everywhere, cute little birds flying around and hanging out at the top, and this adorable little river flowing from, the crack?

But how do you get inside ! I watched the people in front of me as they seemed to step on the rocks in the river to get inside of the crack. *Seriously?* I half felt like it was an extremely bad idea but half felt like a badass climbing through a river to get to a troll cave. So I followed suit and stepped from stone to stone into the canyon.

As soon as I was through the narrow river passageway, I found myself in what seemed like a cylindrical cave that was open at the very top where the light could come in. Thank god the one day it was sunny and not raining was the day I decided to go into a troll grave whose only light came from this opening ; otherwise, I would have been scared shitless.

I felt like I was in *Journey to the Center of the Earth* or something, which was ironic since that legend is based on the volcano nearby. Then I noticed there were people even further up the narrow river that seemed to be coming from another narrow passageway deeper into the cave. Again, I knew in theory it was a bad idea, but there were already other people doing it, so obviously, I had to. I waited until they were done taking their photos before I approached the little river to begin stepping on the stones again. But when I looked down, what I saw was absolutely bone-chilling.

Wedged in between the rocks that I was supposed to be stepping on were carcass after carcass of giant dead birds. I tried not to look at them and their eerie decaying faces, but they were right next to where my foot was supposed to go!

I tried to keep calm and not panic, wondering if maybe they made a mistake on the sign and it was really where birds go to die instead of trolls. *Or maybe the troll kills the birds that try to fly into his cave!* I tried not to think about the fact that if winged-animals got killed in this cave, what chances does a non-winged, slower-moving human have. But I kept stepping on the stones deeper into the canyon because I caught sight of what I thought was a...*could it be?*

Oh hell yes! I found it! The one thing I didn't think I was going to be able to see in Iceland because it was too expensive to book an excursion to one! An ice cave! It wasn't a complete ice cave, but the massive chunk of ice that was spiraling out of the roof of the cave above the small waterfall was good enough for me.

It's not exactly normal to see a waterfall inside a cave either. Most waterfalls are on the outside of the mountains, which is what also makes Rauðfeldar Canyon unique. I couldn't see where the cave led to, and there was no way in hell I was climbing the waterfall to find out, so I carefully balanced myself on the rocks without touching anything to take some pictures of the cave.

I would love to admit that it was all in my head, but I can't deny the bone -chilling feeling I got when I was taking the photos. The temperature dropped drastically and my hands got numb and shaky ; then suddenly I had an extremely creepy feeling that I should not be there. I turned to try to hold out my camera to get a better shot of the cave, then realized the other people were no longer in the cave, and I was completely alone with the dead birds.

"Ok, time to go." I thought, feeling like I was in one of those scary movie scenes when you wonder why the person is going *towards* the murderer. I tried not to panic and run through the river instead of stepping on the stones, mostly because all I could envision was falling on the dead birds and getting stuck in the water, then a creepy troll coming out and killing me.

The heebie-jeebies were in full effect but I still carefully continued stepping on the stones to get out of that damn cave. Once back on solid ground and out in the daylight, I half- ran back to the car, avoiding eye contact with anyone who was on their way into the other-worldly death trap I had just encountered. I was so shaken up that for the first time on the whole trip, I took out my phone to turn on the data roaming to text Nate, but when I looked down at my phone, I realized something strange.

My sunglasses that had been hooked on the front of my shirt, just like they had been when I hiked to waterfalls, climbed basalt rock walls, and did other adventurous activities the past four days in Iceland, were gone. I didn't hear or feel them drop, but at some point, while I was in that damn troll cave, they mysteriously disappeared! Immediately, I decided that it was the troll who stole them somehow, and either way, there was no way I was going to go back in there to look for them. They could rest in peace along with all of the dead birds.

Before I even reached the car, I had already written Nate an obnoxious message describing what had just happened. It sounded like something straight out of a fictional children's horror book, and naturally, he was not the least bit worried, just amused. He didn't even acknowledge my claim that an invisible troll stole my sunglasses right off of my body and instead asked if I was having fun and when my flight gets back to LA. I decided he needed visual proof of my creepy encounter, so I went to download the photos off my camera and onto my phone. But when they finally loaded, they were *all* distorted!

'See! Even the photos are haunted! Not a single one came out!' I typed furiously, sending him three of the twisted, blurry photos.

'Maybe you just need to hold your hand more still?' Was his response. *Ugh.* Why was I wasting my time ? Clearly, he didn't care. Despite how many times he told me he cared about me, I knew it would never be enough to actually commit to me. For the millionth time, I reminded myself that at least I could always depend on him to respond to my crazy messages, no matter what time of day or night it was. But that was it. He wasn't like those guys who would wait hours or even days to respond. If I messaged him, I knew he would immediately respond. Which I guess is what *friends* do. *Sigh.*

224

I put my phone back on airplane mode in fear of racking up a ridiculous bill just because I was so scared of fabled creatures that I felt the need to text my never-will-be-boyfriend. I was tempted to also delete his number once again, but instead, I repeated my usual mantra, *"You are a strong, independent, awesome woman! You don't need players in your life!"* Even though I was purposely ignoring the three texts Triggy had already sent me, professing his inability to focus on anything other than seeing me again. To be honest, I didn't even know how to respond to that since I'm not exactly the sweetest or romantic girl in the world. *#ThisisWhyImSingle*.

Finally, I started driving again, gladly getting as far away as possible from the creepy troll cave and closer to my intended destinations. I passed through endless green fields, some home to even more Icelandic horses, and wondered how many of the properties were owned by Triggy's family. After about forty minutes, I finally got to my next destination.

This was the place that Olaf recommended that I go see, and when I got there, I was extremely glad they did, partially because there was a bathroom. Djúpalónssandur, although impossible to pronounce, was by far one of the most unreal-looking places I had seen in Iceland thus far. I took the path to the left instead of going down to the right where a few other people were going and was treated to an awesome birds-eye view of the entire beach and the jagged lava-rock formations below.

As you can probably guess, the sand here is also black due to the erosion of lava rocks. It crunched as I walked on it with my boots, wandering aimlessly to the left away from any other people. At this point, I was pretty sure all other tourists were going to judge me for being alone, and especially for taking selfies, so avoiding them at all costs sounded ideal. I reached a super alien-ey looking lagoon area with shallow pools in between the lava rock formation that look like craters on another planet, or perhaps where a mermaid would live. I tried to get creative with a reflection shot, but right as I had my selfie stick angled behind me, a couple walked by and stopped to watch me. *Seriously?*

I tapped the remote on my phone to take the shot anyway, then trudged off through the black sand. When I glanced backwards, I realized they had stopped because she wanted a photo there as well. She stood in the same spot and did the same pose, and suddenly I felt guilty for being the one to judge their assumptions when they technically were positive ones.

There were a few more cool lava formations that I investigated and even attempted touching the water to confirm that it was, in fact, freezing. I considered sitting on the black pebbles for a bit, but the thick gray clouds that had decided to make an appearance out of nowhere crushed those plans. The temperature dropped to what felt like below freezing, and rain in the form of mist swirled down to kiss my face. Since I was actually dry for once, I didn't want to go back to my constant state of soggy, so I trudged back to the steps and headed for the car.

Of course, when I got to the car, the clouds had mysteriously cleared out, but I took it as a sign that I needed to get going anyway. I still had a couple more stops I wanted to squeeze in before needing to leave in time for my reservation at the Blue Lagoon. I had purposely passed the next stop on the way to this beach, so at least I knew where to backtrack to get to it, which would at least save some time. All of the other places that I attempted finding took longer because I'd miss the turn off thanks to signs that are impossible for anyone but locals to read.

But I definitely knew how to read the one for Snæfellsjökull, the most famous glacier in Iceland. Snæfellsjökull is where the famous book *"Journey to the Center of the Earth"* was based off of in the beginning. It's actually an active volcano, so technically, it really does go down to the center of the Earth. There were a couple of other big Hollywood movies filmed there as well, and now I'd film mine here too. Even if only a few thousand people would see it on social media.

"That is Snaefellsjokull, a mountain about five thousand feet in height, one of the most remarkable on the whole island, and certainly doomed to be the most celebrated in the world,

for through its crater, we shall reach the centre of the earth." Is what they said in the book slash movie, which again, was partially accurate.

Once again, I noticed some cars driving, so I decided to follow them, but they were heading towards the glacier top of Snæfellsjökull, despite the warning sign that says not to drive unless you have an off-road vehicle. Naturally, I followed them up, but only after the third car similar to mine went. It was scary as hell.

The higher I crept up, the more ice there was on the road, and more than once, my tires slid on them, sending me towards the edge of the cliff. After the third slide, I pulled over and assessed the situation. My heart was pounding out of my chest, and I desperately wanted to turn around, but there wasn't enough room on the narrow, one-car, dirt road. Up ahead, I could see more ice, which meant I would keep sliding, and could possibly get stuck or worse, slide right off the cliff.

A 4X4 truck passed me with ease and shot straight up the road, completely unphased by the slippery ice. My cheeks burned when I saw both passengers look into my window, likely laughing at the stupid solo girl who drove a damn two - wheel drive a rental car up the glacier. Part of me really wanted to get down ASAP, but the adventure addict in me wanted to find out if the white patch up ahead was snow or part of the glacier.

After a few deep breaths to slow my heart from exploding, I kept driving up, slow as all hell, and with my foot on the brake. When I finally got closer, I confirmed that it wasn't fluffy snow at all but patches of icy glaciers that you probably could have ice skated on. If I wasn't alone, I totally would have slid across the patch of glacier I parked near, but something I read on the warning sign about potential thin ice made me think twice about falling down into the center of the Earth.

I carefully parked the car and stepped carefully onto the edge of the glacier for a photo. It was officially the closest I've ever been to seeing snow, and I secretly celebrated the moment. I spun around and around on my toes as if I were a professional ice skater, laughing silently about how fun such a simple joy was. Another big truck passed, with two more passengers who looked at me with raised eyebrows, but they didn't stop or even slow down. They headed straight up to the top of the glacier. I desperately wanted to continue going up, I could even see the top of the volcano-glacier, but I could also see the road was all ice the remainder of the way up. It was a complete bummer, but I decided to go back down to safety. Taking with me the cherished moment of my first almost-interaction with snow. Even though it wasn't actually snow, it was still on an epic volcano-glacier in Iceland. *Winning.*

Once back at the bottom, I pulled up to another make-shift lot that I knew was for Sönghellir; the most famous of many "singing caves" in Iceland. There had been a few cars parked there when I was heading up, but now there were none, which meant once again I was about to go into a creepy cave alone. Hopefully, this one didn't have any dead birds. To be honest, after that last encounter, I wasn't super eager to go in any caves for a while, but I figured I could just run in and run out to see if it really sings.

As I was attempting to just "run in" the wind picked up so hard that it physically pushed me backwards. I could hear the creepy "singing" of the wind through the tunnels of the cave and took both as signs not to go in by myself. *Darn.*

It was somehow already five o'clock anyway, and since I had that lovely long four-hour drive, I really needed to get going. As I drove the last long leg of my Iceland road trip series, I reminded myself constantly to soak in every moment of it. *I can't believe I'm really in Iceland!* I kept repeating as my eyes drank in every rolling hill of grass or towering gray mountain.

Per usual, the ride back didn't seem to take as long as the ride there since the excitement and anticipation diminished. Before I knew it, I was making the roundabout turn towards Keflavik, where the Blue Lagoon is located. I considered stopping at my hotel first to change there, but I was cutting it close on time, and my VIP package said it included a locker as well, so I went straight there.

When I arrived, it was not what I expected. The parking lot was packed, especially with tour buses, which I knew from my research were probably mostly tourists with a long layover en route to Europe. A few airlines, including the one I took here, offered super cheap flights to Europe that had long layovers in Iceland, so tour companies got smart and created short trips to the Blue Lagoon since it's near the airport.

Luckily a couple of them were leaving, but there were still about seven, plus about thirty cars. Suddenly I wished I had just changed at my hotel. The last thing I wanted to do was change in a wet, crowded locker room.

Finally, I found a parking spot, grabbed my purse with my swimsuit in it, and headed towards the entrance. I could tell this was definitely the most developed site in Iceland aside from Reykjavik. There were tall, silver, artistic structures lining the entrance, with an enormous sign that said "Welcome to the Blue Lagoon" in a font you'd expect to see at a luxury resort. But unlike a luxury resort, this was outdoors and surrounded by miles and miles of black lava rocks. As I got closer, I could see some shallow light blue pools lining the walkway to the entrance, which several Chinese tourists had already stopped to take photos of.

They were with a huge tour group, so I took their photo op as my own opportunity to go around them, worried I'd have to wait in line for all fifty of them to check -in. I realized that despite my attempt to go near closing, the Blue Lagoon would likely still look like most photos I saw of it: packed with people.

When I finally made my way inside, I saw signs for two lines: VIP and General Admission. Luckily, everyone had opted for general admission, and I went straight to the front of the VIP line.

"Hello! I have a collaboration with your marketing department ; this is the email." I said sheepishly, not wanting anyone else to hear me in case the staff had no idea what I was talking about and turned me away. The girl at the counter took my phone and read it over several times, clearly looking confused.

"I'm a travel blogger ; I'm supposed to be writing an article about the Blue Lagoon ," I explained as if that would help.

"One moment please," She said, picking up the phone and pressing the extension for what I hoped was the marketing director.

" *Yes hi, it's Sasha from the front desk. I have a woman here who is supposed to be getting a VIP package from marketing? Yes, that's correct. Her name is Alyssa yes.*" She said into the receiver, still staring at my phone as if there were more to read than what she already had. "*Ok. Ok. I see,*" She continued as she now clicked around on her computer. It dawned on me that she wasn't doubting my collaboration ; she just didn't know how to register it in the computer. "*Great, that worked, thank you! I'll let her know.*"

Sasha hung up the phone and handed me back mine with a big welcoming smile. "Thank you for your patience Miss Ramos ; I have you all registered and ready to go!" She said as she pushed back away from the desk and started collecting various items from around it.

"May I please see your wrist? This band will give you access to the VIP lockers, and this chip right here is what will be scanned when you get your two complimentary beverages at any of the bars inside. If you wish to make any additional purchases, you can do it with the band as well, and then you'll make a payment when you leave." She explained as she snapped the blue plastic band around my wrist. "You will also use it to open and close your locker, just follow the directions posted on the walls if you need any help. Here are your two towels, and last but not least," she turned around and opened a drawer from the desk behind her, extracting a beige burlap bag tied with a light blue ribbon. "Here is a small welcome gift from the Blue Lagoon! We hope you enjoy your experience!"

My eyes lit up and a wide smile stretched across my face. I truly felt like a VIP, even if it was just at a tourist destination, and even if I was just getting a free $125 ticket. To me, it was a big step towards my overall goal of one day getting paid thousands of dollars to go to such places and post about them.

As I followed the signs for the locker rooms, I realized there wasn't a separate VIP and General Admission locker room. The VIP-ness simply just had more inclusions like the two free drinks, towels, and Wi-Fi. I was still grateful for it. I definitely didn't just have a spare $125 to spend.

As I pushed open the door to the women's lockers, I was greeted by my worst nightmare; dozens of naked bodies walking around, waiting in line to shower, and shuffling about trying to get to their assigned lockers. Getting naked in public was *not* something I was comfortable with, especially since people tend to stare at my D-cup breasts on my tiny body even when they're fully clothed.

I was a bit shocked and even a little impressed that everyone was so comfortable being naked. *It must be a European thing*, I guessed. Then I saw the massive signs on the wall strictly indicating that it was mandatory to shower without clothes, then with your bathing suit on, before entering the natural pool. *Dammit.*

At least I had a towel. And thank the universe that I opted for the one piece because hardly anyone was sporting a bikini, at least not the types I owned. After finding my assigned locker and figuring out how to open it with the bracelet, I reluctantly started to peel off the multiple layers of clothing I had on. After pulling my base top layer off and getting a strong whiff of the body odor I had doused it with, I had a new appreciation for the "Must shower naked AND in bathing suit"-rule. No way in hell would I want to be swimming in a hot natural pool with people's sweat and *fluids* floating around in it as well.

Once I was completely stripped down and doing my best to cover myself with the hand-towel sized cloth, I tip-toed around a corner to an area of showers that looked less crowded. The floor was almost as gross as the nightclub's had been, mostly because I had to be barefoot and the cold wetness completely grossed me out.

There was no line, but all of the curtains were closed. I started to wonder how long I'd have to wait when one of them flew open and a skinny pale woman with a thick black bush stepped out. She looked me up and down strangely as if it were odd that I was trying to cover myself with the little towel. *It's Iceland, maybe I'm just cold!*

Avoiding eye contact with her and every other human in the locker room, I obliged the rules and showered naked first, then put on my bathing suit, and showered again. I was so beyond excited to get that over with that I hadn't even thought about what it was going to be like hanging out alone in the Blue Lagoon. Of course, that came to the forefront of my concerns when I stepped foot into the inner area of the property. Even with my little towel covering most of my body, everyone was staring. Well, I guess technically, wearing the towel wrapped tight around my boobs wasn't helping me any.

Continuing to avoid eye contact, I pushed open the massive glass double doors that let out to the main natural pool of the famed Blue Lagoon. The traveler in me saw the magnificent sight and bucketlist tick first, admiring the way the milky pale blue water had tufts of white steam rising from it and contrasted beautifully against the stark black lava rocks that form it.

But the realist, the twenty -seven-year old slightly insecure solo traveler, poked her head up to point out that it was definitely crowded, and people were definitely looking at her strangely. So much so that she almost turned her ass around, got dressed, and opted to go have drinks with her sweet Icelandic viking boy instead.

No. Don't let them bother you. I told myself, reminding insecure-Alyssa that they could just be looking at me because they like my towel or my hair and not because it was strange that everyone else was there with a friend, significant other, or family.

Looking around, it became evident that most people left all of their belongings in their lockers, including towels and phones. I not only had my towel but also my camera on the selfie stick *and* my phone. There was no way I was ready to start swimming around with my selfie stick yet, I had fully intended on drinking those two free drinks first, but I was nervous of leaving it unattended. I looked around for somewhere to stash it and found a silver chair in line with several others that seemed to be unoccupied. Reluctantly, I removed my towel and bundled the camera up inside of it, then positioned it under the chair so it looked like just a gross wet towel. There was zero percent chance I was going to leave my phone though. I'd rather take the risk of getting it wet in the lagoon.

As much as I tried procrastinating standing up and heading into the crowded pool, the freezing outdoor weather convinced me to just get it over with. I tiptoed over to the closest entry point, which was a smooth ramp with a metal handrail that a group of young couples were hanging out next to. It wasn't ideal walking past the type of people who I secretly wished to be; a couple traveling with friends, but at least it was better than the judgy older people who straight up scoffed when they saw me. Just as I was growing some balls and getting excited about the warm thermal water, I slipped. On my ass. Straight up slipped and fell in front of the group of couples.

Luckily my ninja skills got me back on my feet in mere seconds, no thanks to anyone, but my ego was bruised, battered, and broken. And my ass cheek likely would be too. I attempted a lame laugh and pretended to focus intently on my phone, examining every millimeter of it for any molecules of water, even though I had lifted it high over my head instinctively because you know, broken bones are less tragic than a broken phone.

There was a small bridge to my left that was the perfect place to escape the stares and whispers from my embarrassing fall and coincidentally led to the swim up bar! Not surprisingly, it was mostly men waiting in line, but at least the water came up to my rib cage, so I felt a little bit more concealed.

Speaking of the water, it was so fascinating! The reason why it's a milky light blue color and warm is because it comes from geothermal seawater that originates six thousand feet beneath the surface, which then travels through porous lava, and finally becomes a blend of sea and fresh water that undergoes mineral exchange near the surface where concentration occurs.

The concentration process includes sedimentation, which mixes in the active ingredients; silica, minerals, and algae, which is what gives the Blue Lagoon its healing effect. The active elements have been researched and proven to have anti-aging effects and also to help treat people with psoriasis!

I wondered if any of the people who judged the way I looked or the fact that I was alone would have expected me to know such scientific facts. *Or that I have a Bachelor of Science degree in biology.*

When it was finally my turn, I ordered one Chardonnay and one waterproof phone pouch. If I could drink my white wine, have free Wi-Fi, *and* use my phone while in the Blue Lagoon, this was going to be one hell of an experience.

The girl behind the bar scanned my VIP bracelet and I collected my goods, smiling to myself about the small accomplishment. Before turning back into the crowded pool, I secured my phone safely in the pouch, then logged into the Wi-Fi using the free code they gave me. At least now, I wouldn't feel so awkward being alone since I could text my friends. Maybe I'd even video call some people, so it was known that I did in fact, have friends. Like a good daughter, I texted my mom first to see if she was available. She immediately replied that she was, but to wait five minutes so she could get some of her co-workers at the Homeless Center together so they could see Iceland too.

While I waited, I drifted slowly along the edges of the Blue Lagoon, examining the peculiar color change of the black to white rock. By the time she called, my first wine was almost empty, and since she was at work, I decided I should probably hide the cup anyway.

"Welcome to the Blue Lagoon!" I said dramatically as I answered, turning the phone so that she and the six faces behind her could see the steamy pool.

"*Wowwww!*" They seemed to say in unison with giant smiles plastered across their faces. *Ah, the power of technology.* I knew my mom was so proud of me for traveling, especially by myself, and that she also got asked quite often if she worried about me doing so. Here was her proof that not only was I completely fine and safe, but also having a fabulous time!

"Is that ice on your eyebrows?!" She yelled at the phone as if it was necessary to hear her better. I squinted at the thumbnail video of myself, then used my free hand to touch my eyebrow.

"Ha! I guess it is! I forgot how cold it is outside because it's so hot in the pool!" I laughed, genuinely shocked that ice had started forming on my eyebrows. It must have been extra shocking for her and the others who were currently in hot, humid South Florida.

I gave them a mini -tour of the corner of the Blue Lagoon, which I was swimming around in, feeling more and more confident just by merely having their faces on the screen. When her co-workers finally trickled away and she shut her office door, I divulged that there was a swim -up bar with great wine that I knew she would love if she was there with me. Actually, if my mom was in the Blue Lagoon with me at ten PM, there would be a ninety-nine percent chance that we would both already be white-wine-drunk and covered in the mud they give you for face masks.

When she finally had to get off the call, I made my way back to the swim up bar to get my second free drink. I went to the same nice bartender girl as before, and noticing I was by myself, she filled the cup all the way up to the rim.

For once, I let my Resting Bitch Face relax and slid with a smile through the lagoon, sipping my extremely chilled wine and marveling at how excited my mom was to get to see the Blue Lagoon. It was the perfect end to my trip, and it would only continue to get better if I ended up meeting up with Triggy.

"How much?" *The fuck?!* My enchanting train of thought was completely derailed as I looked to my immediate left to see the source of such a degrading question.

"EW!" I shouted involuntarily upon seeing the snickering faces and lingering eyes of what seemed like Middle Eastern men. They kept walking as they laughed and puckered their lips at me. Shocked, disturbed, hurt, and downright fed up, I stormed off to yet another less-populated area to drink my wine in peace and video call the one person I knew would make me feel better; Nate.

Unfortunately, it seemed like now even more people were watching me, especially the ones nearby who heard either the "How much" or the very loud "EW ." It may have all been in my head, but I could have sworn almost everyone was whispering about me.

Before attempting to call Nate, I decided it might help if I covered my face in the silica mud. Then I would just blend in with everyone else and no one would judge or bother me. I stuck my hand in the tub of creamy goo that was at one of the many mud-stations and smeared the cold, thick sediments all over my face, neck and chest. I checked my reflection on the screen of my phone and satisfied with my new concealment, drifted over to the natural rock bench under the water, perching myself on it so I could make the call.

As expected, he answered right away, "What in the world is on your face?" Nate laughed from the bed of some hotel he was in, somewhere in the world. I couldn't remember which country he was in this time, but I knew we had similar night hours, except I was way farther up north, hence why it was still light where I was but dark for him.

"It's a mud mask. I'm trying to hide my face so that people stop staring at me and thinking I'm a prostitute or something." I admitted dryly, taking a big sip of my wine. This threw Nate into a fit of laughter.

"I hate to tell ya this, kid, but even with the mud on your face you look attractive." He replied smoothly. I wasn't sure whether I should be flattered at his somewhat compliment or annoyed. Regardless, I decided to keep the jokes rolling.

"I just don't get it! Is it *so* weird that a quote, un-quote *pretty girl* is traveling alone?!" I hissed with a dramatic eye-roll and another big gulp of the wine. I was expecting a joke in return, or maybe some sort of comfort, but instead, he said point blank:

"I mean yeah. It kinda is." I knew he was serious because his shoulders shrugged up and he stopped smiling for a milisecond before he started laughing again. Right then and there, something sparked inside of me. I don't know why it took Nate telling me to my face that people probably thought it was strange that I was traveling alone, but I realized I was definitely sick of it. Sick of the LA guys accusing me of having a rich old guy paying for my trips, sick of tourists I didn't even know automatically assuming I'm a sex worker, sick of everyone in general having an unsolicited opinion about my desire to travel. *I just want to see the world and not have to wait for someone else to do it, dammit!*

"Well, maybe if *you* would ever travel with me, I wouldn't have this problem!" I shot back at Nate, suddenly unrealistically blaming him for why I was there alone. It was partially true, he could *easily* have met me in Iceland, or anywhere else in the world for that matter, but per usual, "something came up ."

"One day, one day!" He laughed in response. That was his typical answer to my never-ending complaint about why we weren't traveling together if we both had jobs that required us to travel, and allegedly he did want to be with me. According to him, it was because he always had business deals that didn't include bringing a guest. But I wasn't an idiot, I've seen plenty of rom-coms to know that male business travelers are more than capable of bringing their partner, and the ones who chose not to take them were usually the ones who wanted to remain to appear single. Obviously, that was the case with Nate ; I just couldn't figure out if it was because he wanted the single women of the world to continue swooning after him or because of the more likely situation – his "non-girlfriend" was still in the picture. Whenever I was forced to think about the entire fucked up situation, it hurt. He knew he had me on a string and continued yanking at it ever-so-slightly, just enough to keep me dangling but never enough to actually get close. The pain from the thought of him never actually traveling with me, plus the multiple stings from the random people who in return, assumed I was a sex worker because I was alone, was too much to handle.

"I'm going to write about it. On Huffington Post. I'm over this shit." I announced boldly. He laughed once again and said something along the lines of, "That'll really rile people up," but I wasn't paying attention. I didn't want to talk to him anymore. I didn't want to talk to anyone. I wanted to write about the way I was feeling and let the whole world know about it.

Ignoring the last remaining stares and whispers from the patrons of the Blue Lagoon, as well as the sign in the locker room that urged everyone to wash off before leaving, I pulled my clothes on right over my wet bathing suit and bee-lined for my car. When I had first arrived, I made a mental note to try and find the marketing manager to thank them for having me before I left, but I was in full -on rampage mode.

I got to Keflavik Inn, and although it was only ten forty-five, the owner and son were already gone from the front desk. Secretly I thanked my lucky stars that they were because I definitely was not in a happy, chatty mood.

Like a silent tornado, I rampaged up the stairs to my room, and quietly unlocked the door, shutting it without a sound. Then, I did what any normal woman would do and threw myself onto the bed, screaming into a pillow and punching the poor thing repeatedly. Once I was finally done taking my anger out on the fluffy rectangle, I grabbed the nearly full bottle of red wine and filled my *single* wine glass all the way up to the rim. Then I downed half of it and re-filled it again. I kicked off my boots and peeled off the partially wet clothing, then the soaking wet swimsuit. Looking at my too-thin-because-can't-afford-food frame and massive boobs in the mirror, I scoffed in irritation. So basically, my whole life, men have only seen me as a piece of ass, and now I realize that's all most people assume I am as well, and I'll probably never get credit for the fact that I'm actually smart or OH! The fact that I've worked my ass off to travel the world. *Just awesome.*

I felt like absolute shit, but that was just fueling my fire. Ignoring the pings coming from my phone indicating incoming messages, I downed the entire glass of wine like it was water, re-filling it with the last remaining contents of the bottle. I was going to voice how I really felt to the world, and the wine was going to help me.

After pulling on a dry pair of leggings, socks, and long-sleeved shirt, I grabbed my laptop and the full glass of wine and settled into the wooden chair on the balcony. I clicked open the draft platform for Huffington Post and let my fingers fly furiously over the keyboard. About twenty minutes later, I was done with both the post and the wine, and with a smirk on my face, I hit the publish button for the most obnoxiously titled post I had ever written in my life: *Yes, I'm Pretty and I'm Traveling Alone.*

My phone rang for the third time inside. I had ignored it the first two times because I was *in the zone* and also because after all the emotions I had encountered in the last few hours, I didn't want to talk to anyone, including Nate and Triggy. As cute as Triggy was, and as much as I wanted the company, I would feel like a hypocrite going to hang out with him after writing an entire rant about how I *wasn't* traveling solo to look for a man.

Just out of curiosity though, I checked my phone. To my surprise, it was my mom, so I answered immediately.

"Oh my god, you aren't going to believe what happened after I got off the video call with you!" I blurted, hot tears building up in my eyes as I prepared to cry to my mom like a little girl who got teased at school. But there was silence on the other end of the phone where I had been expecting an eager response.

"Mom?"

"Hi hunny. I hate to tell you this, but you might want to fly here tomorrow instead of LA...to say goodbye to grandpa." She said softly. For a completely different reason, the tears that were welling up exploded from my eyes. It couldn't be. He had finally just told me, "The thing he loves the most that I do is travel," after years of me feeling like I needed to get married and pop him out some grandkids. My biggest fan, my only male adult family figure, my partner in crime, who I was convinced would live to one hundred, was dying.

"Are -- are you sure? He's not just being dramatic again?" I whimpered, hoping this was just another one of his stunts to get my mom to give him his red wine or take him to the casino.

"I'm sure Alyssa. Come home if you can, I know he'll want to see you."

Suddenly blackness surrounded me. Nothing existed besides my laptop and the multiple tabs I had already pulled up to find the next flight out of Iceland to freaking Florida. I'd spend my last remaining savings if I needed to, just to get there in time to say goodbye to one of my favorite humans.

As expected, the prices were painful; a whopping four hundred dollars for a one-way direct flight to Fort Lauderdale International airport that left in just a few hours at four in the morning. Without thinking twice, I purchased it, immediately getting an overdraft notification from my bank but ignoring it along with everything else that was trying to come at me. For some reason, I kept getting multiple emails from the same unknown address indicating some sort of notification but I couldn't be bothered with what it was about, assuming it was spam.

My head spun. What if my grandpa died before I got there? What if I didn't have the chance to say goodbye? And to tell him that I was officially determined to become a professional travel blogger and see the whole world?

The thought was sobering and cleared my mind to telepathically will him to wait for me. We had a connection, just like I did with my mom, where I could see them in my dreams when something was wrong and vice versa. I willed him to see me and begged him to wait.

I needed to be at the airport in two hours, which was plenty of time to pack since I only had my one carry-on. Apparently, I couldn't focus though because it ended up taking me close to an hour to do it. I caught myself several times re-folding the same dirty shirt, staring blankly at the wall, envisioning all the happy memories I had with him. Like all of the time he would grow his beard out just because he knew I found it so amusing to trim it with scissors. Or the time he somehow acquired an

240

old boat and despite me having three other siblings, decided to name it after me using the only nickname anyone has ever given me; "M'LO ." It was an abbreviation for the names of the women who created me, my mom, her mom, and my dad's mom.

Then there was the time that I got to keep the runt of the baby chickens we hatched in my fifth grade elementary school class while learning about reproduction. It had a lot to do with the fact that my parents had just finally gotten divorced, and my mom was suddenly preoccupied with being a full-time working single mother, but I got to "raise" the chick in my room, which resulted in it thinking I was its mom. A few months later, it turned out to be a Chinese fighting cock. Beautiful bird, but attacked anyone who stepped foot in our backyard so badly that my brothers would come running inside with bloody legs, and a broom had to be kept next to the door.

One day, I noticed my chicken was missing and searched the yard frantically for it for hours. Just when I thought the foxes had finally gotten it, my grandpa drove up the long driveway to our backyard unexpectedly. The drive from Hialeah to our home in Jupiter Farms was about two hours, so it was a bit strange to see him there. He got out and opened the trunk, and to my extreme surprise and delight, he pulled out a rabbit! It was a big rabbit, and it wasn't friendly, but it was immediately replaced by what I thought was the death of my chicken. Turns out he and my mom had secretly arranged for him to capture my chicken and trade it in Hialeah for a more docile animal, like a rude rabbit. They tried to further fix the problem by getting my younger brother and I two *actual pet* rabbits, and the three of them ended up giving us about fourteen bunnies. It was every child's dream and every newly single-parent's nightmare.

Between the memories, the packing, and one very long, much-needed hot shower, I had no time or desire to check my phone or laptop for incoming notifications. In fact, I had almost completely forgotten that I had even posted the obnoxious article. I was sure it would get at least a couple of mean comments, just from the title alone, so I avoided even looking at my emails as well.

With just five minutes until two AM and my designated time to head to the airport, I realized I'd be leaving much earlier than the hotel owner expected. It would be insanely rude of me to just leave without checking out or saying bye, so I decided to do the most polite thing possible and write her a note. In the perfect cursive that my grandpa taught me before it was even time for me to learn how to read or write, I thanked her profusely for her hospitality and let her know that I was leaving early due to a family emergency.

I snuck quietly down the steps of the Inn and left the note on the desk where she always stood to check-in guests, hoping she would see it as soon as she came down in a few hours. Then I whispered a silent goodbye and thank you to the first place that believed in me to do a job that I once had only dreamed of acquiring.

In just twenty minutes, I had gotten to the airport, and in another thirty minutes, I had easily returned the rental car, retrieved my boarding pass, and gone through security. There weren't many people flying to Florida from Iceland at four in the morning, apparently.

Since I had an hour before my flight actually left, I decided to log onto the free airport Wi-Fi to see if there were any updates from my mom. I had been confident sitting on the chair in front of the gate that I would get there in time but couldn't help but be sure.

After in-putting my email information for the free pass, I was bombarded with several pings per usual. From what I could see, none were from my mom, so I guessed that was a good sign, but then one in particular popped up and just stayed on my screen. It was from Nate.

"I can't believe you actually posted that article! You have some BALLS!"

My stomach dropped and my heart started to race. What the hell did that mean?! He was the one who said it would be funny if I posted it! Or did he say it would be bad? Shit! My mind was so discombobulated that I couldn't even remember what he said, not even six hours ago!

"*What? Why?! You said it was a catchy title!*" I immediately responded as the vision of my dream to become a travel blogger blew up into a million pieces. *I just sabotaged my whole career! Everyone is going to hate me!* I wanted to cry and could feel the tears coming.

"*It is! It's just ballsy! At least you're getting some new followers though!*" He replied instantly. Even though it was through text, it sounded to me like he was talking down to me. Almost as if...he was jealous? What was he talking about with new followers?

I realized I hadn't checked my social media since before I hit 'Publish' on the post and tried to think if I even linked any of my accounts on it. Realizing I had just updated my author's byline to include my Instagram, I checked that reluctantly first.

"Ohhhh shiittttt!" I gasped. I couldn't believe it. There was no way. In just a few hours, I had gone from one thousand to three thousand followers and had over one hundred comment notifications. I tapped on the last photo I posted that only had ten comments the last time I checked. It now had one hundred and seventy -five. Assuming they must be all negative, I decided to ignore them and wait until after I had said bye to my grandpa. The last thing I wanted was to feel angry when I only had little precious time left with him.

"*Your blog is also offline. You must be getting a lot of traffic! Hey there's no such thing as bad publicity!*" He said, verifying my assumption that somehow he might be jealous of my sudden attention. Of course, he didn't need to do it in a way that automatically insinuated that it was all negative comments and interest, but he did.

"*Now boarding, all passengers for Flight 241 to Fort Lauderdale. Now boarding, ALLLL passengers.*" A sleepy yet somehow whimsical voice announced over the microphone.

Shit shit shit! How was this all happening at once ? Was I seriously about to get on an eight -hour flight with no service and no way of telling if A) My grandpa was still alive and B) If I was going down the gutter, or dare I say, *going viral?*

"Oh wow, have you seen the comments on the article?" Nate continued, making my anxiety grow tenfold. *Yep. Career. Over.*

"I'm actually about to board a flight to Florida to go see my dying grandfather, but hey, thanks for the support!" I tapped the necessary buttons to block him before he could respond and sent one last text to my mom, telling her I was boarding and that I should be there by the time she wakes up. Sadly, she responded, meaning she wasn't getting any sleep, and said, *"Safe flight! He's waiting for you!"*

Tears poured down my face again, and I tried my best not to make eye-contact with the attendant taking the tickets at the gate. For all she knew, I could just be sad to be leaving Iceland, and it could have nothing to do with the fact that one of the great loves of my life was dying, another was making me feel awful about myself, and I might very well have destroyed my dream job just as I was attaining it. But I took a deep breath. I held my head high. I put my phone in Flight Mode, and I ordered two glasses of wine. Maybe this was all just a terrible nightmare that would end when I woke up.

Chapter Eight

Going Viral and in a Spiral

It was impossible to sleep on the plane, obviously. No amount of alcohol could have placated me from thinking about all of the terrible things that were currently happening while I was trapped in a metal tube without Wi-Fi. I was certain the world thought I was a shallow, narcissistic bitch who wrote an unwarranted sob story, and even more certain there would be comments like, "LOL you're not even attractive!" or "You give women a bad name !" Luckily I also knew these comments would come from the many people who only read article titles and not the actual content. Proving that the term "click bait" was a very real, very successful thing.

More importantly though, I was sure my grandpa was waiting for me. I could feel it. I had been telepathically trying to project to him the entire flight, begging him to just hold on a little longer so I could say goodbye and that I loved him.

It felt like an eternity had passed when we finally hit the ground and began taxi-ing to the terminal in Fort Lauderdale. Nervously, I took my phone off airplane mode, promising to only read the messages from my mom. But the second my data connected, my phone literally exploded with notifications. Like it was physically vibrating non-stop and in all directions. Keeping my promise, I exited out of all of them, at least until I was off the plane in case I needed to scream or something, and tapped my text messages open to text my mom.

'Just landed! No checked bags, so go ahead and pull around in twenty.' I wrote, trying to muster some excitement about seeing my mom; however, the double depressing news of the past twelve hours made it impossible to feel anything but absolute torment.

I pressed my forehead against the seat in front of me and stared at my phone screen, waiting for her to respond. And also waiting eagerly for the announcement chime to ding, indicating we could get off, and I could check the thousands of notifications that my closed email and social media apps were portraying in their ever-anxiety-invoking little red bubbles. There was only the number six in the red notification bubble for Whatsapp, and I partially guessed most were from Nate. Maybe he had something encouraging to say. Unable to contain myself under his spell, I opened Whatsapp, ignored the multiple messages from Triggy, and went straight to the two from Nate.

'You might pass me in followers soon!' The first text said. I checked for the time that he sent it . It was just after I took off. I tried to remember how many followers he had the last time I checked, I thought it was about three-thousand, and that was about how much I had increased immediately following the post. So if he wrote that eight hours ago then...

'Jesus, maybe I'll write a ballsy viral article!' The next message said. It wasn't encouraging at all and didn't make me feel better. It made me feel like the only reason why he thought I'd get new followers was because I wrote something controversial, not for the actual context of the message.

Wait a second. Did he say, *Viral?*

Ding! The chime overhead sounded, indicating that we could all get up at once and see who could get their bags and get off the aircraft first. Normally I waited patiently for the people ahead of me to get off and even block the people behind me from stampeding ahead of them, but this was an urgent matter. What the hell did he mean by '*viral article*'?

In one swift, with a strategic movement that I had been plotting in my head already the entire time I was waiting to get off, I moved from my window seat, across the two empty seats next to me, yanked my carry-on down from the overhead, and walked with it in one hand while carrying my seatbelt bag on the other shoulder, clutching my phone. Everyone was still just standing up by the time I reached the door, and I lied to the flight attendant about having to pee like a racehorse.

Once on solid ground, I dropped my carry-on to its wheels and started making a mad dash for the exit doors where my mom was picking me up. If I went straight there first, I would have time to just peek at my notifications while waiting for her.

The distance seemed longer, even though it wasn't even crowded, and the escalator down to ground level moved just as slowly as the people on the plane. I couldn't wait for it though, so I picked up my carry-on and flew down the metal steps.

When the automatic doors slid open, I was greeted by the expected gust of hot, humid Florida air, which immediately made my cool clammy skin feel sticky. It was extra uncomfortable since I was still in my thermals from freaking Iceland, but not as uncomfortable as not knowing what was being said about me on the interwebs and not knowing if my grandpa was still alive or not. My mom's white Prius was nowhere in sight, so I spun my hardshell carry-on against a concrete column and sat on it like a make-shift stool.

Finally, with my breath held inside my pounding chest, I tapped open the icon for Instagram.

"HOLY FUCKING SHIT!" I yelled, accidentally louder than I anticipated, which caught the attention of an elderly couple several feet away. "Sorry!" I yelled with an awkward wave as they looked at me in fear as if I had a psychological disorder that caused an outburst.

247

I couldn't believe what my eyes were seeing on the screen. And in case they were wrong, I dragged my finger down on the screen to refresh the homepage of my Instagram profile.

But that only caused the "31k" I had seen initially to refresh to "32k ."

Thirty-two *thousand* followers on Instagram! There had to be some mistake! When I left Iceland, I was just about to pass Nate's impressive three thousand mark, and by the time I landed, I had surpassed it ten times?! That explained the less-than friendly texts, but I didn't care anymore, it was true! I had gone viral, literally overnight! It was finally my turn to shine.

There were over two-thousand comments on the last photo I posted and hundreds of direct messages, but I didn't dare read any of them yet. I knew for a fact there would be at least one hate message for every positive one if there were even any positive ones at all but there had to be right? Why else would so many people follow me? I vowed to wait to read the comments until after I saw my grandpa. Even if there were some negative ones, that bold "32k" was more than enough to put an enormous smile on my face. I looked up and around eagerly again for my mom's Prius, but it still hadn't arrived. *Ok, I'll just take one quick peek at my emails, just in case there's something from Huff Post.*

Slowly, I tapped open the icon for my email and again, was thrown into shock. Typically when I submit a guest article for Huffington Post, it takes a couple of hours to receive the response email that either says, "Congratulations, Your Article Has Been Published on Huffington Post!" or "We're Sorry, But Your Post Has Not Been Approved." I'd gotten the first one several times, including just before leaving Iceland, but what I was now seeing was just absolutely unfathomable.

'Toutes nos félicitations! Votre article a été publié sur le Huffington Post!' I'm sorry, *what?!* I saw the words "article" and "Huffington Post ," so I clicked on it immediately to see if it was the unthinkable. Sure enough, the link took me to the French platform for Huffington Post, where my entire article had been translated to French and posted already for all of France to see.

Quickly, I tapped back into my inbox to examine the several other similar subject lines, and sure enough, they were the same thing; in Portuguese, Spanish, Italian, and Arabic. The article had gotten re-published in seven other countries. I couldn't believe it. I had really gone viral.

Before I could get to the other enticing emails, many of which had the words "interview ," "TV ," and "producer" in the subject line, a car horn honked in front of me. I leapt up so fast and excited that I nearly forgot to even grab my carry-on.

"MOM! YOU ARE NOT GOING TO BELIEVE THIS!" I screamed, running over to her as she rounded the backside of the car with a big smile, ready to hug me and help me with my luggage just like she always did when she had to pick me up from an airport.

"What is it, hunny?" She said sweetly, with excitement purely formed from mine. Despite her smile, I could tell her eyes were puffy from crying, so before I could explode with the good news, I asked about my grandpa.

"Wait, first, how's grandpa? Did I make it in time?" No amount of good news would be enough to make me happy if I hadn't made it in time to say goodbye.

"He's hanging in there. He can't talk and has been mostly sleeping, but I told him you were coming and he perked up a bit, so I'm pretty sure he's waiting for you." She said with a tone of defeat.

"Well, let's get going, I'll tell you my news in the car." This brought life back to her face, and after throwing my bag in the trunk, we both got in the car and drove off into the early morning sun. We both knew we only had the hour -long drive to talk about my travels and success since it tended to irritate some of my siblings, so she pried for the gossip as soon as we were off.

First, I read her the article. She laughed when I announced the sub-heading "No, I'm not a prostitute ," and said "*Yeah!*" when I read the part about not having rich parents and having grown up poor with a single mom and three siblings. She had no idea what I was going to divulge next though.

"So right before I took off, Nate told me I had "balls" to write that and might even surpass his three-thousand follower account soon. Guess how many I have now?" I asked her, knowing she was probably more concerned that Nate had pissed me off once again. My mom and I have the type of relationship where we're more like friends than parent and child, so naturally she knew all about every time Nate got my hopes up about traveling then bailed at the last minute or broke my heart for various other reasons. Although she wasn't the biggest fan of his at all because of all the pain and stress he caused me, she would remind me that it's at least nice to have someone to talk to all the time who understands the type of lifestyle I have and want. She also has drunkenly admitted a few times that she secretly thinks we're going to end up together in the future though. But I'm pretty sure she was just trying to make me feel better about subconsciously knowing that would never happen.

"Hmmm, three thousand five hundred?" She asked, likely genuinely thinking that was close to the right answer.

"Thirty-two thousand." I said casually, holding the phone up to show her my Instagram.

"Oh my GOD! That's unbelievable!" She shrieked, swerving the car a bit to the side as she yanked the phone from my hand to see it with her own eyes.

"That's not all!" I continued, "It got translated and re-published on Huffington Post in seven other countries!" I blurted, reaching over and switching to my mail inbox to show her the subject headlines. She moved the phone closer to her face and started to scroll on her own. "Ma! No phone and driving!" I objected, yanking it back from her. I swear, all those commercials that target young people to stop texting and driving are really missing their main perpetrators!

"Wait a minute!" She wailed, trying to grab it back from me, "Did you see you have an email from Inside Edition ?"

"No, what's that?" I asked absently, scrolling through the long list of unread emails to find what she had seen. Not being able to afford cable for so long left me clueless the names of networks, shows, and therefore usually, the news.

"It's a national news station! Open it, open it!" Her excitement through her otherwise very sad current reality warmed my heart. I tapped it open, scanning it first in case it was something bad.

"Holy shit. It's a producer! They want to interview me! They -- Oh." Excitement sent my heart pounding wildly until I read the last sentence asking how soon I could be back in LA.

"What? Why'd you say *Oh*!" She asked, looking back and forth between the road and my face.

"It's an in-studio interview. They want to know how soon I can be in LA." My voice was low, and the disappointment was evident. I'd have to decline the offer. There was no way I was going to leave my grandpa for a couple of seconds on the news.

"Well, email them back and see if they can do it by video! Or, ya know, just tell them your grandpa is dying and you'll be back when you can." She smacked the steering wheel with that last semi-sarcastic statement, forcing a laugh out of me even though I felt bad about it. I nodded and responded right away with both bits of information.

After hitting send, I kept scrolling and tapping on the subject lines that stood out. Ones that said "Interview Request ," "We Want to Feature You ," "You've Been Published On ," and "You're an Inspiration ." I immediately deleted any that were even remotely close to, "You're a disgrace ," "Haha, You Think You're Pretty !" "Boohoo Poor You ," and so on and so forth. Clearly, some people didn't get my amazing sarcasm. *Whatever.*

I read all of the good ones aloud, thoroughly impressing both my mom and myself. I knew she didn't fully understand the magnitude of what this could all mean for my career and life, but I appreciated her excitement. We both agreed to get it all out now since we'd have to suppress it once we got to the house. At least if a certain one of my siblings was there. It made me sad thinking about how I couldn't openly talk about my life or success, especially since I knew my grandpa would want to hear about it. But I vowed to tell him anyway, as soon as I had a moment alone.

When we finally turned onto the long dirt-road driveway of my childhood home, I instinctively pushed back against the seat as if I were trying to prolong confronting it. Not only was I dreading seeing my grandpa in what I knew was going to be a frail, deteriorating state, but I just hated being home in general.

To adolescent-me, the town was a trap. Tons of fun at times, with the weekend sandbar parties, my backyard "keggers," and the fact that I could get into the "hottest" nightclubs with a fake ID. But it was the same thing every week, over and over again. No one ever left, you just grow up and stay in the same place and keep doing the same things. You're conditioned and made to believe that you should graduate, preferably from college, then get a full-time job, get married, have babies, and buy property where you grew up. For most people, that's totally normal and exactly what they want. Then there's the black sheep of the world like me who one day just randomly breaks up with their almost-fiance, quits their 9-5 job, goes to L.A. for a weekend, and never comes back.

That fear of being trapped in my hometown, combined with my "daddy issues" from seeing my dad abandon a family of five was probably why I started working as a waitress when I was thirteen, and by the time I was fifteen, I was a shot girl or bottle waitress in nightclubs, making almost as much money as my mom, because I wanted to save up to get the hell out of there, and never have to depend on any guy. At least I was currently proof that I succeeded at that.

Aside from feeling like the town was a trap, there was also the fact that I was convinced the house is haunted and built on some Native American burial ground or something, which made it cursed, or maybe actually the whole town was. Because I've never heard of or experienced so much death anywhere else. Before I even graduated highschool, thirteen people that I knew had died. If you ever visit Jupiter, Florida, you'll think I grew up in a privileged little beach town where everything is sunshine and cocktails. That's exactly true, so it's a bit strange that so many young people I knew died. Or is it? Many people would agree that when you have everything, you either want more or get bored, and that's why people turn to drugs. Out of the thirteen people I knew who died in highschool, only one was from a car accident. The majority were prescription pill overdoses, suicides, and even two murders. That's right, murders. One of them was a guy that I dated, who got shot by a guy that I worked with at an Italian restaurant over a drug deal gone wrong, supposedly. To me, it was like it was only a matter of time before another person you know dies, or maybe even you. Again, it's one of the many reasons I always felt I needed to get out of there. I didn't want to get trapped there forever or die there.

It didn't help that I was here to witness the death of yet another person I care about. At least now I know I can easily hop on a flight and get out of there. And I'm pretty immune to the sad feelings of death and more programmed to celebrate their lives. So much so that I may or may not have my own funeral-party fully planned out and my living will written. Something my mom thinks of as both responsible and incredibly depressing. Anyway, I was braced for my grandpa's death. I knew I'd still get to see him in my lucid dreams every now and then anyway, like I do with my grandma.

We pulled up onto the concrete carport into the same spot that my mom had always parked in. I breathed a sigh of relief that it was the only car there. I wasn't trying to see anyone else besides my grandpa right now.

"So, he doesn't look like he normally does, I don't want you to be shocked." Mom said, her voice now shaky rather than excited. I nodded, remembering with a shutter the way my grandma looked just before she passed.

I followed her silently through the cluttered garage, into the hallway of the back den, then through the heavy door that led to the main part of the house. It was the same as it always was; sunny, decorated in typical Florida fashion, but always a bit too quiet. And no matter what time of the year, it was *always* hot.

253

My eyes scanned the TV area to the left, where I was used to walking in and seeing my grandpa rocking on the recliner chair, watching some random TV show in Spanish. I always hated seeing him like that because we both knew he was just passing the time before it was time to go. He wasn't supposed to even be staying with my mom, but an unspoken-about fall out with family in Miami resulted in him moving out of their house and into my mom's. To any onlooker, my mom's house wouldn't seem like a terrible alternative, except at least at my family in Miami's house, there were always multiple people there to keep him company . They would take him to his favorite place almost every day; the Hard Rock Casino. At my mom's house, there was no one there during the day besides my cat from college, Charlie. In fact, she had to hire a day nurse to come take care of him since she worked nine to eleven hours per day.

It was in that chair and room that he said his last real words to me just after my Cuba trip when I stopped in Florida on my way back to LA. A phrase that will stick with me forever. After years of constantly asking me when I was going to get married and give him a grandchild, he finally said to me, "That's what I love that you do the most, travel."

We turned right into the large cozy country-themed kitchen with the window overlooking the front porch, which is typically the scene of many of my lucid nightmares. I dropped my heavy purse on one of the high-chairs at the breakfast bar and swiveled my carry-on next to it and out of the way.

To my surprise, my mom grabbed one of the massive bottles of cheap Sutter House red wine from next to the refrigerator and handed it to me, "Here, we can have a last glass of red wine with him." She said, which surprised me even more considering just a month ago she was hiding the big bottle of wine from him because the doctors said it was accelerating his heart problems. Of course, when he told me this, I went and found it and gave it back to him, thoroughly pissing off my mother, so again, seeing her willingly give it to me to give to him was surprising. And of course, indicative that it was really the end.

I took the heavy bottle and continued on into the formal dining room, reaching inside the cream -colored China cabinet that matches the table for three wine glasses.

"Oh, he can't use that." My mom whispered, taking one of the glasses away from me and putting it back. "We've been having to give him water using one of those sponges they use at the hospital." I knew what she was talking about because it's what I used to have to use with my college boyfriend when he finally came out of a three -month chemically induced coma after having emergency brain surgery from getting punched in the temple after a bar fight.

We continued on the dark wood floors that were always impossible to sneak by on because they amplified any step and into the long hallway of the four bedrooms. My old room, which was now my grandpa's room, was the first door on the right.

"Grampa?" I said softly, pushing open the door to see him lying weak on my old bed. My heart immediately shattered. He was the toughest, most durable man I knew, and seeing him there, limp and almost lifeless, was more painful than anything anyone could ever say to me.

"Ahhh!" He made a noise that sounded like he wanted to talk but couldn't as he turned his head, and tried to reach his hand out. I immediately ran to his side and took his hand. "I'm here grandpa! I flew all the way from Iceland to see you!" His eyes were completely ice blue now from his cataracts, but I knew he could still see me. He managed a weak smile and squeezed my hand.

"And look! We brought you wine! Mom's finally letting me give it to you! You have to drink it with a sponge though.." I spoke to him as if everything was normal, and we were having a regular conversation. My mom held the two wine glasses as I filled them to the top and dipped one of the sponges on a stick in mine. "Here you go, salut para una vida con abajos y arribas, pero mucho amorr." *Cheers to a life with ups and downs, but a lot of love.* I said, carefully sticking the wine-soaked sponge in his mouth. He bit down on it with his gums and laughed. This automatically made my mom burst into tears.

"I'm sorry, I just haven't seen him move in days," she stammered, moving closer to his side and rubbing his shoulder. "I knew he'd wake up for you, the apple of his eye."

"Cheers to you grandpa! We love you mucho" I said, tinking my glass with my moms and raising it to him, which made him smile the best he could.

"I'll let you have a moment with him ; I need to go blow my nose," My mom whimpered as she left the room, taking the massive glass of wine with her. Once she was gone and I could hear her walking into her room, I scooted closer to my grandpa to tell him the news that I so desperately wanted to tell him before he passed away.

"Grampa, guess what? I did it!" I started out, not sure exactly what to say or if he'd even understand me.

"I wrote an article and it went viral ; it got re-posted all over the world and now news outlets are calling to interview me!" He smiled and squeezed my hand. "I'm going to become a travel blogger grandpa! I'm going to go see the world!" He squeezed my hand harder and shook it up and down. I knew if anything, he understood that last part. The excitement must have taken most of his energy because shortly after, he started to doze off again. I crawled next to him on the bed and held his leathery, shriveled hand, letting myself doze off as well and purposely ignoring the constant buzzing coming from my phone.

The next morning, my grandpa's day nurse came running into the kitchen, wailing wildly in Spanish. My grandpa was gone.

Immediately my mom and I embraced, crying silently in each other's arms. She leaned back and held me by the shoulders, "You should go back to LA."

"What? No mom, I'm going to stay a few days and be here for you." I insisted, having already made the decision.

"I'll be fine," She said, clearing her throat, "All I want is to see you shine, and this could be your opportunity!"

She went on to explain that due to my grandpa's extreme gambling habits in the past few years, he had left us a lot less money than expected. She said she was going to put each of my siblings' shares in a trust for them, so they didn't blow it all at once but was giving me the option to have it right away to use for whatever I needed to succeed, whether it was travel or new gear.

Obviously, I wanted to immediately take the twenty-five hundred dollars and go travel for two months, but I also wanted to invest in this being a long -term thing. So I decided to instead invest the money in a one-bedroom apartment that I could rent out on Airbnb in order to make money while traveling. If only it were as easy as it sounds.

Chapter Nine

Will Camp for Rent Money

When I got back to LA the next day, I was scheduled to go straight from the airport to the station where Inside Edition was filmed. It was my first time being in an actual TV studio and the experience was exhilarating. The producer lady introduced me to the entire team, explaining who was a camera guy, who was a sound guy, and then finally, who the host was. He was a sweet older man who was so fascinated by my story and the interview that he decided right then and there to do more with it. The next day he and a camera guy drove half an hour with me to one of my favorite waterfall hikes just outside of Hollywood to get footage of me hiking and jumping off a cliff into the water.

I was sure that the interview on Inside Edition and the dozens of interviews on internet media platforms were going to immediately launch me into getting paid travel blogging gigs, but low and behold ; it didn't. At least not right away.

I did go through with getting a one-bedroom apartment in West Hollywood, which ended up costing the entire amount my grandpa left me. To me, it was worth the investment because it was pretty much the only place I had found that had a landlord who was Ok with me renting it out. I invested every last penny I had in refurbishing it and making it appealing for guests. My friends all helped me repaint the entire inside of it, and we added trendy details like a giant white decal of a map with the words "Travel the World" above it.

It immediately started getting booked but there was one teeny tiny problem; since I didn't have any reviews, I couldn't charge as much as I expected I would be able to. I had to charge such a low amount at first that I barely even profited enough to cover the rent. OH! And I had to figure out how to not be there so that I could rent out my room!

In my head, AKA my dream world, I'd be getting travel collaborations right away after I went viral, so I'd simply travel for free while profiting from renting out the apartment. But again, it didn't happen that quickly. So I had to improvise.

First, I went on a fifteen -day camping road trip around Arizona and Utah so that I could rent my place out, just in order to be able to pay the rent on it. At the time, that trip was a nightmare, but little did I know that even eight years later, it would still be one of my most-read blog posts, and some of the most popular images on Google, with thousands of people replicating my exact shots.

I had made the plan for the solo road trip and posted it on my newly popular Instagram. To my surprise and excitement, a male aspiring blogger who found me because of the viral article reached out to say he was going to be nearby at Burning Man and would love to join me if I'd like the company. At this point, Nate and I were still in our typical limbo that consisted of him constantly making me feel like, "If I just do this, we can be together," but I waited and waited, only to be told to keep waiting. It felt like we were together with how much we talked and how intense our feelings were, but according to him, we weren't. I thought the new internet fame and success, plus the grownup one-bedroom apartment would definitely convince him to finally move to California like he always said he would, but he didn't. He still wouldn't travel with me either, but I felt bad about asking other guys to go, so I just kept going solo. But after inviting him on the road trip and him declining "because he has a business trip", I told him I was going to accept this motorcycle-blogger guy's request to join me.

Long story short, it was a complete and utter catastrophe that I could probably write an entire book about.

Although this motorcycle guy was undeniably cute, well, from what I could see in his many shirtless, six-pack-ab photos, I had a really weird feeling about him. We agreed to meet in Vegas after he went to Burning Man, but the day of, he told me he might have to cancel because his motorcycle broke down, and then he got robbed by people at a "crack house" he accidentally stayed at. I wasn't surprised when he asked if it would be Ok to just drive in my car with me. Reluctantly, I said yes, because it was too awkward to say no, even though I knew this meant I wouldn't be able to just leave him if I wanted to. Nate obviously was not thrilled at all about this and suddenly had time to come meet up with me and this random biker guy.

Anyway, what happened with the biker was that as expected, he was not happy with my lack of interest in him. He told me I needed to be more present and that I wasn't as exciting as I seemed online, without knowing that the entire time I was also getting bitched at by Nate for being on a roadtrip with a random guy. Nate's solution, per usual when I seemed remotely interested in someone else, was to randomly drop in when he knew I was with another guy. Even if it meant paying hundreds of dollars to fly to the tiny airport in Page, Arizona.

But before Nate even got there, things were getting scary with the motorcycle guy. Our first stop was Havasu Falls, and although we only had the day to see it, he tried to insist on doing the five -hour hike into it rather than paying $80 for the helicopter. I didn't have it in my budget either, but there's no way we would have had enough time, so we negotiated taking the helicopter in and potentially hiking out. As we walked to the falls, he told me his life story, which involved a completely unexpected revelation that he used to be a male stripper. Suddenly everything started to make sense. The whole "I don't care about being famous but I have a blog and take shirtless photos on Instagram"-thing. The "I want to meet up but could you give me a ride"-thing. And of course, trying to put me down with things like "You're not present" and "you only care about taking photos of yourself" when I was trying to focus on driving us safely, getting my content for my budding-career, and figuring out how to fit a third person in my already packed Mustang. But of course, I wasn't allowed to say anything about him back.

When he started trying to put me down about taking photos of myself for my blog as I was attempting tri-pod photos in the park, I couldn't take it anymore, so I asked him, "Why do you care so much? And why do YOU post photos of yourself shirtless on Instagram if you don't want the attention or to be famous?" He actually walked ahead of me and left me looking for him in the canyon, right when the rains were picking up. I actually didn't even find him until the flash flood was getting so bad that Havasu Falls looked like a gushing explosion of chocolate milk rather than the tranquil blue waterfall you typically see in photos.

"We're not going to be able to hike out!" I yelled over the sound of the thundering waterfall.

"Yes, we can! We'll just sneak around the guard gate!" He yelled back, thoroughly convincing me that he might either be crazy or just not have any concern at all about his or someone else's life. And that tiny fact is what made me always question his disappearance in India a few years later.

As he went to try and sneak around the guard gate, the woman working in it from the reservation desk came running out to stop him.

"What are you doing?! You can't hike out during a flash flood! You'll die! You have to take the helicopter, NOW!" She screamed. And so , after scrounging up the last remaining cash we both had, we got air-lifted out.

He was obviously not happy about it at all. But nowhere near as not happy as when I told him I needed to pick up Nate from the Page airport the next day and that he would be joining us for a couple of days. To be completely honest, I had no idea how that was going to work out and no idea what to do. I obviously wanted to be there traveling with Nate over this stripper-turned-spiritual-survivalist who was more gas-lighty than uplifty. But I had no idea how I was going to pull it off. Finally, I told him and explained my idea that I would give him my tent to use since his got stolen at Burning Man, and I would stay in a hotel with Nate.

He was so not-happy that he basically laughed in my face, grabbed his backpack from my car, and stormed off down the road with his thumb in the air, apparently planning to hitch-hike the rest of the way, or maybe the way back to Vegas.

When Nate finally landed, I told him that when I told the guy he was coming, he left. Nate simply laughed as if this was all part of his plan. Although slightly worried that this guy might get murdered or something trying to hitch-hike, I was so incredibly happy to finally be back with Nate, and even more so, getting to travel with him. Even if he wasn't the easiest person to do that with.

We finally got to the main area of Page at around ten PM, where I knew there were two main chain hotels. We pulled into the first one and immediately looked at each other with concern upon seeing four massive Chinese tourist buses. Nate ran in to see if there was a room, only to reappear seconds later with the information that all of the hotels in Page had been completely booked out for this Chinese tour group.

" There are a couple of campgrounds here ; we can just camp in my tent." I suggested, to which he immediately replied, "Absolutely not." I used my wits and finally found an Airbnb about an hour away. It wasn't ideal and definitely looked like a haunted house, but it at least had a bed and bathroom, even though it was shared. It was actually Nate's first time ever staying in an Airbnb. He was much more used to bougie hotels.

The next morning we got out of there as soon as we woke up and spent the day exploring Upper and Lower Antelope Canyon. It was basically my dream come true; traveling with Nate, having him take photos of me and I of him. We even took a few photos together even though it was only because the

262

guide insisted on taking them. It only got better because Nate had found and booked the most expensive hotel in the area, which was a resort on Lake Powell. After camping for several days, it felt like heaven to shower, do my hair, and be treated to a nice dinner and wine. How naive I was to think that the remainder of the trip would be this dreamy.

"So tomorrow, I thought we could go paddleboarding on Lake Powell!" I chirped, biting into a delicious piece of seared tuna.

"I gotta fly out early tomorrow, sorry kid." He said casually, not giving the slightest fuck that he had just shattered my heart once again.

"Wh-what? You just got here!" I rebutted, dropping my fork.

"Yeah but I gotta get back to Seattle for a business thing. You know I'd love to stay." It was the same excuse, in a different location.

"You ALWAYS say that! You can't just drop in every time I'm with a guy, scare him off, then leave me by myself! I wasn't planning on camping by myself, Nate!" I was a bit too loud and it made people turn to stare, but I didn't care. This was absolute bullshit.

"You're always mad at me!" Again, his typical response.

"You always screw me over!" Was always mine.

He left first thing in the morning. Alas, once again, I was left to travel solo because of him.

But unlike Iceland , Cuba, or even Panama, I felt *really* alone. And even a bit scared. Unlike most people, the U.S. feels more dangerous to me than any other country. It's the only place I've been where   I feel there are so many people with psychological disorders or drug problems that make them have a desire to do evil things to other people or flat out just be unfriendly. I was terrified of the idea of camping by myself, and it didn't help that for some reason, the U.S. somehow has the worst cellular service almost in the entire world. Seriously, I've been on the world's most remote islands and there was better reception than a lot of places in the U.S.

Do not cry over him again, get your shit together, and get going. I refused to let him get me down again. So I packed my few belongings up, took any free item I could find from his fancy hotel room, and was back on the road towards Page. I had a collaboration to fulfill.

Two weeks before the roadtrip, I had reached out to as many businesses as I could to try and get collaborations. From camping gear to camper vans, I emailed over fifty companies to try and get whatever I could to make a little extra cash, or at least get some free stuff so I didn't have to spend my own money on it. Only two people were interested, and one of them was Lake Powell Paddleboards, who had agreed to give me a free paddleboard rental for the day in exchange for a blog post.

It wasn't much, but considering that it was one of the few things I could get, I was extremely grateful for it. As I drove up to the gravel parking lot for the shop, I wondered how the other emails were doing that I had sent out the day before leaving for this trip. I had spent the entire day, literally fourteen hours, emailing every tour company and hotel in about six countries that were at the top of my bucketlist. I had made what would have been a resume for a normal job, but instead of work and education, I replaced it with follower counts and press outlets I had been featured on. It was just a little something I thought would make people take me more seriously. *Little did I expect to be speaking about how to make one (now called a Media Deck) at bootcamps and travel conferences a couple of years later.*

But I couldn't get enough service for my email to load without Wi-Fi and realized I had been too distracted by Nate to have used it at the hotel. Oh well, I guess I'd have to just enjoy the *present* moment!

Nervously, I approached the door to the paddleboard shop, having my rehearsed greeting ready to go; '*Hi, I'm Alyssa, I'm a travel blogger who is supposed to be doing a collaboration with you?*'

When I entered the small, crowded shop, I saw an older man behind the desk, already eyeing me suspiciously.

"Hi, can I help you?" He said loudly.

"Hi! My name is Alyssa, I spoke to someone about --" I started with my recital.

"Ah yes, the *travel blogger*," he said slowly, studying my appearance, "We've had a couple of you reach out for these *collaborations*, but usually, they never end up giving us what they say they will." He added, which came as a shock to me.

"What? Really? Like they don't write the blog or post a picture?" I blurted, full honesty in my voice.

"Nope." He said, still eyeing me skeptically.

"That's ridiculous, I'm sorry to hear that . That gives travel bloggers a really bad name. But I can assure you, I am very grateful for this opportunity and I will have a blog post up by tomorrow." I said boldly and proudly.

"I know you are. I saw your website. It's very impressive. I liked your article about traveling alone too." He said, finally smiling. I blushed, not realizing that my very obnoxious article would be actually read by the businesses I was pitching to.

"How much time do you have? And do you have your own camping gear?" He asked as he started to shuffle items behind the desk, pulling out a map of the lake from a stack of several.

"I'm flexible, I can get the board back in a couple of hours if you need it. And yeah, I'm camping, so if you happen to know of any good campsites nearby that are still available --" I said, assuming having the board for the whole day was a bit much.

"No, I don't need the board. I have a great adventure for you if you're up for it." He waved me over to the counter where he had placed the map, pen in hand over it.

"If you drive towards the area where you do the Antelope Canyon tours, there's a turn off just after the entrance for Lower Antelope Canyon," He explained as he drew a star over a thin line on the map, "Turn left there and go all the way down until you get to the boat ramp, then park in the lot to the left. Then, carry the board and your camping gear down to the boat ramp area, and to the right of it is a little shore area that you can load the board and your gear on." He drew lines and circles as he spoke. *What exactly is he about to propose I do with a paddleboard and my camping gear?*

"Start paddling towards the middle, but be careful because sometimes boats speed through there. Oh, and the current starts to pick up, so be sure you keep paddling through it, towards the island on the other side ; it's called Antelope Island." He explained nonchalantly, circling it on the map and writing the name out.

"Drop your gear off there, it should be safe, and then you can head to the slot canyons on your board," He drew a line from the island all the way down a long portion of the lake and into a turn-off that then zig-zagged through canyons. "If you're feeling bold and don't mind getting dirty, you can walk through the muck at the very end, which will take you into the very very end of Lower Antelope Canyon that's only accessible by the water! You'll have the whole place to yourself! Just be sure to leave well before sunset, so you have enough light to set up your tent." He finished drawing lines and then pushed the map towards me.

"So, so I just camp on the island?" I said nervously, half wondering if I was even capable of doing that and half wondering if it was legal.

"Yeah, it's a great experience! It'll make for a great blog post, I want to make sure we look good ya know?" He said with a wink.

"You, you think I can do it by myself?" I squeaked. I expected him to expect I'd just paddle around in the sun for a few hours, not go on an extreme excursion and then camp on an island by myself.

"Sure, why not? You went to all those places on your blog by yourself." He said as he simultaneously yelled for someone in the back to come load the paddleboard onto the roof of my Mustang.

Alright well, I guess I'm doing this.

I listened intently as the young shop assistant explained how the roof rack works and how to get the board on and off of it. The damn thing was almost as long as my car, and to be

266

honest, I wasn't fully sure I'd be able to even carry it by myself. But I obviously wasn't going to let anyone know that.

Following the directions to the parking lot was easy, but as expected, what was not easy was unloading and carrying the paddleboard. It was so heavy that I basically had to let it fall off my car and then had to make two trips to get it and my camping gear to the lake. Speaking of my camping gear, I had wasted a solid twenty minutes trying to decide what was essential to bring with me since I had limited space on the board.

The first of my essentials was a styrofoam cooler I had splurged on at the grocery store before I got there, which I filled with essentials like wine, more wine, and some perishable food like veggies and cheese. I also bought easy -to -make food like tuna and bread and got bold with buying firewood and a flame thrower. Hopefully, all the times I went camping with my brothers when I was a child would pay off tonight.

For my camping gear, I brought both my regular blue tent and also the cute pink castle tent I dubbed as "my closet ." I brought my sleeping bag, utensils, and a flashlight. That should be enough. More importantly, I used one of my plastic space-saver packing bags to vacuum seal my laptop so I could bring that to write my blog post when it got dark outside, I put my phone in its waterproof case that hung around my neck and slipped my selfie stick through the front of my bathing suit so that the camera hung from the string in the front.

I had just finally finished loading everything onto the board when a boat started to pull up onto the ramp. It was full of young people, drinking and having a good time. My cheeks burned and my stomach twisted, feeling a pang of embarrassment that I was by myself. The boat had brought a wake with it, and I stumbled about to pull the board higher up onto the shore so it wouldn't be rocked. The only possible worse thing that could happen to me right now was if all of my stuff fell into the water.

The small waves had a big impact on my board, so I decided to sit on it and wait for them to pass. And also for the people to pass because I was too embarrassed to be seen struggling to get the board in the water, not to mention getting on it, standing up, and potentially tipping everything over.

"Are you paddling your gear to go camp on the island?!" A loud voice suddenly announced from the dock above me. I squinted to look up and saw two of the guys examining my situation, both holding a can of beer.

"Oh, uh, yeah. I'm just waiting for the waves to stop." I said nervously, hoping they weren't going to ask if I needed help.

"That's badass!" He yelled.

"Do you need help getting in?" The other asked. *Thanks but no thanks.* Truth be told, I did want help, but I also didn't want to be seen as weak or incapable , especially to myself.

"I'm Ok, thanks!" I smiled and tapped the top of the cooler, suddenly wishing I had a cover up on.

"Enjoy! The lake is beautiful today! *Hey guys, hurry up so she can get going!*" The first guy said to me and then yelled at his friend who was backing a giant pick-up truck towards the boat. This made the rest of the friends look at me, including the girls, who I'm pretty sure didn't appreciate the two guys stopping to talk to me.

When they were finally gone and the water was calm again, I carefully walked the board into the water until it was thigh-deep. Next would be the most important balancing act of my life. As if I were competing for a gold medal in a gymnastics routine, I used my arms and upper body strength to lift my entire body up high enough until I could easily get my knees on the board. My arms shook under the weight of my body, and so did the board, which made me try extra hard to keep my balance. When both knees were stable, I used my arms again to control the weight distribution, and rose to my feet, slightly shaking. It felt like being on a trapeze high above the ground and came complete with that weird feeling in your stomach like you're about to fall. After wobbling a bit, I carefully dunked the paddle into the water on my left and pushed it back using my core strength in order to keep my balance. The board easily moved forward, and again when I switched to the right.

Oh yeah! I got this! I cheered myself on as I glided farther and farther towards the middle of the lake. Luckily there were no boats on it, and I took that opportunity to take the selfie stick out from my bathing suit and take a few shots and videos.

Shit! The selfie stick clunked down on board after falling through my suit when I was trying to replace it with one hand. My heart skipped a beat as I foresaw it sinking down into the dark abyss of Lake Powell. But it didn't, thank god, and I quickly yet carefully bent down to get it, just as a speed boat was approaching in the distance. *Shit shit shit!*

Instead of standing back up, I knelt down, first securing the stick and camera to the top of the bundle on the front of the board and then getting my paddle ready to brace myself against the oncoming wake. The boat was going fast, which meant the waves were going to be big, which meant there was a good possibility of tipping over. But I remembered my days paddleboarding in Florida and knew that if I just pointed the nose into the wave, I should be able to just go over it rather than remaining parallel to it and potentially getting knocked sideways.

As I braced for it, the boat suddenly slowed and someone yelled "*Sorry!*" as they passed. I saw the boat already far in the distance as the rolls of water approached. I paddled hard into them, going up and then down gracefully. *Thank god.*

Realizing more boats were bound to come, I got back up and paddled as fast and hard as possible to get to the island. It was *way* farther than it looked both on the map and from the parking lot. When I finally approached the shore of it, I wanted to jump off and kiss it. My arms burned from paddling and so did my skin from being in the blazing sun longer than expected. Carefully, I stepped off the board and pulled it onto the sandy shore, taking the bag with my laptop off of it first and placing it far away from the water.

I should be recording this, I thought, realizing how ridiculous I probably looked. Before continuing, I unlatched the selfie stick from the front and set the tripod foot up in the sand facing the shore.

"Hey everyone! I'm Alyssa from My Life's a Travel Movie, and today I'm going to be *camping* solo on Antelope Island! I've just paddled all of my gear across Lake Powel and now it's time to find my own beach!" I said to the camera, then left it on to record myself unloading and explaining what I brought.

"Most importantly, lots of wine!" I said to the camera, twisting off a mini bottle of Sutter Home chardonnay and downing almost half of it in one gulp. I continued to walk around the small island with the selfie stick behind me, explaining to the camera why I liked or disliked each little enclave I found to set my tents up in.

When I finally found one I liked, I hid my stuff in a nook and set off to go see the slot canyons so I'd get back well before dark to set up.

Just like the distance to the island, the entrance to the slot canyon was even farther than I expected. My biceps felt like they might look like Popeye's by the time I was done, and I had already spent way more time than anticipated. But the views were undeniably breathtaking, and hardly anyone else was there.

The earthy-orange canyon walls towered high above me as I navigated the calm dark waters on the board. The waterway started out wide then continued to get narrower and narrower, which I assumed meant I would soon hit the end where I could hop off and explore the lesser known part of Antelope Canyon. But as I got closer to the end, the water became filled with a strange layer of what seemed like hay mixed with mud. Or maybe it was cow shit because that's definitely what it smelled like.

There was a kayak with a couple stuck in the muck and laughing wildly. I guess it would be entertaining if you weren't trying to get through shit alone.

"Is the slot canyon near?" I yelled out to them with strange confidence that I didn't even know I had.

"Yeah! It's just around the corner but it's almost impossible to get through with the board, you'd have to swim through it!"

The guy yelled back. *Swim? Through this shit?* Judging by their clean appearance, I guessed they opted not to attempt it.

"Thanks!" I yelled back, continuing to paddle through the strange muck.

As I rounded the corner, I could see the end and the crevice to the left that I was told to walk through, although it might go up to my waist with mud. I tried my best to paddle closer to it, but the clumps of water-soaked earth made it nearly impossible. I used my paddle to break the chunks of dirt apart to get closer, and each time, I imagined a giant mud-hippopotamus emerging up suddenly and taking me under.

I don't know why it was so terrifying, but I did know there was no way I was going to swim through this thick, rancid-smelling shit. Did I desperately want to see what was in the slot canyon? Yes. Did I want to potentially get stuck in it alone and die? Nope. I got a weird vibe similar to the one I felt in the haunted troll cave in Iceland and immediately started to try and back out of the crap. It had re-surrounded me from behind even though I had made a path farther into it. This creeped me out even more and made me fight extra hard, despite my burning arms and aching hands, to get out of it.

When I was finally free, I saw another kayak with a couple in it rounding the corner, which instantly calmed me. At least if a mud-hippo attacked me, there would be witnesses.

"Hey! What's back there?" The girl in the front yelled.

"A lot of muck! It smells like shit! I couldn't get through it!" I yelled back, feeling slightly like a failure.

"*Oh fuck that!*" I heard her announce to the muscular guy behind her, making me smile and not feel so bad about not wanting to swim in it.

"Yeah, someone told me you can walk through the mud to get to the slot canyon but there's like twenty feet of the floating crap before you can even get to it." I explained as I paddled closer and used my free hand to point to the area.

"I'm good, we can go back." She said to him, her animated honesty making me laugh. "Thanks girl!"

As I paddled back the way I came, trying to go as fast as possible since it was already three PM, I realized they didn't act like it was strange at all that I was alone. Or at least it didn't show. I smiled to myself, appreciating the small win.

Finally, I turned the last bend to the wide part of the canyons, and to my extreme surprise, a two -level river cruise boat was coming through it. I didn't even know such a thing existed, but it was clear it was part of a tour, and specifically, the Chinese tour that had taken over all the hotels in town. I must have fulfilled the visual expectations they had co me for because the entire group crowded the railings on the top deck to take photo after photo of me. I wished there was a way to at least send one of them to me since all I could manage was my typical wide-angle selfie of my back. Not going to lie though, it was a great photo since I was able to get the entire water way and canyons with me on the board in the middle.

After what seemed like hours, I finally made it back to 'my beach' around four, which gave me at least three hours of light left. I realized I was starving, so I decided to first set up the tent and then make some lunch.

Quickly I realized though, that I hadn't set up the tent by myself before. The motorcycle guy helped me and basically did it on his own, so how hard could it be? I set up my tripod stick and put the camera on time-lapse for two seconds, knowing fully well that it might take about ten minutes and I definitely did not have enough space on my SD card for that.

Connecting all the sticks and sliding them into the frame of the tent was easy. I thought I was home free and super cool for doing it by myself so quickly. Until it was time for the final click of all the pieces, which I realized is what Motorcycle guy always needed my help with. It was a two-person tent, which meant it needed two people to set it up; one to try and hold all the legs of the frame out, and the other to pop the connector of the top so that the whole frame stays together and doesn't collapse. I didn't have enough arms to do it all.

But I kept trying and trying and trying, I even brought it closer to the rocks to try to get higher to pop the top. I tried putting it upside down, on its side, on an angle, but nothing was working. Finally, I got inside of it and pushed the connector as hard as I could with one hand while attempting to hold two of the sides out with an arm and a leg, and magically, it all popped into place. Making for one hell of a time-lapse video. *Little did I know that what I thought was an informative solo camping video would go viral with almost a million views a couple of years later.* But for entertainment purposes of course.

Once my tent was up, I proceeded to create a "Cooking in the Camp Kitchen with Alyssa" show, where step by step, I showed the camera how to make tuna salad. *Enthralling, I know.*

It turned messier and smellier than I thought (think onions and tuna in heat with no sink), so I decided I should probably dunk in the lake to wash up. The sun was starting to set and I hadn't seen a boat go by in a while, so boldly, I opted to go in naked, something I'd literally only do if I was on a deserted island, which I was, so I did.

It was beyond liberating not having to worry about anyone staring at me, being able to feel the freedom of being naked in nature. Well, until a boat came speeding around the lake bend. Fear flushed through my entire body, and had I known what a panic attack felt like, I would have definitely thought I was having one. The boat slowed down and seemed like it was approaching, and it was too late to run out of the water without the people on it seeing my bare ass. *Shit!*

My main fear about camping alone on the island honestly was getting attacked and raped. It's sad to say that, but it's the truth. In fact, that's usually my only fear when I'm traveling solo; experiencing a man force himself upon me. The fear doesn't come from nowhere of course. Too many times, I've been mistaken as or treated like a sex worker, whether it was an honest mistake or just some jerk trying to break me down. I know what it feels like to want to only kiss someone, but when things heat up and they want more, having to say no repeatedly and even sometimes be forceful. I know what the sound of my voice sounds like when I get truly scared someone isn't going to stop, and I know that most men will immediately back off when they hear it. I know I'm capable of putting a grown man in a headlock because I've done it twice when saying no wasn't enough. But I also know either of those times they could not have backed off, and that's what I dread most of potentially happening in the future. And what better opportunity for a predator than to find a naked woman alone on an island.

"*Look at the pink tent!*" I heard a woman's voice yell excitedly. *Phew.* It was reassuring not just to hear there were women on board but that the reason why they had slowed down was to get a better look at my tent castle. I sunk down lower in the water just in case though. Praying they didn't want to hop off for a closer look.

"*We should get one of those for Bella!*" I heard her continue. Double-phew. They had kids, and the only damage that could potentially be done was to my ego for being a grown adult woman with a children's tent.

Somehow my bobbing head went unnoticed in the water where I was pretending not to notice them anyway. I breathed a sigh of relief when they accelerated off onto the glassy waters towards the boat dock , although that didn't make me feel entirely great either. All of the boats were getting out of the water . None were planning on camping like I was, which meant I was about to be completely alone. With that thought suddenly at the forefront of my head, I did one more look around for any other boats or humans and when the coast was clear, I made a mad dash for my towel on the shore. I decided I should probably attempt to make a fire *before* it gets dark so I don't have to worry about it when it gets really dark.

I dried off and put the only outfit I brought onto the island on; jean shorts, a halter top, and a pair of flat ankle boots. If I was going to go camping, I at least wanted to look the part. I found a spot near one of the smooth boulders that looked like it had had several camp fires on it in the past and set up my bundle of firewood. I knew from camping with my brothers that you need some sort of kindle to start the flames, so I did a quick march around the rocks to collect small twigs and dead brush.

"Alright, I shall now attempt making a fire!" I said to the camera when I finally had my little stack of wood and kindle set up. I lit the flame thrower only for it to immediately be extinguished by the light wind. *Shit!*

Click click click. Click click click. No matter how many times I clicked the flame on, it wouldn't stay lit long enough to light my branches of kindle. Maybe they needed to be smaller. I quickly yanked them out of the pile and stomped on top of them in circles. All while the camera was still rolling of course. Once they were crushed up, I arranged them under the triangle of wood logs and tried again.

Click click, whooooosh! Finally, a little flame started, and I used my hands to shelter it from the wind so that it would spread to the logs. It felt like it took ten minutes, but finally, the logs were ablaze and my campfire was as photo-worthy as ever!

"I did it!" I yelled to the camera as if it was my friend, "I built a fire!" I continued, smiling like a lunatic and pointing at the flames, "...for myself."

As I squatted next to the flames, feeling the comfort of the heat, I also felt the discomfort of being alone at night creeping up like a sleep-paralysis monster. Before I knew it, darkness had descended and it felt like things were moving all around me. Thank god for iPhone flashlights. But wait, would that attract predators ?

I decided the best possible idea was to extinguish the fire and lock myself in my tent. I don't know why I thought locking the zippers of a tent together would prevent someone from simply slashing it open with a knife or something, but it gave me a tiny bit of comfort. That is until the wind really started picking up.

It was so loud that I couldn't concentrate on the blog post I had attempted to start writing on my laptop, and I had to opt for a downloaded episode of Sex and the Ci ty with the volume all the way up. After the third episode and all of my wine later, my eyes felt heavy, but my brain was on high alert. The wind had continued to pick up and at a shockingly random rhythm. It literally seemed like someone was smacking my tent from all sides, but it was so random that I knew there was no way it could be a human , though it definitely sounded like one.

Maybe I can just quickly paddle back to the boat dock and sleep in my car. I thought —several times. But let's be serious, the only thing scarier than being inside the tent would be being *outside* of it, on a pitch -black lake. *NOPE.*

I checked the time for the trillionth time and gained a little more confidence. It was four -thirty in the morning, only about two hours until sunrise. *You got this.* Except I didn't 'got this' because my laptop and phone were both about to die, which meant I'd have to lay there wide awake listening to the sounds of a ghost trying to pummel my tent with me inside of it.

Let's just say the remaining two hours was like a two -hour long panic attack. I tried my best to wrap myself in the sleeping bag and turn towards whatever direction it felt like the wind-intruder was coming from. Which, obviously, was difficult since it felt like literally all directions. Did I mention that I forgot to check the ground for rocks before setting up the tent? Not fun finding out there's a bunch of rocks in the sand because you keep getting stabbed with them while you're attempting to sleep.

But let's be serious. There was a zero percent chance I was going to sleep. Which sucks. Because I suck when I don't sleep. If you ever catch me after a long flight where I didn't sleep the entire way in an attempt to watch every free movie and get every free meal, it's not pretty. I had inherently decided that I need a minimum of eight hours of sleep since I was in highschool, and I fully blame it on my sleep interruption from lucid dreaming every night and also my extreme reluctance to be told what to do.

Light? I must have either dozed off for a few minutes or started to un-buzz from the wine because suddenly, there was a pale light seeping through the bright blue fabric of my tent. It wasn't bright enough for me to *not* be terrified of what was outside though, so I pulled the sleeping bag up closer around me and kept on waiting. It's *rare* that I ever get up for sunrise, and even though I had the perfect opportunity to pretend like I did it on purpose, I dreaded seeing it from the point of view of

276

a person who hadn't slept all night. Nope, those days are long over.

Finally, a ray of real freaking sunshine shone through the wall of the tent, and I scrambled about to unlock myself out of it. The zipper sounded obnoxiously loud in comparison to the stark silence of dusk. When I finally pulled back the door-flap, my breath was taken away by the delicious colors I saw and also the fact that there was now absolutely zero wind. Like, why couldn't there have been zero wind all night? Anyway, the palette of juicy orange and pink that painted the sky reflected sharply on the flat glassy surface of the still lake. The sand looked more red than it had in the afternoon light yesterday and -- *what the hell is this?!*

As my eyes made their way across the entire real estate of sand I had claimed as my camping spot, I counted about seven different types of animal footprints. Most looked like small rodents, a couple were birds, and there was one *very* distinct slither that I knew was a snake. I started to question if the wind was really all that was touching my tent throughout the night. As much as I wanted to make a mad-paddle to the other side and get the hell off the island, I calmly made a video of all the animal footprints first, then proceeded to film myself exiting the tent while singing, *'We are the champions.'*

I didn't bother filming the packing session. But let's just say it took one -eighth of the time to get that shit down, onto my board, and back across the lake than it did getting there. What *wasn't* as fast or easy was getting the damn paddleboard back up onto the roof of my car. No matter how many times or angles I tried, my arms just weren't strong enough. Finally, I figured out that if I slid it nose first from the hood of my car up onto the roof, I could somewhat get it back up there. It was facing the wrong direction, and it had made a bunch of scratches, but it was up there and secure. Thanks to all of the random things I used to tie it to my car.

When I finally reached the Page Paddleboard shop, I prayed out loud that the owner wouldn't be there. Hell no, I did not want to talk about my night of terror and why I hadn't slept because I was scared of the wind and small rodents. Luckily it was seven freaking AM in the morning, and only the shop assistant kid was there.

"Wow, you're up early! Did you have fun?" He asked, starting to pull at the random things I had tied around the board to secure it. "The roof rack is tricky, you did a good makeshift job!" He added with a laugh that I couldn't tell was mockery or simple amusement.

"Yeah, it was easy to get down, but not to get back up, sorry ," I mumbled, feeling slightly embarrassed but more focused on getting the hell out of there.

"All good! Well, I don't think you have a bill or anything, so you're good to go!" He said rather enthusiastically for that early in the morning but I was grateful for it . It was better than a cup of coffee.

With a new sense of pride, bravery, and get-me-out-of-here, I sped off on the empty highway, north towards Utah. If I moved quickly enough, I could make it to Bryce Canyon *and* an epic looking waterfall I saw on social media that, from my research, is an hour farther than Bryce. It was a stretch to do alone, but if I could handle one night on a deserted island, I felt like I could handle a few extra hours of driving.

Thanks to my little detour fiasco with Nate, I was almost a full day behind, which would have been fine had I not set my heart on finding the gorgeous waterfall I had seen in photos. But I couldn't *not* try to go see a waterfall. Especially when chasing waterfalls is my top favorite hobby.

After camping alone on the island, I didn't feel much like going through the ridiculous tent-set up process right away. Well, that and I was also in desperate need of some actual sleep and I knew camping alone again would guarantee that wouldn't happen. I checked my phone for the two-hundredth time since I had been driving from Lake Powell towards Bryce Canyon, but shocker, still no service.

The road seemed never -ending and there was barely anything civilization-wise as far as it stretched. But I still kept going because I could have sworn I saw one or two random hotels on the map when I had the service to check it before I left. I was just hoping I didn't pass them, which I guess would be hard to do since there was literally nothing else on the sides of the road.

Oh thank baby Jesus! As I drove over another hill, I could see the bold 'MOTEL' sign up ahead. It looked literally like every nightmare you could possibly have about a creepy hotel in the middle of a desert, but the sun was setting and if I didn't stop now, there was a chance I'd be sleeping in the car. The motel was one level, all dark brown, and with mostly sketchy - looking vehicles in the lot. I know it's weird to stereotype cars, but they were the kinds that you see in literally every murder movie. I pulled my Mustang up next to an old VW hatchback -- the kind with faux wood paneling on the outside and checked my surroundings for humans *or murderous-incest-made-mutants from the Hills Have Eyes*. There wasn't a soul sight, so I made my way to the building labeled Reception.

"Um, hi, I'd like a single room. If you have one?" I mumbled to the older woman behind the desk who was eyeing me up and down suspiciously.

"You heading to Bryce Canyon or something?" She asked as she clicked around on the computer, not taking her eyes off of me.

"Yeah, well, I want to try to go to Lower Calf Creek first but need to make sure I have a place to sleep." I admitted, checking the time. This knowledge seemed to appease her and she raised her eyebrows in approval.

"Alright, we got one single left, you'll have to share a bathroom and it's forty-five dollars." She said, more telling me than asking me if I wanted it. It was definitely not in my budget, and the idea of sharing a bathroom wasn't ideal, but to be fair, the campgrounds weren't much cheaper and I had to share a bathroom there as well. She turned away briefly, then turned back with a laminated color map of the area. "If you get up around seven AM, you can make it to Lower Calf Creek before it gets busy," she explained matter-of-factly as she traced the route with her wrinkled index finger, "It's about an hour hike each way," this new fact made me cringe slightly due to lack of time," but then you can get to Bryce just as it's opening when there are not too many people there yet as well." She traced her finger back towards the motel, stopping at the big brown mass that represented Bryce Canyon.

"Oh wow, thank you!" I said breathily, digging through my seatbelt bag for my wallet. I handed over my debit card reluctantly, hoping it had enough funds in it to cover the room, and watched nervously as she ran it through the machine. I let out a deep sigh of relief when the old machine started spitting out my receipt.

"You traveling alone?" She asked finally as she tore off the receipt.

"Y-yeah. Well, my...*boyfriend* was with me but he had to leave to get back to work." I lied on so many levels.

"Well, you'll still enjoy it, it's a beautiful area!" She said suddenly warmly. "Here's your key, it's room one-oh-nine, you can enter through that door over there," she said, pointing in the distance. "Oh and breakfast is on us, it's from six AM to ten." She said with a smile, eyeing my body as if I had an eating disorder. It reminded me suddenly that I hadn't eaten all day and was actually starving. I hoped there were some chips or nuts in the room but highly doubted it. I'd have to splurge to order something from their restaurant.

For not being a morning person, it sure as hell was easy to wake up at the crack of dawn all of a sudden. Maybe because I was constantly finding myself in the same *"Please be light out soon so I can get the hell out of here"* thoughts.

It was barely five AM, but I decided to get up and get dressed anyway. That only took about fifteen minutes, so I started working on another blog post until breakfast started at six. *'10 Stops on the Ultimate Arizona to Utah Roadtrip'* I titled it. Not knowing at all whatsoever that in a few years, it would be one of my top read and shared posts of all time.

Of course, I left out the whole dramatic debacle with the motorcycle guy and then Nate. Making the blog post purely about information, tips, and the epic photos I managed to get with my selfie stick and action camera. What I really wanted to write was about how incredibly scared, hurt, angry, yet

280

exasperatingly happy I was through it all. Such a strange mix of emotions. Does that make me bipolar? Or maybe more like quad-polar.

I expected to be the first person at the dimly-lit wood cabin restaurant, but to my surprise, there were already several couples and families in it. This was both reassuring that I wasn't the only person staying there and awkward because I was definitely the only solo person. So awkward in fact that I almost opted out of a free breakfast that I desperately needed. I decided to pretend like I was doing something super important on my phone while I ate as much as possible. Dodging everyone's inquisitive stares.

It took about two hours to get to the parking lot of Lower Calf Creek, and I enjoyed the majority of the scenic drive up until I got there. When my car shut off for some reason. *Fuck.*

Frantically I re-started it over and over again, immediately wondering what in the actual hell I would do if it didn't start back up. I *still* didn't have service, so I wouldn't have even been able to call for a tow truck. Not to mention, I was literally in the middle of nowhere. Miraculously it started back up on the twenty-seventh try, and I continued on to the lot even though I probably should have driven back towards town in case it really was dying.

But I had just gone four hours out of the way for this damn waterfall, so there was no turning back now. I parked my car and graciously stretched outside in the golden sunlight. There were only a couple of other cars there and the entire area was quiet aside from the chirping of birds and buzzing of insects. Instantaneously I felt rejuvenated and alive even if my car was not.

I packed my typical hiking essentials into my backpack: my camera and pink selfie stick, a portable charger, and my water bottle. I swung it onto my back and set off with a big smile on my face that was for no one but myself.

'Aaaahhhhh' I breathed out loud as I inhaled the sweet smell of nature and basked in the gentle warmth of the rising sun. Plants of all shapes and sizes towered above me on either side of the dirt trail, many exhibiting beautiful flowers in purple and yellow hues. Moments like these were why I pushed myself so hard to do the things I do. Moments like these were what I was literally living for. I marched the entire one -hour hike with a smile on my face. Well, except for the four times my mind wandered to the thought of getting back and my car being completely dead.

After about fifty minutes, I started to hear a comforting sound; people laughing wildly and water crashing to the ground. *I made it!* I picked up my pace excitedly, getting that weird unnecessary anxiety of finally getting to the grand event and not having enough time or light to enjoy or photograph it.

But when Lower Calf Creek came into view, my breath went out of view too. Not that breath is visible, but you know what I mean. In the clearing ahead of me was a tall half-moon cliff, with a perfect stream of water falling down the middle of it. On either side of the waterfall was some sort of fungus growing from the moisture, making what looked like a rainbow color on either side of it. Below was a shallow pool that the water dropped down into, but to be completely honest, I had no idea where it went after that.

My eyeballs felt like they were having an orgasm, and my body involuntarily moved closer and closer until I was at the banks of the small and shallow pond below. There were only about three couples there and one small family, so it was empty enough to fully enjoy. *Why did I not bring a bathing suit ?*

The business-woman in me did first-things-first -- got the photos. The ultra-wide lens of my action camera easily got the entire area in the shot ; otherwise, there would be no way to capture it all. Then I put the camera away, rolled up my leggings as high as they would go, and swished my feet through the shockingly icy water from the falls. I wanted to stay there all day and was jealous of the couple I saw sitting and enjoying the view with all the time in the world. If I wanted to make it to all of the sites on my list, I would need to leave in approximately ten minutes. I made a mental note to come back here one day when I was successful and not rushed for a time due to the threat of lacking money.

After a few more minutes of enjoying the view, a few more figuring out where the hell the water *goes*, and a couple of minutes sighing heavily that I couldn't freeze time, I set off for the hour-long hike back to the car. The hike back involved way more anxiety. Literally, all I could think about was what I was going to do if my car wouldn't start. I thought of several ideas and solutions, as I typically do when I'm panicking, ranging from waiting for someone to come to the parking lot and asking to use their phone to walking a few miles to get to a gas station to use a phone.

When I finally got to my car and turned it on, my worst fears all came true. My car was dead, and even after twenty-seven more times of trying to start it, it wouldn't budge.

"You need a jump miss?" The sudden noise scared the crap out of me and I jumped sideways in the driver's seat as if a bear were about to attack. An older man and his wife were peering at me from a few feet away, clearly noticing my struggles. Meanwhile, I had been freaking out so much that I didn't even notice they had approached.

"Y-yeah. I think so?" I sniffed, wiping the sweat, snot, and building tears from my face. "I don't know what happened, I've been driving for days and now it just suddenly died!" I wailed, mostly at the steering wheel.

"May I try?" The man asked, shuffling closer to me as his wife looked at me with sincere pity. I nodded and jumped out of the driver's seat as he slowly and stiffly crouched all the way down to get into my low-set car.

"Thank you." I sniffed to the woman, who smiled and patted my back maternally.

He wasn't able to start it after a few tries, which he seemed to expect, so he got out purposefully and backed their heavyduty pickup truck next to my out-of-place sports car. He pulled out jumper cables, attached them to his engine, then popped the hood of my car and attached the other end to mine. I watched the entire process carefully, trying to memorize what he was doing in case I needed to do it again in the future.

"Alrighty! Can you get in and turn it on when I say go?" He yelled from the driver's seat of the pickup.

"What if it explodes?" I yelled back, envisioning the power of the giant truck causing my little car to fly into the air in flames.

"It won't! This is how you jump a car ma'am!" He yelled back with a laugh.

Even with his reassurance I was definitely convinced the car was going to blow up, but I went into the driver's seat and turned the key in the ignition anyway.

Vroom vroooooomm! It turned on! I couldn't believe it! I wasn't going to have to walk miles on the highway to get to a phone after all! I jumped from the car and thanked them both profusely, getting in response a mixture of amusement and sympathy. I told them about my plans to continue on to Bryce Canyon and then Zion before heading back to LA and they gave me a couple of tips, mostly for avoiding my car dying again.

It was fortunate that one of the tips included driving for an hour or more to reboot the engine because that was how far away Bryce Canyon was. I was behind schedule, so I wouldn't get much time there but I didn't care, as long as my car wasn't dead and I wasn't stuck in the middle of nowhere. I didn't even know what Bryce Canyon was before I did my thorough research before the trip on National Parks in Utah, so admittedly it wasn't at the very very tippy top of my list. I was much more determined to get to Zion, although now that I was solo, I wasn't quite sure I'd have the confidence to hike alone there.

When I finally arrived at Bryce Canyon it was already two in the afternoon. I had intended on getting there at twelve because I knew the sun would start to make shadows on the canyon around two-thirty, according to my research. I also knew I needed to leave no later than three- thirty in order to make the six -hour drive to Zion in order to find either a hotel or campsite before it got dark. Online it said all the reservable camping spots were taken, so I was planning to try my luck with an open-reservation one, or depending on how tired I was, I would just look for a hotel. I assumed there had to be a lot near Zion, given its popularity.

I parked my car, praying that it wouldn't die again, and walked to one of the many lookout points inside the national park. It was drastically different from what I had just seen in Lake Powell, Antelope Valley, Havasu Falls, and the Grand Canyon.

Bryce Canyon has these peculiar giant reddish-orange rock formations jutting up from the base of the canyon. It looks like something you'd expect to see on Mars, not in the middle of nowhere in southern Utah. I saw a cool area without a guard rail that would make for a great wide-lens photo, so I sat down, hung my feet over the edge, put on a hat to hide my disgusting dirty hair, and reached my selfie stick out behind me. Almost immediately, a family walked behind me with parents who snickered 'Selfie!'

It was almost enough self-esteem shattering to deter me from continuing on down into the canyon, but not quite. I hadn't driven an extra four hours to get scared off by a Boomer who hadn't caught on to the explosive selfie trend yet. *Get back to me in a couple of years when literally everyone is using them.*

With a massive eye-roll, I got up and continued down the dirt path that led into the canyon but unfortunately, I didn't make it all the way down. A cat call whistle and creepy wandering eyes all over my sports bra cleavage made me retreat. I was breaching my allotted time limit there anyway. Any longer and I'd be driving at night on a road that was known for accidents caused by deer running in the road, and the last thing I wanted was to hurt Bambi.

I'd been driving for about an hour when I finally got one bar of cell service. I immediately pulled over so I could try to reserve a camping site near Zion. I'm not entirely sure why I thought the most popular National Park in the area was going to have availability, but yep. Nope.

Frantically I started searching for a hotel instead of using my typical hacks and tactics: zooming in on the map and looking for the bubbles with the lowest price. Except, there were no bubbles near Zion. In fact, there were only a total of two and the closer one was about three-hundred dollars for the night. The farther one was an hour north of Zion, which was an hour out of the way, and an additional hour earlier, I'd have to wake up in the morning in order to be one of the first people in the park. I could take my chances and try to go to one of the campgrounds anyway to see if any of the reservations didn't show up, but if that didn't work, I'd be sleeping in my car. So I booked the farther hotel for fifty dollars and set off.

Night had fallen about an hour before I got to where the directions for the hotel were leading me. The roads were empty, and creepy mist lingered at eye level. Scenes from literally every horror movie where a girl is driving alone at night in the woods played in HD in my mind, not helping the situation at all. Oh, and I quickly understood the "like a deer in headlights" analogy and why there were so many accidents on this road. I had to slam on my brakes about twenty-eight times because of all the deer that decide to just jump out in the middle of the road when a car is coming. It definitely did not help my rising anxiety about the situation. Another thing that did not help the situation; when I finally got to the address of the hotel, it was an empty parking lot.

My heart started pounding and my stomach twisted into a knot. I tried to click on the website for the hotel but my one tiny dot of cell service would not allow it. Instead, I tried calling the number listed on the booking site. Shocker, it wasn't a working number. I drove slowly around the empty lot, in case I was just missing it in the dark, but nothing was to be seen except a run down car with a man in it , which was enough motivation to immediately leave. I started driving back towards the highway, tears in my eyes due to the failure and fatigue of driving for so long and so late. Deer were all over the roads by this point. And as much as I love seeing a cute deer in the daylight, seeing them suddenly pop out on a dark road at night with creepy reflective eyeballs and avoiding hitting them is like a nightmare zombie apocalypse video game. Finally, about an hour later, I saw a very brightly lit gas station with several cars in it. It was at least comforting to know I wasn't the only person driving right now.

I pulled in and racked my brain for a solution. The only thing I could think of was to call the booking website and complain, so I did. To my extreme surprise, one of their customer service agents actually answered the phone in the middle of the night. And after telling them my story, again to my extreme surprise, they booked me at the nicer hotel, which apparently had a last -minute cancellation. So all was good in solo travel paradise again.

The nice hotel made me realize how much I'd been roughing it. I wasn't sure if the front desk clerk was suspiciously eyeing my disheveled appearance or just the fact that I was arriving alone in the middle of the night. I didn't have the energy to care. All of my worries melted away anyway when I reached my room.

The brightly lit white-marble bathroom had a rainshower head, which I stood under with scorching hot water for close to twenty minutes. The queen size bed had a cloud-like comforter and six squishy pillows that made me pass out the second my head sunk into them. All of this made me wake up late and miss being the first person at Zion. At that moment though, it was worth it.

When I finally got to Zion at around eleven AM, it still wasn't too crowded, which surprised me. I had to take a shuttle from the parking lot, and the close proximity to other humans got me a few unwarranted evaluations from families and couples, so I decided to wear my camera around my neck in an attempt to look more like an avid hiker and photographer. To my surprise, it seemed to work, and I felt a lot less judgy looks and even a few more smiles and nods!

Unfortunately, my camera died ten minutes after I started one of the hikes, but it made me feel so much more confident about hiking solo that I continued to wear it around my neck anyway. The hike was beautiful. To my delight, it started with a circular waterfall and then zigzagged through tall bushes of flowers that smelled like nature-scented air freshener that you'd buy from an expensive home decor store.

I wasn't entirely sure where the hike was leading to ; I just kept following it since it's where most people seemed to be heading. It started to zig -zag sharply up in a long series of switch-backs, which made my legs burn and my brain contemplate this decision, but I tried to have fun with it. Since no one was around, I pulled out my phone, which shockingly had service, and started doing Instagram Stories, so that other people could witness the ridiculousness I was getting myself into. Doing the Stories made me forget how long and how far I had been hiking because suddenly I was at another set of switch-backs, except they were much narrower, steeper, and clearly led to the top of the mountain. *I climbed a mountain?!*

I'm not going to lie ; it was brutal and felt like the suicide exercises they made us do in middle school where you run back and forth on the basketball court until your legs can't take it anymore. But the reward was glorious. At the top of the switch-backs were several people sitting down, enjoying the view, or more likely; resting their legs. It seemed like they all were looking at me as I emerged solo, so I kept walking towards what looked like an information sign.

Well. It was kind of informative. It had the yearly count of how many people have died climbing up to the summit and several warnings of what not to do if you're going to attempt it.

As much as that rattled me, there was another important piece of information that stood out; at the very top it said 'Welcome to Angel's Landing.'

I knew damn well about Angel's Landing, but I did not know that's what I was hiking! To be honest, when I looked up the hikes to do in Zion, although it said Angel's Landing was the best, it also said it was the highest and took the longest to do; about six hours, and I didn't think I would have that sort of time. Apparently I did because I had made it to the base of the summit. A couple passed me, and I realized they were heading to climb all the way up to the highest point.

I'd never seen chains nailed to the side of a mountain to help people climb it before and questioned whether I had it in me or not to attempt climbing it by myself. At least if I fell there would be a lot of people below to call an ambulance or something. Or maybe I should just focus on not falling.

The born-adventurer in me strode towards the metal ropes confidently and just started climbing like I actually knew what the hell I was doing. In full honesty, it was terrifying, and I had to keep telling myself not to look down. Finally, I made it.

The first clearing was a flat space with only a couple of other people on it. I spun slowly around to soak in the three-sixty degree views of the giant ripples in the earth below me. I looked back down where I had climbed and saw how stunning the mountain range looks from above it. With confidence and adrenaline levels on high, I sat down, untangled my topknot from its hair tie, extended my selfie stick, and took one of the most epic aerial view shots I've ever taken.

"There's an even better view up there!" A sweaty guy said as he started descending from where I had just climbed up.

"Oh! Thanks!" I mumbled back, shocked and grateful for a tip rather than a whisper.

Carefully, so as not to fall off the side of the mountain, I scrambled to my feet and continued the easy incline hike up to the very very top of Angel's Landing.

When I got there, it was like I had really just climbed up into heaven. Not only were the views absolutely stunning, but the vibe from the brave adventurers who had also climbed up was so docile, peaceful, and grateful. There were only about six or seven others, but they all sat with satisfied smiles and wide eyes as they took in the majestic views. You could see the entire mountain range and valleys that make up Zion. It was surreal to see how serene it was, especially since just a few days before, while I was escaping the flash flood in Havasupai, several people were swept away and killed here in Zion while hiking the Narrows. I closed my eyes and took a moment to acknowledge them and send hope that they passed quickly and while doing something they loved.

Although I didn't have much time, I sat down like the others to take in the views and the moment. I couldn't believe I had just accidentally climbed to the top of a 69,480 foot mountain.

"Hey! Do you want me to take your picture there? It's a really great shot from here!" A guy who was sitting with his friend behind me said. Oh good, this must be where all the cool, nice travelers are.

"Really? Yeah, that would be great! Thank you so much!" I blurted excitedly, handing my selfie stick and action camera over to them. I awkwardly did a couple of poses as they counted one-two-three and told me where to move so that you could see the whole background in the picture. *My dream come true.*

After talking to them for a bit about where they were from in India, and a few more minutes of sitting and admiring the view, I forced myself to get up and get going, knowing fully well it was going to be a very very long drive back to LA.

As I was starting to walk back down, two young girls passed me, but as they did, they looked almost excited? They whirled around, both gasping and one asked, "Oh my god, are you Alyssa? From My Life's a Travel Movie ?" I smiled but before I could answer, the other one said, "We saw your Stories that you were here! We were wondering if we'd run into you!" And then my ego blew up and I was at a loss for words. It was the first time complete strangers had stopped me in a completely random place to say hi and that they follow me on social media. *Little did I know that this was about to start happening more frequently than I would ever in a million years expected.*

Thanks to that little interaction, plus the accomplishment of climbing a freaking mountain, and the kindness of the people on it, I had a whole new level of not just confidence but purpose. During the entire three -hour hike back down, I manifested the shit out of what I want in life. *I am going to travel the world. I am going to become successful as a travel blogger. I am going to make a difference in the travel industry.* I said it over and over again, even out loud, and before I knew it, I was back at my trusty Mustang and ready to go.

Chapter Ten

Hey Look Ma, I Made It

Seven grueling hours later, including a stop in Vegas for lunch, and I was finally back at my apartment in West Hollywood. I badly wanted to just shower and crawl into bed, but since my BnB guest had just left that morning and left everything incredibly dirty, I had to clean everything first. Luckily I had picked up a well -deserved bottle of white wine on the way home.

While I waited for my bedsheets to wash, I finally pulled out my laptop to check my email, now that I actually had functioning Wi-Fi and enough energy. What I was expecting was the typical spam from social media notifications, maybe some random articles from my mom, and if I was lucky, a few more interview requests from people who had seen all the hype around my viral article.

But when I scrolled through the subject lines of the dozens of unread emails, I had to double -check that I wasn't in one of my lucid dreams. I literally couldn't believe my eyes. Slowly, as if savoring the moment while simultaneously bracing myself for a kind decline, I opened the first one.

"Hi Alyssa San! Thank you so much for reaching out! We would love to host you for three nights at Park Tokyo Hotel. Can you please let us know the dates you are coming?"

My jaw dropped. It was a five -star hotel in Tokyo, one of the many I had pitched just before the roadtrip. I starred it as important and went on to the next, and then the next, and the next.

By the time I had gotten through them all, I had offers for three hotels and one sushi cooking class in Japan, a four -night stay at a beach hotel in the Philippines, and four resorts and villas in Bali. In total, they would all cover my accommodation for a month's worth of traveling in Asia. All I'd need to do was buy the flights.

But that wasn't all. After opening the rest of the emails, something even more incredible happened. For the first time, tour companies and hotels had reached out to me first to ask if I wanted to come there for a collaboration. By the time I was finished reading them all, I had offers to hike the Inca Trail to Machu Picchu in Peru, take a trip to the Bolivia Salt Flats, and learn how to surf in Costa Rica.

A little drizzle of drool started pooling at the side of my mouth from how long it was widely spread open in an enormous smile. More wetness was leaking out of my eyes. Then it was flowing. And soon, I was full -on crying and shouting with joy.

"Yes! I did it! I fucking did it!" I screamed as I jumped up and down on the worn couch. It was enough euphoria to fill the holes in my heart that Nate had left. Speaking of which, should I text him to tell him the good news? Or would he just get my hopes up about meeting me somewhere then bail last minute? My brain knew the answer, but my heart couldn't resist. After texting him about my new trip plans in Asia, he immediately responded saying he'd love to meet me in Tokyo, and he was pretty convincing about it. But he had been pretty convincing about a lot of trips that he never came through on. I decided to not even let myself believe he'd actually come and forced my brain to focus on the work and logistics.

None of these trips would be without massive risk. And that risk had a lot to do with money. After some intense flight searching and hacking, I calculated that I'd have just enough money to afford the flights for the three trips in South America and then for the three -country trip to Asia for a month, OR my share of rent on the apartment in case I didn't get it fully rented out. I couldn't do both.

I had to make a choice. Keep the stability of a home, side hustle work, my dog, and all of my friends. Or give it all up temporarily to fulfill my wildest dreams, and travel full time almost for free, working my way to becoming a full -time travel blogger, which would hopefully get me paid to do collaborations like these in the future. Ideas started whirling around my head about how to make that happen; I'd immediately start pitching to businesses for paid collaborations where I'd take photos of their products in the epic destinations I was going to. I'd emphasize it would be a win-win situation for them because they'd get the photographer, "model," dreamy location, and audience, all for one low price. Plus I'd casually include links to all of my recent press features.

I smiled to myself. Who knew that by mustering the courage to travel on my own, and that by not letting what other people say about my dream to be a blogger deter me, that my life was going to completely change, and feel like I was living in a never -ending movie?

It was settled then. Yes, I was a woman traveling alone. And yes, I was going to go nomadic and become a full-time travel blogger.

To Be Continued.

Made in the USA
Middletown, DE
20 November 2023